Guide Me, Savior

365

TIMELESS DEVOTIONS
FROM PORTALS *of* PRAYER®

Edited by Erik Rottmann

CONCORDIA PUBLISHING HOUSE · SAINT LOUIS

Copyright © 2006 Concordia Publishing House
3558 S. Jefferson Avenue
St. Louis, MO 63118-3968
1-800-325-3040 · www.cph.org

Library of Congress Cataloging-in-Publication Data

Guide Me, Savior: 365 Timeless Devotions from Portals of Prayer /
edited by Erik Rottmann.
    p. cm.
   ISBN 978-0-7586-0799-7
1. Devotional calendars—Lutheran Church—Missouri Synod.
2. Lutheran Church—Missouri Synod—Prayer-books and devotions—
English. I. Rottmann, Erik.
   BV4810.P575 2004
   242'.2—dc22

                        2004006700

1	2	3	4	5	6	7	8	9	10
15	14	13	12	11	10	09	08	07	06

Preface

Here is the second volume in a series that revisits *Portals of Prayer*, this time focusing on the decade of the 1950s. I have treaded more lightly here than I did in the first effort, in most cases allowing each author to make his original point with only minor revisions in vocabulary. A few devotions have undergone more drastic revision, mainly for the sake of making sure the Gospel is clearly proclaimed in each case. As before, citations have been added for quoted verses that do not appear in the assigned readings. Unlike before, all verse quotations have been updated to the English Standard Version of the Bible.

I suggest the following usage of this book:

• As taught in the Small Catechism, begin your devotion with the sign of the cross and the invocation, the Creed and the Lord's Prayer.

• Ask God to open your eyes that you may see wonderful things in His Word (Psalm 119:18).

• Using the printed devotion as a doorway to God's Word, read and reread the assigned Bible passages as many times during the day as you are able.

I sincerely thank my wonderful assistant Rachel Riordan for her dedication in helping me with this task. Her careful attention to detail has lightened my load considerably and I hope she will be able to tolerate future projects with me. I offer this volume to my beloved brothers in the Sedalia Circuit of the Missouri District LCMS, as a token of my appreciation and affection for each of them.

The LORD be with you!

Pr. Erik Rottmann
Reformation Day

De Colores, Carol

We hope you enjoy reading this and you also enjoy Lutheran Cursillo 149.

May our Lord be with you.

In Christ's love,
Don + Joni Dunn

Special Days

The Sinless Made Sin

For our sake He made Him to be sin who knew no sin, so that in Him we might become the righteousness of God. 2 Corinthians 5:21

Sin has estranged us from God. And the wages and penalty of sin is death—until Jesus was made to be sin for us. On Him was laid the iniquity of us all. He was penalized for the wrongs we have done. Since then no one need remain estranged and live in hiding from God, in a doomed state, and be lost.

By making Jesus to be sin for us, all blame is taken from our shoulders. This makes us righteous before God by substitution. To us is credited the perfect holiness of Jesus. He fulfilled the Law for us. God sees us through Jesus, and we are washed and cleansed and made acceptable children of His household of grace.

This deliverance and salvation is ours by faith. Beneath the cross of Jesus we find healing and life eternal. God reconciled and redeemed the whole race of men through Calvary's sacrifice, but only those enjoy this eternal peace who stand by faith under the cross and look up to the pierced Savior.

Nothing is of greater importance than this truth that the sinless was made sin for us, for none of us can save his soul by the accomplishments of his hands. Only Jesus could do this, because in Him was no sin, and He was no sin, and He is God made flesh. Now we can sleep in peace each night and face the judgment and eternity without fear.

Thank You, Father, that You made Your Son to be sin for me, that I may be Your righteousness. Amen.

A Human Question and a Divine Answer

Then Peter said in reply, "See, we have left everything and followed You. What then will we have?" Matthew 19:27

Peter asked a question that many a person has asked about some project in which he has been requested to take a part: "What is in it for me?" Many a Christian has been inclined to ask: "What am I going to get out of following Jesus?"

Today, Ash Wednesday, the beginning of the holy season of Lent, we are reminded of how our Lord was willing to suffer for our redemption. We recall how He said His followers would have to suffer much for His cause. He told the disciples they would be delivered to the councils, scourged in the synagogues, brought before kings and governors, and persecuted for His and the Gospel's sake.

How wonderfully our Savior answered Peter by telling him and us that for any earthly losses a Christian profession may bring, there will be divine, heavenly compensation. He mentions that whosoever has forsaken earthly things, even relatives, for His sake, shall not lose out but be a hundred times blessed—with eternal life.

This Lenten season reminds us that any seeming sacrifice we make in faith for our Lord is insignificant compared to the loss He suffered for our sake. And in Him, we gain every good and eternal gift from God!

Thank You, Jesus, for having suffered all things for me. Keep me mindful and thankful of Your great gifts during this Lenten season and always. Amen.

The Upper Room

"And he will show you a large upper room furnished; prepare it there." Luke 22:12

On the night Jesus was betrayed, He gathered His disciples in the Upper Room. Here He instituted the Lord's Supper. The Passover meal preceded the giving of the Sacrament. Why? Because on the morrow He was to be the real Passover Lamb of God, offered up for the sins of the whole world. Out of this Passover meal, the Old Covenant, would come the New Testament, the Covenant of Grace, in and through which Christ gives His body and blood.

Having finished the Passover meal, Jesus took the bread and the cup, saying, "Take, eat; this is My body" (Matthew 26:26). "Drink of it, all of you, for this is My blood" (Matthew 26:27–28). He is giving Himself that you and I might have remission of sin. At the Lord's Table our souls find peace. Yet we go so seldom to have this forgiveness sealed and assured to us!

Jesus urges us to show forth His death until He comes. Every time, then, the church administers the Lord's Supper, it confesses that Jesus is coming again. Each Communion invites us to make ready for His return. So today, on this Holy Thursday, we shall ascend to the Upper Room to receive this blessed Sacrament and thereby strengthen our faith in the forgiveness of all our sins and obtain the blessed assurance that we are at peace with God.

Friend of sinners, make our hearts ever ready to receive Your Supper worthily. Amen.

White as Snow

And He said to him, "Truly, I say to you, today you will be with Me in Paradise." Luke 23:43

These glorious words were spoken by our crucified Savior to one of the malefactors. This criminal admitted that he deserved to be crucified. He rebuked his impenitent partner, the other malefactor: "Do you not fear God, since you are under the same sentence of condemnation? And we indeed justly, for we are receiving the due reward of our deeds" (Luke 23:40–41).

If we examine ourselves under the eye of God as to our past, we find that our conscience will convict us of many sins of thought, word, and deed. "If we say we have no sin, we deceive ourselves, and the truth is not in us" (1 John 1:8).

However, this penitent sinner by the grace of God had a change of heart. He heard the rulers under the cross scoff: "He saved others; let Him save Himself if He is the Christ of God, His Chosen One" (Luke 23:35). "Let Him come down now from the cross, and we will believe in Him. . . . For He said, 'I am the Son of God'" (Matthew 27:42–43). He heard the prayer of Jesus for His tormentors: "Father, forgive them, for they know not what they do" (Luke 23:34). The Holy Spirit gave this sinner faith, enabling him to say, "Jesus, remember me when You come into Your kingdom" (Luke 23:42).

To this penitent sinner—and to all sinners—Jesus spoke full pardon when He said, "Truly, I say to you, today you will be with Me in Paradise."

Lord Jesus, think on me
That, when the flood is past,
I may th' eternal brightness see
And share your joy at last. Amen. (LW 231:4)

Dead and Buried

For You will not abandon my soul to Sheol, or let Your holy one see corruption. Psalm 16:10

On His last journey to Jerusalem Jesus told His disciples: "Everything that is written about the Son of Man by the prophets will be accomplished. For He will be delivered over to the Gentiles and will be mocked and shamefully treated and spit upon" (Luke 18:31–32). "Christ died for our sins in accordance with the Scriptures" (1 Corinthians 15:3).

Helpless and hopeless women such as Mary, the mother of Jesus, and others with John, stood under that cross on which the Prince of glory died. God in His providence, however, saw to it that His beloved Son received an honorable burial. Joseph of Arimathea, who had been a secret disciple of Jesus, went in boldly to Pilate and asked for the body of Jesus. When Pilate knew from the centurion that Jesus had actually died, he gave the body to Joseph. Joseph and Nicodemus, wealthy members of the Sanhedrin, brought fine linen and a hundred-pound mixture of myrrh and aloes, reverently took the body of Jesus from the cross, tenderly wrapped it in the linen, and laid it in Joseph's new sepulcher that had been hewn out of a rock, "where no one had ever yet been laid" (Luke 23:53). Then they rolled a great stone to the door of the sepulcher and departed.

There our Savior rested until the third day, without seeing corruption. We have the glorious assurance, "Since we believe that Jesus died and rose again, even so, through Jesus, God will bring with Him those who have fallen asleep" (1 Thessalonians 4:14).

O Jesus blest,
My help and rest,
My tears flow to entreat you:
Make me love you to the last,
Till in heav'n I greet you. Amen. (LW 122:7)

The Easter Sunrise

And very early on the first day of the week, when the sun had risen, they went to the tomb. Mark 16:2

The rising sun of Easter revealed Jesus risen from the dead. The tomb was empty, and before long Mary Magdalene, Johanna, Salome, and other women saw the living Jesus. That same evening, the disciples, hidden behind closed doors, saw Jesus again, who identified Himself by His pierced hands and feet.

The risen sun of Easter dispels the gloomy shadows of sin and death. The guilt of transgressing against the will of God hangs over us and fills the soul with fear of the judgment to come. The Lord promises peace and forgiveness. God is reconciled through His cross. Christ's resurrection proclaims to sinful man that He has defeated the powers of hell and set us free. Therefore, death holds no terror for us believers, who pass through its shadows to live in God's presence forever. "If a man dies, shall he live again?" (Job 14:14). The risen Jesus says, "Because I live, you also will live" (John 14:19).

Jesus rose at the rising of the sun. This brightens our day, makes life more cheerful, and makes death a homecoming to be forever with the Lord.

So long as I remain in the pilgrimage of this life, O Lord, let me never forget the resurrection homecoming You have promised me. Amen.

Easter Sunday

We Are Glad He Ascended

Therefore it says, "When He ascended on high He led a host of captives, and He gave gifts to men." Ephesians 4:8

Homecomings are, as a rule, happy events. Jesus' homecoming to heaven was no exception. His ascension marked His return to the glory He left some 33 years before when He became our Brother. Furthermore, it represented the conquering climax in His long struggle with Satan and his evil angels. Thereby, "He led a host of captives."

We rejoice with Jesus on this important day of His ascension. As we think of His holiness and the beauty of His being, we know that heaven is His rightful place of residence. We are glad He ascended, even as we rejoice over the good fortune of anyone who is dear to us.

But we are glad also for ourselves. Before ascending, Jesus promised His people here on the earth that He would be with them even until the end of time. He declared further: "If I go and prepare a place for you, I will come again and will take you to Myself" (John 14:3).

A third reason for rejoicing today is found in the words "and He gave gifts to men." A direct result of Christ's ascension was the imparting of gifts for the building up of the church. The apostle Paul lists these gifts in a later verse: "He gave [gifts to] the apostles, the prophets, the evangelists, the pastors and teachers, to equip the saints for the work of ministry" (Ephesians 4:11–12).

Our pastors are God's gifts to the church. They are indeed frail human beings, but the message they proclaim is not frail. It is "the power of God for salvation to everyone who believes" (Romans 1:16).

We thank You, Lord, for every faithful pastor You have given Your church. Amen.

Ascension Day

Pentecost

Therefore I want you to understand that no one speaking in the Spirit of God ever says "Jesus is accursed!" and no one can say "Jesus is Lord" except in the Holy Spirit. 1 Corinthians 12:3

Today is the Festival of the Holy Spirit, the third person of the Holy Trinity.

Was it really necessary for Him to come for the purpose for which He did? "God so loved the world, that He gave His only Son" (John 3:16). Jesus, through His perfect obedience and His sacrificial death on the cross, completely atoned for the world's guilt. Is not the warmth of this love so powerful that it should thaw cold human hearts and awaken in them faith and love?

The Word of God speaks of man as "dead in the trespasses and sins" (Ephesians 2:1). Therefore, "the natural person does not accept the things of the Spirit of God, for they are folly to him, and he is not able to understand them because they are spiritually discerned" (1 Corinthians 2:14). Our catechism echoes this truth: "I believe that I cannot by my own reason or strength believe in Jesus Christ, my Lord, or come to Him."

Without the activity of the Holy Spirit there would not be a kingdom of grace. Not a single person would benefit by the atonement. The story of Bethlehem and Calvary would be an impenetrable mystery to all alike.

We today thank God for saving us by sending us His Spirit. He has gone all the way to assure to us forgiveness and life in its fullness.

Come, Holy Spirit, from above
With Thy celestial fire;
Come and with flames of zeal and love
Our hearts and tongues inspire. Amen. (TLH 232:4)

The Blessing of the Lord

The LORD bless you and keep you; the LORD make His face to shine upon you and be gracious to you; the LORD lift up His countenance upon you and give you peace. Numbers 6:24–26

Today is Trinity Sunday, the day the church reflects on the great mystery of the Holy Trinity. One of the earliest Bible passages teaching this doctrine is this benediction, which God gave to Aaron.

For more than three thousand years the children of God have heard these words in their church services. In the Old Testament the priest spoke this benediction over the congregation. To this day these are the last words spoken by the pastor in many Christian services.

In commanding the use of this benediction by the priests, the Lord said: "So shall they put My name upon the people of Israel; and I will bless them" (Numbers 6:27). God promised that when the priest spoke this blessing over the children of Israel, He Himself would guarantee its fulfillment. "I will bless them," He said.

When we hear these words spoken over us at the close of our worship and leave our church, we should take from them the certainty that God the Father will go with us to keep us and to give us all we truly need for our life on this earth; that God the Son will go with us to keep us in the favor and the grace of God; and that God the Holy Spirit will go with us to give peace to our hearts by the daily assurance that our sins have been taken away by the grace of God and by the work of the Lord Jesus Christ. The doctrine of the Trinity is hard to understand but wonderful to believe.

Lord, let Your blessing rest upon us and ours always. Amen.

Our Daily Load

Blessed be the Lord, who daily bears us up; God is our salvation.
Psalm 68:19

Not a day without a blessing: 365 days, 365 good things. Is that the record in our ledger? Even if yesterday brought only one good thing—which hardly seems possible—is not one blessing deserving of thanksgiving? Who among us thinks we have received only one blessing a day? Must we not say with David that He daily loads us with things good for us?

We think of the Christian man who tells us that having read the message brought to St. Paul in his day of seemingly unanswered prayer, "My grace is sufficient for you" (2 Corinthians 12:9), he burst into laughter, saying, "I should think it is, Lord." It is as if the Lord should say to a worrying little fish: "Drink away, little fish, there is an ocean of water"; or to a troubled little mouse: "Eat on, little mouse, here is a granary of corn"; to anxious man: "Breathe away, O man, here are My heavens of fresh air." He daily loads us with good things.

We are grateful for daily food; God satisfies us with the bread of life and eternal waters. We thank God for help in time of danger; He delivers our souls from destruction. We praise God for health; He bestows eternal life. We are happy because of peace; He offers us His friendship. What a load of blessings! Yes, "His mercies still endure, Ever faithful, ever sure" (*TLH* 570:1).

Lord, grant that every day I will bless You. Amen.

Daily Devotions

Power with God

*For does not my house stand so with God? For He has made
with me an everlasting covenant, ordered in all things and
secure. For will He not cause to prosper all my help and my
desire? 2 Samuel 23:5*

At the end of his career King David is penitently aware
that he has not measured up to his responsibilities. His record
of outstanding achievements is stained with sins that have
deeply offended God and tragically limited his influence as a
father and as a ruler.

But there is the light of confidence in his fading eyes.
Forgiveness, peace, and life are his because of an everlasting
agreement God made with him. Nothing in it was left to
chance. Every detail was carefully planned. The heart of it from
which all promised blessings flow is the coming of one who is
both God's Son and David's descendant. He is to achieve for us
a full salvation from sins, a full salvation of righteousness and
its eternal joys.

As we today cross the border of one year into the unchart-
ed paths of another, our eyes are lifted to Him who has made a
contract with us, one that rests upon the complete atonement
made for us by our Savior. It guarantees to us forgiveness,
peace, and the power adequate for every task and every experience that lies ahead.

*Guide me, O Thou great Jehovah,
Pilgrim through this barren land.
I am weak, but Thou art mighty;
Hold me with Thy pow'rful hand. Amen. (TLH 54:1)*

His Title Is Christ

Simon Peter replied, "You are the Christ, the Son of the living God." Matthew 16:16

At the angel's command, Mary and Joseph gave our Lord the personal name "Jesus." Peter and his fellow disciples later used the title "Christ" when answering His question, "Who do you say that I am?" (Matthew 16:15). "Christ" is Greek for the Hebrew "Messiah" or "Anointed One"—the One who is the main theme of Old Testament scripture, the One in whom the great anointed offices of the Old Covenant—prophet, priest, and king—would be fused, the One who was anointed with the Holy Ghost and with power.

Undoubtedly because of the wrong ideas people had about the Messiah, Jesus seldom referred to Himself with that title. But when the high priest demanded, "Are you the Christ?" (Mark 14:61), He confessed before the whole Sanhedrin, "I am" (Mark 14:62). For this claim He was nailed to the cross.

It was not as though men had failed to recognize Him as the Christ. Bethlehem angels announced the birth of the Christ. Wise Men searched for the Christ. Simeon rejoiced to hold the Christ. John the Baptist pointed to Him as the Christ. To all these Jesus would say what He said to Peter, "Blessed are you, Simon Bar-Jonah! For flesh and blood has not revealed this to you, but My Father who is in heaven" (Matthew 16:17).

May the heavenly Father fill our hearts with His Holy Spirit that we may rightly behold Jesus the Christ—our Prophet, our Priest, and our King.

O Lord Christ, rule our hearts with Your perfect Word and Your saving grace. Amen.

Never Against Us

What then shall we say to these things? If God is for us, who can be against us? Romans 8:31

God for us! Three little words, yet big with power to brace our heavy hearts. For with God as our ally in life and companion in death there is no problem, power, or pain that shall destroy us because all things have already been won for us by Christ. God and I are an unbeatable majority against the persistent and unnumbered legions of life's miseries and grief.

God for us! Life is worth living and death is safe dying. God is for me, and I can laugh at the coffin and the grave. God is for me, and I need never crucify myself between those two thieves of happiness—regret and worry. How can I resurrect the ghost of yesterday's guilt when it lies chained forever in the empty sepulcher of my living Lord? How can I fear tomorrow when the Shepherd who laid down His life for me is preparing my pasture before me and pursuing me with His goodness and mercy?

God for us! I can lay sorrow to rest. For the only real tragedy that men can experience is to be coffined without the Lord. With God for me, I need never endure that unendurable fate. With God for me, the suffering of this present pain is always outweighed by the glory to be revealed in me. That is why I can face this New Year just begun without fear and misgivings. God is for me!

Lord Jesus, help us to be permanently happy in the knowledge that You are our Friend in life and in death. Amen.

My God

O God, You are my God; earnestly I seek You; my soul thirsts for You; my flesh faints for You, as in a dry and weary land where there is no water. Psalm 63:1

Moses groaned under "the burden of all this people" (Numbers 11:11). Paul was oppressed with the "anxiety for all the churches" (2 Corinthians 11:28). These responsibilities vanish into insignificance, however, when compared with those resting upon the heart of God. He upholds this vast, unmeasured universe with the word of His power. He satisfies the desire of every living thing. Daily the prayers of millions rise up to Him as they cast their care upon Him.

This is not mere wishful thinking, born out of an overpowering sense of weakness and helplessness. At the very heart of our life stands the cross of God's only-begotten Son. We hear the ever-faithful God say: "Fear not, for I have redeemed you; I have called you by name, you are mine" (Isaiah 43:1).

From this the inspired apostle draws the conclusion: "He who did not spare His own Son but gave Him up for us all, how will He not also with Him graciously give us all things?" (Romans 8:32).

Therefore, I seek Him early. As each new day dawns upon me, I lift my eyes to Him who is mine in a deeper and larger sense than is possible in any human relationship. As a new year begins to unfold before my eyes, I face it with my eyes confidently fixed upon Him who has taught me to say:

Lord, You are my shepherd; in You I want for nothing. Amen.

The Sufficiency of God's Grace

But He said to me, "My grace is sufficient for you, for My power is made perfect in weakness." Therefore I will boast all the more gladly of my weaknesses, so that the power of Christ may rest upon me. 2 Corinthians 12:9

The grace of God includes all the goodness of our heavenly Father, showering upon us blessings unmerited and unnumbered.

God's grace is sufficient to save us. "For by grace you have been saved through faith" (Ephesians 2:8). Salvation is altogether of God's grace. It is "not a result of works, so that no one may boast" (Ephesians 2:9).

God's grace is sufficient to enable us to live the Christian life for which we have been "created in Christ Jesus" (Ephesians 2:10). "And God is able to provide you with every blessing in abundance, so that having all contentment in all things at all times, you may abound in every good work" (2 Corinthians 9:8).

God's grace is sufficient to prosper us in our daily calling. "But by the grace of God I am what I am, and His grace toward me was not in vain" (1 Corinthians 15:10).

God's grace is sufficient in sorrow and suffering. We have not been promised exemption from sorrow and suffering, but we have been promised the sustaining power of God's grace. Paul's "thorn . . . in the flesh" (2 Corinthians 12:7) was not removed, but he was assured: "My grace is sufficient for you."

O God, how matchless is Your grace to save and keep us! Increase our faith, we beseech You, that our lives may be rich with the praise of the glory of Your grace. For Jesus' sake. Amen.

Eyes That See

And the Word became flesh and dwelt among us, and we have seen His glory, glory as of the only Son from the Father, full of grace and truth. John 1:14

This is the Festival of Epiphany. It centers the attention of Christendom upon one of the most fascinating events in human history.

Wise Men, somewhere in the Orient, scan the evening sky and with the trained eyes of science discover an unusual star. But with the eyes of faith they recognize in it the message from God that the long-promised Messiah has come.

A long journey through dreary desert and populous areas leads them to the crib of Jesus. Physical eyes behold a child in humble surroundings, dependent upon the loving care of His mother. The God-given sight of faith sees in Him the only-begotten of the Father, full of grace and truth, and pays deep homage to Him.

Many today stress the eyes of science at the expense of faith. They measure Jesus the same way they measure things and people otherwise coming under their observation. As a result they reduce the immeasurable One to another human being, better and greater than others, but still only a human being.

The eyes of faith behold in Jesus the answer to the cry of the sin-burdened and helpless heart—God's own Son, who was made flesh in order that He, as our Substitute, might fulfill the Law, which we have broken, and pay the full penalty for our sins on the cross.

We worship you; we bless you;
To you alone we sing;
We praise you and confess you,
Our holy lord and king. Amen. (LW 282:1)

The Morning Star

"I, Jesus, have sent My angel to testify to you about these things for the churches. I am the root and the descendant of David, the bright morning star." Revelation 22:16

One of the brightest lights in the heavens is the morning star. Its name is derived from its function, namely, the ushering in of a new day. It is the last star shining as the new day begins.

On His throne of glory, our blessed Savior calls to our world of today and tells it that He is the Morning Star. He really and truly brought a new day to our earth. Our world lay in deepest darkness. Men lived in the dense darkness of unbelief, sin, and evil. They were all on the way to destruction. Then came Jesus as the only Savior the world ever had. He took upon Himself all the sins of all men, paid the price for their redemption, and gave them His own perfection as a gift.

Living in the new day always helps us to remember that our Morning Star in heaven will sometime usher in for us the perfect day of heaven. "I will come again and will take you to Myself" (John 14:3). This He promised, and we know He will keep the promise. Like David of old, we say, "In Your presence there is fullness of joy; at Your right hand are pleasures forevermore" (Psalm 16:11). What a glorious Epiphany indeed!

O Morning Star, shine the light of Your grace brightly upon us. Amen.

Our Friend

And I came to the exiles at Tel-abib, who were dwelling by the Chebar canal, and I sat where they were dwelling. And I sat there overwhelmed among them seven days. Ezekiel 3:15

Ezekiel was instructed by God to be His voice to a rebellious Israel. Being a patriot as well as a prophet, he was deeply distressed over his mission. He speaks of himself as being "in bitterness in the heat of my spirit" (Ezekiel 3:14). At the command of God he now went to the exiles at Tel-abib. For seven days he sat where they sat, in order to see, to hear, to understand.

Jesus, sent by His Father into a sinful world, could also say of Himself, "I sat where they were dwelling." At the beginning of His early career He was a Child among children and later a young Man among young people. In the days of His public ministry He was a Guest at a wedding. He was the Friend of the sick and the handicapped. He entered the house of mourning. He discussed divine truth with the Samaritan woman as well as with the learned Nicodemus. He spent hours of relaxation and refreshment in the highly regarded home of Mary, Martha, and Lazarus. Over the protest of shocked Pharisees, He entered the dwelling of a despised publican.

He sat where they sat. No wonder the people heard Him gladly. He understood. He sympathized. He was able to meet their deepest needs.

Jesus still is accessible to all, regardless of age, position, or race. He knows what is in each of us. Extending the arms of mercy, He invites: "Come to Me, all who labor and are heavy laden, and I will give you rest" (Matthew 11:28).

Thank You, Lord, for sitting where I sit and walking where I walk. Amen.

Children of Light

You are all children of light. 1 Thessalonians 5:5

The Christian Church is the community gathered around the one true Light, which is Jesus Christ the Lord. Members of the church reflect the brightness of Christ as the moon reflects the sunlight. Jesus even calls Christians "sons of light" (Luke 16:8).

As the children of light, Christians naturally reflect their relationship to Jesus, just as the moon reflects the light of the sun. There is nothing artificial or strained about this reflection. When people are filled with the forgiveness of Christ's love, the confidence of His presence, and the hope of His return, they radiate the joy and beauty of His life.

However, Paul reminds us that as sons of light we walk in a world of darkness. Cut off from Him who is the Light, we become shadows in the darkness of this world of death. We cannot hope to give light for ourselves or by ourselves. Without Him we would not have a flicker more of hope than the rest of the world.

So long as we are in communion with the Light, we reflect light in the darkness. It is essential, therefore, that we maintain our communion with Him through Word and Sacraments, from which we take the light He offers. When we have Him, we know that it is the God who commanded the light to shine out of darkness who now shines in our hearts to give this light of the knowledge of the glory of God in the face of Christ (2 Corinthians 4:6). When we have Him, we know we have the light that the darkness of the world could not put out.

Lord Jesus, keep our hearts aglow with the brightness of Your light. Amen.

What Is Man?

I praise You, for I am fearfully and wonderfully made. Wonderful are Your works; my soul knows it very well. Psalm 139:14

Christmas and Epiphany place a tremendous importance upon man in the scheme of the universe. God's beloved Son becomes man for our sake. Angels pour out of heaven in uncounted numbers to bring the news to frightened shepherds. The starry firmament aids in directing men from the East to His crib.

What is the answer? The psalmist says, "I am fearfully and wonderfully made." When God created man, He formed him out of the dust of the ground and thus in material and structure related him to the animal world. But He also breathed into him His own image and thus related him to Himself.

One evening two astronomers were studying the sky through a telescope. One remarked, "Compared with all this, man is but an insignificant speck." "Yes," the other replied, "but man is still the astronomer." Jesus, however, saw something vastly greater in man than the mind that has given to us "the marvels of modern science." He said: "For what does it profit a man to gain the whole world and forfeit his life?" (Mark 8:36).

He saw that soul lost in sin, doomed to eternal punishment in hell. Infinite love and mercy, therefore, moved Him to become one of us. He bore our guilt. He carried our sorrows. We are now children of God through faith in Him. Therefore, we can confess in faith, "I am fearfully and wonderfully made."

For all the blessings of body and soul I thank You, Lord. Help me to live to Your glory. Amen.

January

Jesus Is Baptized

And when Jesus was baptized, immediately He went up from the water, and behold, the heavens were opened to Him, and He saw the Spirit of God descending like a dove and coming to rest on Him; and behold, a voice from heaven said, "This is My beloved Son, with whom I am well pleased." Matthew 3:16–17

In *Old Yeller* a young man named Travis Coates was left to take care of his father's farm when the father left for the cattle markets. They shook hands and parted. Travis later commented that it was the first time he had ever shaken hands like a man. He felt solemn and important in a way he had never felt before. Best of all, the confidence thus expressed by the father gave Travis the security that he could handle all that needed to be done.

One senses this same sort of mutual confidence at the Baptism of our Lord Jesus. The Father had committed to His Son the task of salvation, which no creature could accomplish. The Son faced the temptations and dangers of His mission alone and untried. At His Baptism He gives evidence to the Father and to the world that He desires "to fulfill all righteousness" (Matthew 3:15). Knowing the cost, He here consecrates Himself to all the Father had sent Him to do. The Father, too, expressed His confidence: "This is My beloved Son, with whom I am well pleased."

The moment was important to both. The Baptism was assurance to the Father that the Son was fulfilling the eternal decrees of His love. The Son was comforted by the confidence of the Father. The moment is likewise important to us, who receive the benefits of the determination of Father and Son to fulfill all righteousness for us. Here at His Baptism, the Son of God gathers up all of our sin upon Himself, that by His death we might become the righteousness of God.

Lord Jesus, may Your Baptism be to us the assurance that You have fulfilled all righteousness for us. Amen.

Jesus Obeys

And He went down with them and came to Nazareth and was submissive to them. And His mother treasured up all these things in her heart. Luke 2:51

Mary and Joseph were agents of God's providential care for His Son. They reared Him in the traditions and training of a God-fearing Jewish household. They guided and aided Him in His development. They attended His every want. They were the vessels of the Father's love for His Son. Jesus returned their love with His love and obedience. Through them He returned His love to the Father.

Jesus' obedience in little things—those things His mother and Joseph called for—was a prelude to greater things that demanded His obedience in the wilderness of temptation, in the trials of persecution, at Gethsemane, and at Golgotha. Yet even on the cross He did not forget His mother Mary, to whom He had given the first signs of His perfect obedience. To her He gave a last tribute of His esteem as He arranged for His disciple John to attend her. His perfect obedience continued from Nazareth to Calvary and ended with the cry, "It is finished" (John 19:30).

Jesus rendered this perfect obedience in all things for us who have been disobedient even in little things. He became man—one of us—and was obedient before His Father. His simple, unwavering obedience does more than chart the course for our own obedience to God. His obedience unto death atones for our disobedience, that we might receive from Him the crown of life.

Lord Jesus, grant that we find daily joy in returning our love to You in faithful obedience. Amen.

A God's-Eye View

So she called the name of the LORD who spoke to her, "You are a God of seeing," for she said, "Truly here I have seen Him who looks after me." Genesis 16:13

Hagar was fleeing from Sarah. She who was to be the ancestress of a mighty people was leaving the Land of Promise for the idolatry of Egypt.

The angel of the Lord appeared to her and called for her return. Deeply impressed and grateful, Hagar named the place, "You, God, see me." God saw her in His justice. He saw her in His love that would save her from the tragedy into which she was fleeing with an unborn child.

"You, God, see me." There is great comfort power in this truth. It places a restraining hand upon us when we would leave the path of promise for the path of curse. It sustains us when the battle of life seems to be going against us. It gives us courage, the same courage that enabled Luther to write to his friend Phillip Melanchthon in the dark days of the Reformation: "I am against those worrying cares which are taking the heart out of you. Why make God a liar in not believing His wonderful promises, when He commands us to be of good cheer and to cast all our care upon Him, for He will sustain us? Do you think He throws such words to the winds? What more can the devil do than slay us? Christ has died for sin once for all, but for righteousness He will not die, but live and reign. Why, then, worry, seeing He is at the helm? He who has been our Father will also be the Father of our children."

Faint not nor fear, his arms are near;
He changes not who holds you dear. Amen. (LW 299:4)

Acceptable Worship

*Let the words of my mouth and the meditation of my heart be
acceptable in Your sight, O LORD, my rock and my redeemer.
Psalm 19:14*

This is the prayer of one who has stood reverently in the
temple of nature, where everything articulates glory. The heavens and the firmament in universal language speak the praises
of their Creator.

He notes that God has also established a character and a
course for man. He reveals them in a Law that is perfect. Man,
loving God with all his heart and his neighbor as himself, would
have been the brightest star in a universe of divine glory.

But man sinned. He chose his own path and thus defeated the destiny God had in view for him. The psalmist includes
himself and prays for cleansing from Him whom he calls his
Strength and his Redeemer.

We are painfully aware how little we have reflected the
glory of God in what we have thought, spoken, and done. There
were some bright spots in whatever we did out of faith, according to the Ten Commandments, for the glory of God and the
welfare of our fellow man. But there still was much, very much,
for which we ask God's forgiveness for Jesus' sake.

As our thoughts turn toward the house of God and His
worship in which we shall soon participate again, we pray that
God may take from our hearts thoughts and attitudes that
interfere. We pray that the words spoken and sung by us may be
the voice of a believing and loving heart.

*Unseal our lips to sing Thy praise,
Our souls to Thee in worship raise,
Make strong our faith, increase our light
That we may know Thy name aright. Amen. (TLH 3:2)*

Jesus Is Tempted

Then Jesus was led up by the Spirit into the wilderness to be tempted by the devil. Matthew 4:1

Our Lord's temptations were inevitable. The fallen angel who had won victory over the first Adam became a pretender to the throne of man's heart. To maintain his position of dominance it was necessary for the tempter to destroy the Prince of Peace sent by the Father to reclaim the loyalty and love of men. The victories of Christ over the devil maintained the innocence of the second Adam needed for victory over death.

What Christ overcame we, too, can overcome. By His victories, He secured benefits for us, His disciples. Each attempt of the tempter to make Him fall marks an assault on His humanity, launched in the hope that the man Jesus would fall into sin. Each of Jesus' victories is a victory for His humanity. Each victory of His humanity is a victory for our humanity, for He shared in our humanity (Hebrews 2:14).

Jesus now gives us His victories as the means to conquer our temptations. We walk in His footsteps, but we also walk in His power. The news of His death-and-resurrection victory over Satan is the help we need in time of temptation. Through Him we learn to know what temptation is. Through Him we have the powerful Word by which the tempter gets silenced and shunned. As Luther rightly wrote about the devil in his famous Reformation hymn, "one little word can fell him (*LW* 298:3)." In Jesus we have assurance that the devil has no hold on us and that "the ruler of this world is judged" (John 16:11). With this assurance, all fear of the tempter gives way to confidence in Christ, who already won all things for us.

Lord Jesus, enable us to overcome temptations. Amen.

His Name Is Our Name

When he had found him, he brought him to Antioch. For a whole year they met with the church and taught a great many people. And in Antioch the disciples were first called Christians.
Acts 11:26

The persecution that followed the stoning of Stephen scattered most of the believers from Jerusalem, the center of the mother church. Wherever they went, they shared the Gospel, mostly with Jews.

Outwardly the new disciples looked no different from their friends and relatives. But inwardly and spiritually they were vastly different because they believed in Christ and patterned their lives after His. "And in Antioch the disciples were first called Christians." The name is a happy choice, for the disciples of Christ are no mere followers. Paul would say they are wedded to Christ by faith. As a bridegroom gives his bride his name, so Christ, the heavenly Bridegroom, gives His bride, the Church, His name.

Furthermore, the disciples are intimately bound to Christ through Holy Baptism. Paul says that in Baptism we "put on Christ" (Galatians 3:27). We are "christened," we say. Paul would say, "Christ in you" (Colossians 1:27) or "Christ is formed in you" (Galatians 4:19).

"Christian" symbolizes more, therefore, than local church membership. It signals that the Father in heaven has numbered us among His sons and daughters, that He has filled us with the righteousness of His Son, and even that He has declared us to be "little Christs." That is what we each are, made so by the miracle of God in Baptism.

Blessed Lord Christ, whose name is above every name, help us to keep Your name holy. Amen.

January

The Fruitful Branch

"Abide in Me, and I in you. As the branch cannot bear fruit by itself, unless it abides in the vine, neither can you, unless you abide in Me." John 15:4

All the vine possesses belongs to the branches. Jesus, to whom we owe our life, completely gives Himself for us and to us: "The glory that you have given Me I have given to them" (John 17:22); "Whoever believes in Me will also do the works that I do" (John 14:12). All His fullness and all His riches are for us, as believers.

All the branch possesses belongs to the vine. The branch does not exist for itself, but to bear fruit that can proclaim the excellence of the vine.

What a glorious image of the calling of the believer, of his complete consecration to the service of his Lord. Every power of his being, every moment of his life, every thought and feeling belongs to Jesus, that from Him and for Him he may bring forth fruit.

For this is the *purpose* of the union. The branches are for fruit. "Every branch of Mine that does not bear fruit He takes away" (John 15:2). As the believer enters into his calling as a branch, he sees that he has to forget himself and to live entirely for his fellow men. To love them, to seek them, and to save them, Jesus came; for this every branch on the Vine has to live as much as the Vine itself. It is for fruit, much fruit, that the Father has made us one with Jesus.

Lord Jesus, how great my need, but also how perfect my claim, to all Your fullness. As my Vine, bear me, nourish me, use me, and fill me to the full to make me bring forth fruit abundantly. Amen.

The Divine Word

"Do you not believe that I am in the Father and the Father is in Me? The words that I say to you I do not speak on My own authority, but the Father who dwells in Me does His works."
John 14:10

We employ words to express ourselves. We reveal ourselves, our personalities, our characters in our words. So does God. He revealed Himself in the Word, which began creation: "And God said" (Genesis 1:3). God expressed Himself, and an infinite universe revealed Him—His perfection, infinity, power, and majesty, His wisdom, providence, and goodness.

In the midst of all this beauty and perfect glory stood man, in whom God had expressed Himself best, for man was created in the image of God. But man dared to believe that the perfect expression of God was imperfect and incomplete; he wanted to be as God. His sin was to doubt God's expression; his dreadful curse ever since is that he cannot read God's expression in the creation.

Therefore, God spoke again in a new expression as Man to men. Jesus Christ is the very embodiment of this divine Word. He grew up among men and among their temptations and tragedies, speaking to them of the love of the Father in heaven, speaking what the Father wanted them to hear. And they crucified Jesus for what He said.

Yet in the crucifixion the Word made its fullest and best expression. Dying for and at the hands of guilty man, He arose. The Word could not be destroyed. This is God's Word for and to man. In Christ, the Word, there is life. And this Word is now ours eternally.

Father, increase our trust in Your Word, the Christ. Amen.

Ears to Hear

"He who has ears, let him hear." Matthew 13:9

In the parable of the sower, our Lord shows the varied reactions of people to the proclamation of God's Word. Note that He first of all describes three classes of hearers who receive no enduring blessing from the hearing of God's Word. This is tragic but true. Although the message of God's grace in Christ Jesus reaches them, they go through life into eternity without saving faith and hope.

Then Jesus mentions a fourth class of hearers. They receive the Word into their hearts and this living faith bears fruit.

Our Lord, as a good teacher, speaks plainly in this parable. He concludes with this striking statement: "He who has ears, let him hear." We must realize He is directing these words to us this day.

Our Creator has given us ears to hear. In our home God's Word sounds in our ears. In our church His saving truth will be preached for us.

What an important message God has for us in our Bible! He shows us that we are transgressors of His Law, deserving of His wrath and judgment. But God has more to tell us in His Word. He wants us to hear of His love and grace for us sinners, explaining that "God so loved the world, that He gave His only Son, that whoever believes in Him should not perish but have eternal life" (John 3:16).

We thank You, Lord Jesus, for alerting us to hear Your Word with faith. Amen.

The Blood That Cleanses

But if we walk in the light, as He is in the light, we have fellowship with one another, and the blood of Jesus His Son cleanses us from all sin. 1 John 1:7

Sin separates men from one another. An angry deed or dishonest act can destroy a friendship.

Sin separated men from God. "All we like sheep have gone astray; we have turned every one to *his own* way!" (Isaiah 53:6, emphasis added). When men go their own way, they go away from God because God's way is in the light and man's way is in darkness.

But God is faithful. He keeps His Word. He is not willing that any should perish in the dark night of his wandering away from God. He called us out of darkness into His marvelous light. We whose souls were black with sin are now purified.

How was this extraordinary change brought about? This was not a miracle performed by men. It was an act of divine mercy, an act that took place on Calvary.

There from the holy wounds of Jesus came forth the blood of God in the flesh. His blood is the price for our pardon. Christ's blood is also the source of our daily purifying. By His blood we are kept clean for righteous living.

There is a fountain filled with blood
Drawn from Immanuel's veins,
And sinners plunged beneath that flood
Lose all their guilty stains.

Dear dying Lamb, Thy precious blood
Shall never lose its power
Till all the ransomed Church of God
Be saved to sin no more. Amen. (TLH 157:1,3)

God's Love

But God shows His love for us in that while we were still sinners, Christ died for us. Romans 5:8

Many attempts have been made to define love. Some say love is an emotion, a feeling deep within us, something that rises from our heart. They are correct. Others say love is more than the appreciation of something beautiful, such as an interesting landscape, a delicate flower, a precious gem, or an artistic building. Often a good feeling rises in the heart when we see or experience kindness, understanding, gentleness, trustworthiness on the part of our fellow man. They are also correct in their use of the word love. In still another sense, love describes that personal attachment we have for our family or others dear to us.

But when the Bible speaks of God's love, it means something entirely different. God's love is not awakened by anything man does. It is there already. The love of God is an attitude God has toward man, a desire to save him. The unusual character of God's love is pointed out by Paul when he writes: "But God shows His love for us in that while we were still sinners, Christ died for us." Sinners we are, who deserve nothing but punishment for our wrong. But despite this, God loves us and executes a plan by which we may be saved, giving His Son into death for us. Loving the unloving and the undeserving is the essence of God's love.

O Lord, lead us to a deeper appreciation of the love You have showered upon us. Amen.

Whom God Forgives

Whoever conceals his transgressions will not prosper, but he who confesses and forsakes them will obtain mercy. Proverbs 28:13

Modern psychiatrists tell us that a sense of guilt crowded down into our innermost being makes for mental disturbances. David knew that long ago. He wrote: "For when I kept silent, my bones wasted away though my groaning all day long. For day and night Your hand was heavy upon me" (Psalm 32:3–4).

Some, however, resort to more subtle ways of covering their sins. They assure us that when you are in Rome, you must do as the Romans do. In other words, you are more or less obliged to accept the moral standards of the circle within which you move. Others streamline God's Law to suit their fancy and thus try to develop an easy conscience. Still others speak of sin in terms that tend to soften guilt or remove it entirely.

The result is the same. They shall not prosper before God, who judges all without exception according to His holy Law. They shall not prosper within. A conscience that has been duped may at any time awaken with disastrous results to what seems to be peace of mind.

Why try to cover our sins? The blood of Jesus Christ cleanses us from all sin. For His sake God says to those who frankly and penitently confess their sins and believe in Him as their personal Savior: "Come now, let us reason together, says the LORD: though your sins are like scarlet, they shall be as white as snow; though they are red like crimson, they shall become like wool" (Isaiah 1:18).

Plenteous grace with Thee is found, Grace to cover all my sins. Amen. (TLH 345:5)

Of Course We Are in Love

Do not love the world or the things in the world. If anyone loves the world, the love of the Father is not in him. 1 John 2:15

There are many things in life that woo our hearts and try to make us fall in love with them. There is that evil tug within us to love the wrong thing and hate the good. Our eyes fall in love with the possessions of others and we yearn for them. David lusted after Bathsheba and fell in love with a woman he had no right to marry. We can become so attached to the passing treasures of this world that we no longer possess our possessions, but are possessed by them. However, we gain nothing if we lose our soul's salvation.

We have fallen in love with our God and the treasures He offers us. God's Spirit has wooed and won our hearts, and we have been overwhelmed by the gifts He has given us to prove His love. The brightest jewel of His grace is His forgiveness. We know Him as a triumphant Lord who helps us overcome the devil and gives us strength to live as His dear children.

Let me be Thine forever,
Thou faithful God and Lord;
Let me forsake Thee never
Nor wander from Thy Word. Amen. (TLH 334:1)

Love and Truth Are Twins

I write to you, not because you do not know the truth, but because you know it, and because no lie is of the truth. 1 John 2:21

"Love . . . rejoices with the truth," says St. Paul in the great love chapter of the Bible, 1 Corinthians 13. That is natural because he who loves God must love the truth. He must love God's Son, Jesus Christ, who is the Truth (John 14:6). He must love God's Word, for His Word is truth. And he loves God by "doing the truth."

Love is intolerant of false teaching. It cannot gloss over a doctrine that denies that Jesus is the Son of God and Savior of sinners. It is a miserable form of charity that covers up a damning lie. To belittle the denial of any truth of the Bible is to belittle the truth itself. And those who love God treat His truth with a holy awe.

The only thing love has to hide or cover up is the sins of the person loved. But when love hides, it does not approve. It simply says: I know what God knows about me, and yet He says to me, "Your transgressions are forgiven." I will do the same for my fellow man.

Preserve me in the truth, O Lord, and enable me to speak the truth faithfully to others. Amen.

If Anyone Does Sin

My little children, I am writing these things to you so that you may not sin. But if anyone does sin, we have an advocate with the Father, Jesus Christ the righteous. He is the propitiation for our sins, and not for ours only but also for the sins of the whole world. 1 John 2:1–2

Among the many wonderful expressions in our Bible passage we have a strange statement, "if anyone does sin." God never did want man to sin. God still instructs us that we sin not. But if any man does sin? What then?

God clearly tells us, "the soul who sins shall die" (Ezekiel 18:4). Sin is terrible, for it is rebellion against God and justly deserves His condemning judgment.

How awful for us if God's judgment comes down on us. But there is a way of escape provided for us by God Himself. In Jesus Christ, the righteous Son of God, we have forgiveness of sins. He is the Peace Offering for our sins and for the sins of the whole world. The Bible brings us assurance that the blood of Christ, God's Son, cleanses us from all sins. Not only that, but if any man sin, the same Jesus represents us as our attorney at the bar of justice to win acquittal for us.

"If anyone does sin"—here is something we need to know and believe. How thankful we are that we have this gracious assurance! These truths of God's mercy and grace are written for us that we sin not.

O Lord that pardons iniquity and delights in mercy. Forgive us our sins for Jesus' sake. Amen.

Strength and Weakness

For the sake of Christ, then, I am content with weaknesses, insults, hardships, persecutions, and calamities. For when I am weak, then I am strong. 2 Corinthians 12:10

What is this? Here is a man who says that when he is weak, he is strong. Come now, Paul, let's be serious! Do you not know that might makes right and force forges fame?

Well, regardless of how *we* feel, Paul certainly staked his all on the experience of his conversion, through which—weakly falling to the ground—he was to rise strong in the Lord and become the greatest of the apostles.

We need to be reminded of the weakness of power. Power is weak because it underestimates unseen realities. When dictators (in politics, in the home, or in the church) have their way for very long, they assume they can always "lord it over" weaker folks. Tyrants believe that by making people afraid they can always control them. But then, one day, the people revolt, the children rebel, the church attempts reform. Brute power has failed.

God moves in when human power admits its bankruptcy. He selected an unimposing little nation in Old Testament times to convey His truth. Then God came Himself in the meek and loving Jesus to set at naught the wisdom of this world. Later, the church was at its best when, in its weakness, it trusted God—not politics or wealth—for its strength.

God, our Strength, fill us with Your Holy Spirit that we may face our daily tasks with confidence and honesty. Amen.

Two Lost Sons and a Forgiving Father

*"And he arose and came to his father. But while he was still a
long way off, his father saw him and felt compassion, and ran
and embraced him and kissed him. … But he was angry and
refused to go in. His father came out and entreated him." Luke
15:20, 28*

In this well-known story we have, first, Jesus' graphic
description of the desperate plight of the prodigal son, who
squandered everything he had in riotous living and who
learned by bitter experience that the way of the transgressor is
hard.

The Master's picture of the elder son, too, is keen and
revealing. This son stayed at home; but he had gone far from his
father's heart. He wasted the spiritual heritage that was his; he
was bitter, self-righteous, jealous, unforgiving. They were both
lost sons. The younger was lost in shame, the elder in sham.

The ugly behavior of the two lost sons all the more glorifies the goodness of the father. When he saw the younger son,
the crushed sinner, he ran to meet him and showered on
him the evidences of his loving heart. When he was confronted by the elder, the self-righteous son, the father assured him
that "all that is mine is yours" (Luke 15:31). What a gracious,
forgiving Father!

*How matchless is Your grace, O heavenly Father, to forgive us our
many sins for Jesus' sake! We promise You, with the help of Your Spirit,
more than ever to do Your will. Amen.*

A Safe Refuge

Each will be like a hiding place from the wind, a shelter from the storm, like streams of water in a dry place, like the shade of a great rock in a weary land. Isaiah 32:2

The setting is a dry and arid country in the Orient. The hot winds of the East make shelter and water all-important at all times. Nowhere are rivulets of water more appreciated than in parched areas. When the relentless sun burns down in desert regions, the shadows of a great rock is a welcome place of escape from the scorching heat.

Life also has its hot places, its times of desert thirst, its need of some great rock for shade. Such are the moments when we anxiously look about for help, for relief. Life is very liable to disturbing upsets. There are mysterious, inner hurricanes within when our conscience becomes alive and our mind is tempest-tossed. There come upon us not infrequently gales of temporal loss, of bereavement, affliction, physical pain. They make us conscious of how weak we are.

Such are the moments when we anxiously look about for help, for relief. All our needs are met in Christ. He is our hiding place from our sin-tossed conscience. To the penitent He says, "I have blotted out your transgressions like a cloud and your sins like mist; return to Me, for I have redeemed you" (Isaiah 44:22). Thus He meets the thirst of our souls for living water. And He is also the shadow of a great rock to us when we become weary of afflictions. He assures us that underneath are the everlasting arms to sustain us.

Jesus, Lover of my soul, let me to Your bosom fly. Amen.

Judgment and Forgiveness

Because He has fixed a day on which He will judge the world in righteousness by a man whom He has appointed; and of this He has given assurance to all by raising Him from the dead. Acts 17:31

God judges the world. Christ could tell a story that included the words, "Cast the worthless servant into the outer darkness" (Matthew 25:30). And yet in agony from the cross, He could utter the unmatched words, "Father, forgive them; for they know not what they do" (Luke 23:34).

The balancing of judgment and forgiveness is one of the most difficult things we are called upon to do as followers of Christ. Forgiveness without judgment is a weak thing that destroys moral fiber. But judgment without forgiveness destroys moral values. Strict justice can become unjust. And we have ample evidence today of how law and government can destroy people if not tempered with mercy.

Life and history are a revelation of the inevitable working out of moral principles. The Hebrews were God's chosen people, but this never meant they were excused from God's justice. He is no respecter of persons or nations. And Paul tells listeners in Athens that God "will judge the world in righteousness."

Now if this is true, where does forgiveness come in and what does it mean? God does not stop judging the world. But He now sees us wearing the cloak of Christ's righteousness. Christ meets the demands of moral perfection and thus makes up our deficits. God judges the world, yes; but He does it "by a Man whom He has appointed" to be our Savior.

Jesus, your blood and righteousness
My beauty are, my glorious dress! Amen. (LW 362:1)

Our Ever-Living Intercessor

Consequently, He is able to save to the uttermost those who draw
near to God through Him, since He always lives to make inter-
cession for them. Hebrews 7:25

The Christian faith did not begin with the coming of
Christ. The great thoughts of the New Testament have their
roots at the very gate of the Garden of Eden. The promise of the
woman's Seed who should crush the serpent's head grows
brighter through the centuries. It survived the invasion of foreign armies, subjugation to foreign kings, captivity in foreign
lands.

At the strategic moment in human history, the moment
appointed by God in His wisdom and love, Jesus came. He was
all that God had promised. The prophecies and the ceremonial
system converged in Him as their fulfillment. As the High
Priest, He obeyed. He suffered. He entered the holy of holies in
heaven with His blood. He now stands at the right hand of God
and there pleads for us.

He is, therefore, able to save to the uttermost all that come
to God by Him. There is no sin for which He has not paid the
full penalty. Memories of past transgressions may haunt us.
They may dog our steps into the stillness of the night. But "who
is to condemn? Christ Jesus is the one who died—more than
that, who has raised—who is at the right hand of God, who
indeed is interceding for us" (Romans 8:34).

O depth of love, to me revealing
The sea where my sins disappear!
In Christ my wounds find perfect healing,
There is no condemnation here;
For Jesus' blood through earth and skies
Forever "Mercy! Mercy!" cries. Amen. (LW 360:4)

The Disgraced Sinner

She said, "No one, Lord." And Jesus said, "Neither do I condemn You; go, and from now on sin no more." John 8:11

The case against this disgraced sinner was clear. She had been taken in the very act of adultery. The law of Moses covering her case was clear, too. "Now in the Law Moses commanded us to stone such women" (John 8:5), said the men who brought this unfortunate woman to Jesus.

After a tense and embarrassing silence that served to rebuke both the woman and her accusers, Jesus said, "Let him who is without sin among you be the first to throw a stone at her" (John 8:7). Of course no one dared to throw a stone. Then Jesus forgave her and filled her with hope to mend her shattered life. "Neither do I condemn you; go, and from now on sin no more."

The case against us is clear, too. "Surely there is not a righteous man on earth who does good and never sins" (Ecclesiastes 7:20). The Law also is clear. "For whoever keeps the whole law but fails in one point has become accountable for all of it" (James 2:10). "The soul who sins shall die" (Ezekiel 18:4). Is there forgiveness and hope also for us?

Thank God, there is! Jesus fulfilled the Law as our substitute and did it perfectly. He also took upon Himself our guilt and suffered our punishment by His death on the cross.

Our Father, we confess that our conduct has not always been that of obedient children. We knew what Your commandments expected of us; nevertheless we are guilty of transgressions. Our consolation is that You will forgive us for Jesus' sake. Amen.

The Charm of False Doctrine

O foolish Galatians! Who has bewitched you? It was before your eyes that Jesus Christ was publicly portrayed as crucified.
Galatians 3:1

Sometimes we hear educators speak eloquently about man's great quest for truth. As though everyone truly prized truth as the highest good! In real life we find a different reaction toward truth. It seems that many people find false assumptions and misleading philosophies quite fascinating. They seek not truth, but a lie (Romans 1:25).

This was Paul's tragic discovery among the Christians in the congregations of Galatia. He had preached the truth so clearly it almost seemed to them that Jesus Christ had been crucified for them before their own eyes. They had believed the Gospel and rejoiced in the truth of salvation. Then something occurred that changed them entirely. It almost seemed as though a spell had been cast over them. Paul asked, "O foolish Galatians! Who has bewitched you?" Through false teachers they were led to reject the grace of God and to trust for their salvation in their own keeping of the Ceremonial Law of the Old Testament. Paul had to say to all who followed this false teaching that they had fallen from grace.

Christians today are still exposed to many false doctrines and misleading philosophies. Such anti-Christian teachings frequently seem so reasonable and even filled with sweet sentiment. How important it is that we cling to God's truth revealed in the Bible and not be charmed into doubt and unbelief. Only in Christ we have the Way, the Truth, and the Life.

Heavenly Father, sanctify and keep us in Your truth for Jesus' sake. Amen.

February

The Dying Sinner

And he said, "Jesus, remember me when You come into Your kingdom." Luke 23:42

One of the thieves crucified with Jesus, who had at first also joined in the chorus of blasphemous mockery, now repented of his sins. His repentance was sincere; he confessed his guilt, acknowledging the justice of his sentence: "For we are receiving the due reward of our deeds" (Luke 23:41). His repentance was complete. Turning to the crucified Savior, the dying thief gave evidence of a faith vibrating with trust: "'Jesus, remember me when You come into Your kingdom.' And He said to him: 'Truly, I say to you, today you will be with Me in Paradise'" (Luke 23:42–43).

Here we see all the beauty of the Gospel of God's grace. The dying sinner had done nothing to merit a place in glory; in fact, he had done the very opposite. But in his dying hour this manifest sinner is saved by grace! How reassuring it is to have this complete evidence of the very heart of the Gospel: "For by grace you have been saved through faith. And this is not your own doing; it is the gift of God, not a result of works, so that no one may boast" (Ephesians 2:8–9).

Thank You, Lord, for Your ongoing patience toward me. Amen.

Is Anything Too Hard for the Lord?

The LORD said to Abraham, "Why did Sarah laugh and say, 'Shall I indeed bear a child, now that I am old?' Is anything too hard for the LORD ? At the appointed time I will return to you about this time next year, and Sarah shall have a son." Genesis 18:13–14

Is anything too hard for the Lord? Sarah thought so. She thought it impossible that at her advanced age she should still conceive a child. In this matter Sarah was familiar with the laws of nature that vetoed any prospect of her bearing a child. She did not know (or she forgot) that God is the Lord of nature and its law and can do with them as He pleases. In due time Sarah did conceive and bear a son, and then she knew: Nothing is ever too hard for the Lord (Genesis 18:14).

If we could always remember and apply practically the lesson Sarah learned, then life would be much easier. Often there seems to be an impossible situation in our individual life, in our family life, in our community life, in our congregational life, in the affairs of the nation or in the international situation. Every circumstance seems to shout, "No solution is possible!" And the lips of many people are ready to echo this verdict. At such times let us recall the question of God in our text. Through the death of Christ we reconciled with God. Because of this, the knowledge of His omnipotence becomes for us a source of never-failing comfort, cheer, and strength. Remember this for this present day and you will enjoy this day.

Holy God, we praise your name;
Lord of all, we bow before you.
All on earth your scepter claim,
All in heav'n above adore you.
Infinite your vast domain.
Everlasting is your reign. Amen. (LW 171:1)

More Than Conquerors

But thanks be to God, who gives us the victory through our Lord Jesus Christ. 1 Corinthians 15:57

Victory is a wonderful experience. Thrilling records have been written in the lives of heroes and heroines who, despite handicaps, moved from victory to victory in the glorious successes of life. For most of us history will not record sensational victories. Our life is quite ordinary; still we as Christians have a transcending interest in victory—the final victory over all evil and over death. And this victory we shall have by the grace of God.

All other victories so important in the lives of men are as nothing compared with our victory in Christ. It is victory observed with the shouting of hosannas and hallelujahs by the angelic choirs in heaven. It is the final victory over sin, death, and the devil. It is the victory of a glorious deliverance into heaven with the assured triumph of resurrection from the dead.

Thanks be to God for this victory. He provides it for us through Christ and His gracious salvation. If Christ Jesus had not come into this world to take away the sins of the world, we would still be in our sinful state, dying in tragic defeat under an eternal curse. Yet because Christ has conquered sin, death and the grave, there awaits for us not death, but eternal resurrection life in Him.

We thank You, Lord, for our victory through Jesus Christ, our Savior. Amen.

The Sufficient Christ

For in Him the whole fullness of deity dwells bodily. Colossians 2:9

Most of us feel rather inadequate at times. We develop moods of discouragement. We feel depressed. Life and the problems of life seem to overwhelm us. We may even feel incapable of struggling onward.

Perhaps we dream of how nice it would be to be able to do everything we would like to do. How wonderful if we could find the power to meet every situation of life confidently and successfully.

We can have that power. God made it available to us. It is the power of God in Christ Jesus. Jesus is true God, in whom is found "the whole fullness of deity." That means Jesus has all power, understanding, mercy, and love. What He did for us was of unlimited value. Through faith in His work and mercy, we have become the children of God. Now we need never feel we cannot measure up to the tasks before us. We can say with St. Paul, "I can do all things through Him who strengthens me" (Philippians 4:13).

All this is the case because Christ is able to give us all things. He is the unlimited source of all that we require—forgiveness for our sins, peace with God, love for our neighbor, courage to meet the crises of life, hope for the life that is hereafter. Christ is sufficient to all of our spiritual and material wants and problems.

Lord Jesus, who art All in all, the Fullness of God, fill us by faith with the grace to live fully here and hereafter. Amen.

The Understanding Christ

[Jesus] needed no one to bear witness about man, for He Himself knew what was in man. John 2:25

No one is completely understood by his fellow men. Even those who are nearest and dearest to us do not know every detail and facet of our personality. All of us hide within ourselves some of our likes and dislikes, fears and disappointments, hopes and ambitions. We carefully guard this inner life. It is the secret we keep from others, whether it is good or bad to do so.

At times this causes us sorrow and difficulty. We feel that no one understands us, that no one can understand us. How wrong we are! Perhaps none of our fellow beings can understand us, not even our loved ones, but there is One who does know and understand. It is Jesus.

Jesus understands both our strong points and our weaknesses. He knows our virtues as well as our vices. He knows our sins and our sorrows. He "knew what was in man." Because He knew, He took upon Himself our nature, our form. He humbled Himself; He suffered and died for us. The experiences of men, the joys and the sorrows, the agonies and the drawbacks were experienced by Him. Jesus knows us.

What a comfort this is to us. Our loving Savior, who suffered that we might have forgiveness of sins, understands us and promises us His help. He invites us, saying, "Come to Me, all who labor and are heavy laden, and I will give you rest" (Matthew 11:28).

Lord Jesus, we come to You as to one who knows us. Receive us, forgive us, help us, and give us Your peace. Amen.

February

The Obedient Christ

For as by the one man's disobedience the many were made sinners, so by the one man's obedience the many will be made righteous. Romans 5:19

One of the mysterious traits of human nature is rebellion. Many people do not find a thing attractive until it has been put on the forbidden list. Items that become rare and hard to obtain are often very desirable to people who were never interested in them when they were plentiful. The forbidden fruit seems to be more attractive than what is available to all. This is a strange delusion worked by Satan. He succeeded with it in the case of our first parents, Adam and Eve. He has been successful with it ever since.

Such rebellion is disobedience to God and His Law. Even the desire for the forbidden is wrong. Such opposition to God and His Law is sin, and sin requires payment. God is just and must keep the records straight. He must receive full satisfaction and payment for the violations of His Law. This frightens us because we realize we have become guilty and cannot, of our own efforts, satisfy God's demands.

How grateful we are to hear that our Savior Jesus Christ became our substitute! He kept the Law of God perfectly. By His death He paid for the sins we have committed. By His obedience we are now declared righteous. By faith in Him we are clothed with the righteousness of Jesus. Jesus is our "Advocate with the Father . . . [and] He is the Propitiation [the One who made good] for our sins" (1 John 2:1–2).

Lord Jesus, our obedient, crucified Substitute, may Your blood and righteousness make us the obedient children of God. Amen.

A Human Question and a Divine Answer

The Samaritan woman said to Him, "How is it that You, a Jew, ask for a drink from me, a woman of Samaria?" (For Jews have no dealings with Samaritans.) Jesus answered her, "If you knew the gift of God, and who it is that is saying to you, 'Give Me a drink,' you would have asked Him, and He would have given you living water." John 4:9–10

It was a logical question that the woman of Samaria asked the Savior at Jacob's well, outside the city of Sychar. It was unusual for a Jew to condescend to ask any favors of a despised Samaritan. Jesus satisfied her curiosity, and she received a priceless blessing when she came to know who Jesus was and what He offered her. This apparently "chance" encounter was brought about by the loving Christ, who was always seeking and saving those who were lost.

How intriguing and inviting was the Lord's reply to this woman: "If you knew the gift of God, and who it is that is saying to you, 'Give Me a drink,' you would have asked Him, and He would have given you 'living water.'"

It was a gracious invitation asking this woman to believe in Jesus as her and her people's Savior through faith in Him to have the thirst of her soul quenched so she would never know any soul-thirst again. She did believe, as did many of her townspeople to whom she brought the news of Jesus. All the spiritual need of her soul was taken away when she believed in Christ.

In a physical way we get thirsty repeatedly and need to refresh ourselves often by drinking draughts of cool water. Spiritually, our souls are refreshed when, day by day, we look to Jesus in faith and have communion with Him in His Word and by prayer. In that way we drink of the water of life that quenches soul-thirst and gives us peace in the assurance of eternal life.

Gracious Lord, continue to pour out for me the refreshing water of eternal life. Amen.

When Loss Is Gain

Indeed, I count everything as loss because of the surpassing worth of knowing Christ Jesus my Lord. For His sake I have suffered the loss of all things and count them as rubbish, in order that I may gain Christ. Philippians 3:8

The body of the emperor Charlemagne is said to be buried at Aix-la-Chapelle, sitting in a marble chair and clothed in royal robes. The open Bible rests on his lap, and his finger points to the passage: "For what shall it profit a man, if he shall gain the whole world, and lose his own soul?" (Mark 8:36 KJV).

In a parable Jesus tells of a worldly rich man whose land had just produced a fine harvest that he stored in new barns. Then he said to his soul: "Soul, you have ample goods laid up for many years; relax, eat, drink, be merry" (Luke 12:19). But God said to him: "Fool! This night your soul is required of you" (Luke 12:20). Jesus then explains: "So is the one who lays up treasure for himself and is not rich toward God" (Luke 12:21).

As a young man, Saul felt that having a fine education, a good position, and a lot of influence and power were more important than Christ, whom he hated, and the church, which he persecuted. But when Jesus met him on the way to Damascus and revealed Himself as his Savior, the very things that were gain to Saul, who became known as Paul, he now counted as loss, compared with knowing Christ.

The devil also tries to fool us into believing that the things of this world and of this life, such as social position, education, power, wealth, and prestige, are more important than a saving knowledge of Christ. Many permit themselves so to be fooled, but we dare not. These earthly treasures perish in time. Only the Gospel of Christ, the power of God to salvation, holds blessings for us that last eternally.

Help us, O Lord, rightly to lay up treasures in heaven. Amen.

February

A Heart of Flesh for a Heart of Stone

*And I will remove the heart of stone from your flesh and give
you a heart of flesh. Ezekiel 36:26b*

There were people in the days of Ezekiel who with their
lips cried, "Lord, Lord" but whose hearts were far from right.
They had hearts of stone—cold, hard, dead to spiritual things.
But the Holy Spirit promised by the prophet, "And I will give
you a new heart, and a new spirit I will put within you. And I
will remove the heart of stone from your flesh and give you a
heart of flesh" (Ezekiel 36:26).

By nature all hearts are stony. No power or skill of man
can change the stony heart into one of flesh. We can make some
superficial changes, just as we can paint a stone, or polish it, or
make of it a statue so lifelike that it almost seems ready to speak.
But after all is done, the heart is still what it always was—cold,
hard, dead stone. No religious veneer a person may apply to
himself can change the natural stony heart. As a matter of fact,
we cannot change it no matter what we may do.

What we cannot do, God does for us in His powerful
Word. His Word melts the hardest hearts of stone and turns
them into hearts of flesh. Once our hearts have been made alive
by God's miracle, we become able to love of Jesus, we begin to
desire that God's will be done in our lives, and we walk in a new
manner, pleasing the Lord through works done in faith. None
of these things are possible, were it not for the divine "heart sur-
gery" that God accomplishes for us through His Word!

*"Create in me a clean heart, O God, and renew a right spirit within
me" (Psalm 51:10). Amen.*

Tender Dealings

A bruised reed he will not break, and a faintly burning wick he will not quench; he will faithfully bring forth justice. Isaiah 42:3

Like the proud eagle that cares not for the company of the lowly birds of the valley, the rich, the powerful, and the strong men of this world often find no place for the weak.

Thank God it is not so in the Christian world. There we have the picture of Jesus, the Good Shepherd, seeking the last, carrying a lamb in His arms, and dealing gently with those that are with young. His assurance reads: "The Son of Man is not come to destroy men's lives, but to save them" (Luke 9:56, KJV). To John the Baptist, seeking assurance that Jesus was truly the promised Messiah, our Lord paints this picture of His work: "The blind receive their sight, and the lame walk, the lepers are cleansed, and the deaf hear, the dead are raised up, and the poor have the gospel preached to them" (Matthew 11:5).

Looking out over the years to Christ's coming into the world, Isaiah sees in Jesus a Savior full of loving kindness and tender mercies, who would not break "a bruised reed . . . [or quench] a faintly burning wick." These are pictures of Christ's tender dealings with those who are bruised and hurt by sin, and whose faith is as low as the last lingering spark of fire on a smoking oil wick. Jesus does not cast such out, but heals their broken hearts and fans the tiny spark of faith into a flame again.

Sin-burdened as we are, let us heed His kind invitation: "Come to Me, all who labor and are heavy laden, and I will give you rest" (Matthew 11:28). "Come now, let us reason together, says the LORD: though your sins are like scarlet, they shall be as white as snow; though they are red like crimson, they shall become like wool" (Isaiah 1:18).

Lord, deal with us according to Your loving kindness and tender mercy. Amen.

February

Divine Security

The eternal God is your dwelling place, and underneath are the everlasting arms. And he thrust out the enemy before you and said, Destroy. Deuteronomy 33:27

These words, so full of faith and comfort, are among the last with which Moses, the man of God, blessed his people before he died. The homeless Israelites, on their way to the Promised Land, were divinely assured that they had a secure dwelling place in the "Eternal God," whose "everlasting arms" were ever underneath and round about them to support and protect them.

We, too, are pilgrims on the way to our heavenly home. We, too, have the blessed assurance that the same eternal God is our refuge and dwelling place in all generations and that His "everlasting arms" of help and protection are constantly about us.

God is a Spirit who surrounds and encloses us as a precious refuge or dwelling place. "He is actually not far from each one of us, for 'in Him we live and move and have our being'" (Acts 17:27–28). Because we have made the Lord, which is our refuge, even the Most High, our habitation, there shall no evil befall us, neither shall any plague come nigh our dwelling. His everlasting arms support us, sustain us, and protect us.

God is good. He makes all things work together for good to them that love Him. He can and does turn that which seems hurtful and harmful into eternal good for us. His amazing goodness reached its highest point in the gift of His Son, Jesus Christ, by whose holy life and innocent suffering and death we have been redeemed from sin and death and made the children of God by faith. In our God there is divine security in body and soul for time and eternity.

O Lord, be our safe dwelling place to the end of the world. Amen.

Light Divine

For God, who said, "Let light shine out of darkness," has shone in our hearts to give the light of the knowledge of the glory of God in the face of Jesus Christ. 2 Corinthians 4:6

The first Sunday of the world's calendar began in deep darkness. The earth was dead, cold, chaotic. God, breaking the silence of eternity, said: "Let there be light" (Genesis 1:3). Thus came into being that element of mystery known to us as light.

God also has come to our sin-blighted souls. He saw them dead, cold, chaotic. He sent a light far more sublime than that which radiated upon the world on the first day. It is the light of the knowledge of His glory in the face of Jesus Christ.

The light that shone from the face of Moses when he descended from Mount Sinai was sharp and blinding so that the people pleaded with him to soften it by covering it with a cloth. It was the light of the Law.

The light that was in the face of Jesus was the light of grace. It shone brightly and invitingly when He spoke the unforgettable words: "For God so loved the world, that He gave His only Son, that whoever believes in Him should not perish but have eternal life" (John 3:16). It radiated upon the sick and the handicapped as He healed them. It was most brilliant when He suffered and died on the cross for the sins of fallen mankind.

When we gather for worship in the house of God, this light again shines upon us. It sends its life-giving and life-sustaining rays into our hearts as we listen to God's ambassador unfolding before our eyes the glory of God in the face of Jesus.

Abide with heav'nly brightness
Among us, precious Light;
Thy truth direct and keep us
From error's gloomy night. Amen. (TLH 53:3)

A Subtle Adversary

Be sober-minded; be watchful. Your adversary the devil prowls around like a roaring lion, seeking someone to devour. Resist him, firm in your faith, knowing that the same kinds of suffering are being experienced by your brotherhood throughout the world. 1 Peter 5:8–9

Some people refuse to believe that there is a devil; they often treat anything said about the existence of the devil as a joke. Even Christians sometimes fail to recognize as they should that Satan is real and that his designs and purposes are always evil. "Be sober-minded; be watchful" (1 Peter 5:8).

The devil did not hesitate to assault even the holy Christ. In three separate temptations he sought in a subtle way to persuade Jesus to disobey the will of His heavenly Father. In the Garden of Eden the devil beguiled Adam and Eve; they disobeyed the will of God, and sin with all its evil was brought into the world. Even so Satan now seeks to turn us from the will of God, to persuade us to love the world, and to destroy body and soul forever. Will he fail, as he did in the case of Jesus? Or will he succeed, as in the case of Adam and Eve?

Jesus demonstrated how to resist the evil one successfully. He withstood the tempter with a mighty "It is written" (Matthew 4:4, 6, 7). And the devil abandoned his attacks. Martin Luther knew from experience the power of the Word of God when facing this subtle adversary; he said, "One little word can fell him." Yet this happens only because Christ has first defeated the devil for us. In His Word, not ours, is found the peaceful realization that the devil now has no power over us.

Lord, we pray You, teach us to use Your Word, the sword of the Spirit, in every temptation of Satan, and help us to stand fast in the power of Your might. Amen.

The Sympathetic Christ

And when the Lord saw her, He had compassion on her and said to her, "Do not weep." Luke 7:13

How dreadful it is to bear a load of grief! What a comfort to have the understanding and sympathy of others! Although we feel that no one really understands the full measure of our grief, we appreciate the expressions of sympathy, nevertheless. They give us a certain measure of strength and decrease the terrible sting and bitterness of our loss and disappointment. If it were possible for someone to understand completely the loss and the sorrow we have sustained, our grief might be somewhat neutralized.

There *is* One who understands and who feels with us. It is Jesus, whose heart is one of divine sympathy, or compassion. When Jesus saw the widow at Nain carrying her only son to the grave, He understood completely what grief and sadness was hers. Understanding, He reassured her by telling her not to weep and by restoring her son to life again. What a comforting example for grief-removing sympathy.

We, too, have our grief, our heartaches, and our disappointments, our bereavements. When our heart cries out wildly and our spirits will not be comforted, may we in humble faith and earnest prayer go to Jesus. He understands the meaning of sorrow. He has the power to help in our disappointments. And He knows and feels with us what burdens are ours. His is the same assurance to us, "Do not weep."

Lord Jesus, Sufferer of all sufferings, who understands our sorrows, think on us in the hour of our grief. Amen.

The Convenient Food

"Give us this day our daily bread." Matthew 6:11

"The eyes of all look to You, and You give them their food in due season. You open Your hand; You satisfy the desire of every living thing" (Psalm 145:15–16). The universal cry of humanity, as well as the desire of every creature, may be summed up in this petition, "Give us food."

For the Christian the Fourth Petition of the Lord's Prayer has a special significance. "God certainly gives daily bread to everyone without our prayers, even to all evil people, but we pray in this petition that God would lead us to realize this and to receive our daily bread with thanksgiving" (*Luther's Small Catechism*).

This beautiful petition is an open admission that every good gift and every perfect gift is from above and comes down from the Father of lights. Out of His bountiful goodness He provides for our needs each day. Therefore we should so trust Him that we would ask of Him the food that is convenient for each day. As we pray for food for ourselves, we dare not be unmindful of the needs of others. The fact that we pray, "give us," challenges us to share our bounties with the needy and the hungry. Failure to do so is a denial of the faith.

The daily needs of our bodies should remind us also of the daily spiritual needs of our souls. Jesus is the Bread of life. He is the Bread of God that comes down from heaven and gives life to the world. "I am the Bread of life" (John 6:35), He declares. "I am the living bread that came down from heaven. If anyone eats of this bread, he will live forever" (John 6:51).

Heavenly Father, evermore feed us with the Living Bread. Amen.

A Safe Deposit

But I am not ashamed, for I know whom I have believed, and I am convinced that he is able to guard until that Day what has been entrusted to me. 2 Timothy 1:12

When St. Polycarp of Smyrna was called upon to renounce Christ to save his life from death by burning, he answered: "Eighty and six years have I served my Lord, and He has done me no wrong. How, then, can I speak evil of my King who saved me?"

Standing trial before Nero in Rome, one of St. Paul's complaints was: "At my first defense no one came to stand by me, but all deserted me" (2 Timothy 4:16). Then he adds these comforting words: "But the Lord stood by me and strengthened me" (2 Timothy 4:17). He who once hated Christ is now His most faithful follower. Facing almost certain death, he seems to say: "My enemies may do their worst, they may insult my gray hairs; they may load me with irons; they may burn my body and scatter my ashes, but I am not afraid or ashamed." "I know whom I have believed." His trust, as ours also must be, was in the living Lord. His motto was, as ours should be: "For to me to live is Christ" (Philippians 1:21).

If we have the blessed confidence of St. Paul, we can also share his glorious conclusion. "I am convinced," he declares, "that He is able to guard until that Day what has been entrusted to me." What had Paul deposited with Jesus for safekeeping against the great Day of Judgment? His life and salvation. "There is laid up for me the crown of righteousness, which the Lord, the righteous judge, will award to me on that Day" (2 Timothy 4:8).

Keep me, O Lord, to eternal life through Your Word. Amen.

February

The Awareness of Sin

Wretched man that I am! Who will deliver me from this body of death? Romans 7:24

A cruel form of punishment used occasionally by the ancients was to chain the criminal to a corpse, from which he could not free himself. It was a frightful experience. This appears to be what the apostle refers to as he describes his desperate spiritual condition.

To Paul it was a bitter state of affairs that, with all his earnest endeavors, he continued to be painfully aware of sin in his life. He once complained, "For I know that nothing good dwells in me, that is, in my flesh. For I have the desire to do what is right, but not the ability to carry it out. For I do not do the good I want, but the evil I do not want is what I keep on doing" (Romans 7:18–19). To Paul this was like being chained to a dead body.

Certainly this is not a pleasant thought. But this image is designed to make us each aware of the presence of sin in our lives. This will keep us from being too sure of ourselves. We ever need to keep in mind the admonition, "Therefore let anyone who thinks he that he stands take heed lest he fall" (1 Corinthians 10:12).

How comforting, therefore, to know that our salvation does not depend on any effort of our own to rid ourselves of sin. "For by grace you have been saved through faith. And this is not your own doing; it is the gift of God, not a result of works, so that no one may boast" (Ephesians 2:8–9).

O Christ, . . . to whom save Thee, who canst alone
For sin atone, Lord, shall I flee? Amen. (TLH 380:1)

What a Load!

All we like sheep have gone astray; we have turned every one to his own way; and the LORD has laid on Him the iniquity of us all. Isaiah 53:6

Inasmuch as this text tells us that God the Father laid on the Messiah the iniquity of all of us, each one of us can say: He laid on Jesus not only the sins of others, but my sins too. To this each one of us might add: And how many, many sins I have! Each one must confess: I have my sins of commission and of omission; visible sins perpetrated by the hand, and audible sins by the words of the mouth; internal, hence invisible sins committed by a mean thought, an evil desire, a rebellious attitude toward God, etc. Many sins, altogether too many sins!

Yet not only your sins and mine did God lay on Jesus, but the sins of us all: the sins of all people living on this earth today, plus the sins of the uncounted billions from Adam to the present plus the sins of the unknown numbers still to be born before the Day of Judgment. What a load! What a crushing burden! What agony in Gethsemane and on the cross!

Thank God that we can say: "In Him we have redemption through His blood, the forgiveness of our trespasses, according to the riches of His grace" (Ephesians 1:7).

Lord Jesus, we give thanks to Thee
That Thou hast died to set us free;
Made righteous thro' Thy precious blood,
We now are reconciled to God. Amen. (TLH 173:1)

Soldiers

Share in suffering as a good soldier of Christ Jesus. No soldier gets entangled in civilian pursuits, since his aim is to please the one who enlisted him. 2 Timothy 2:3–4

Christ, the Captain of our salvation, has selected us to be His soldiers. His command is "Follow Me" (John 21:19). Are we ready to follow our Captain in the war against the enemy of our soul's salvation? Do we recognize the enemy? "For we do not wrestle against flesh and blood, but against the rulers, against the authorities, against the cosmic powers over this present darkness, against the spiritual forces of evil in the heavenly places" (Ephesians 6:12)—against the wiles of the devil. Allied with Satan are the world with its temptations and the old Adam in us with his sinful urgings.

Can we be certain of victory against such an enemy? Yes. The struggle may be long and hard as long as we live in this world, but the victory is assured because Christ has already won it for us. Following the example of our Captain, we shall willingly "share in suffering" as good soldiers and really fight the good fight of faith, confessing all the while, "Thanks be to God, who gives us the victory through our Lord Jesus Christ" (1 Corinthians 15:57).

St. Paul, as a good solider of Jesus Christ, gladly suffered the hardships of a bitter campaign to conquer men for Christ. But he also saw the day of triumph ahead. "I have fought the good fight, I have finished the race, I have kept the faith. Henceforth there is laid up for me the crown of righteousness" (2 Timothy 4:7–8).

Teach us, O Captain of our salvation, how to be good soldiers of the cross, that we may please You, who bids us to follow in Your army. Amen.

February

The Everlasting Arms

The eternal God is your dwelling place, and underneath are the everlasting arms. And he thrust out the enemy before you and said, Destroy. Deuteronomy 33:27

This statement brings rich comfort and satisfying assurance to troubled hearts. It suggests the intimacy and tenderness of a solicitous parent drawing his disturbed and frightened child closer to himself in a loving, protective embrace. At the same time there is a suggestion of the absolute strength and eternal security that only the omnipotent God can afford. "The everlasting arms!" "From everlasting to everlasting You are God!" (Psalm 90:2). "In Your hand are power and might, and in Your hand it is to make great and to give strength to all!" (1 Chronicles 28:12). Thank God for these mighty statements!

When grief and disappointment, sin and temptation, sickness and death bring us face to face with our own weakness and our need of something that no human friend nor earthly object can supply, how good it is then to know that He who is the same yesterday, today, and forever, the almighty God, will support us with the everlasting arms of His divine love! When we are weak, we will be strong. God promises that we shall live "underneath . . . the everlasting arms."

I need thy presence ev'ry passing hour;
What but thy grace can foil the tempter's pow'r?
Who like thyself my guide and stay can be?
Through cloud and sunshine, oh, abide with me. Amen. (LW 490:2)

The Greater Freedom

"So if the Son sets you free, you will be free indeed." John 8:36

Today is Washington's birthday. Under him our country started on the fabulous road of the American way of life. This gives us freedom of worship, speech, travel, and the ballot. The history of our nation has been unique among the peoples of the earth, both ancient and modern.

Yet many who live in this free country are nevertheless slaves—slaves of *sin*. "Everyone who commits sin is a slave to sin" (John 8:34), says Jesus. Sin enslaves the *mind*, warping our thinking and leading our thoughts into the basest channels of filth. Sin enslaves our *passions*, making us so unashamed of our fallen desires that we no longer blush. Sin enslaves our *will*. In fact, no brainwashing is so vicious, for it beclouds our appraisal of right and wrong. Sin "unlaws" our behavior, damages our body, injures our character, dulls our conscience, and makes us loveless. Sin sends us to damnation.

To secure for us freedom from the enslavement, guilt, curse, and penalty of sin, Jesus went to Calvary to pay the full ransom price that set us free. By the power of the cross, manifest in Baptism, we are unshackled from the chains of sin and declared children of grace. We are freed to serve Him who made sure our salvation. This is the greater freedom that our crucified Savior alone can give us.

Lord Jesus, keep me close to Your heart of love that I may be eternally free. Amen.

Christ in Us

I have been crucified with Christ. It is no longer I who live, but Christ who lives in me. And the life I now live in the flesh I live by faith in the Son of God, who loved me and gave Himself for me. Galatians 2:20

We are a part of a generation that thought it could exist without God and without obedience to His will. Such godlessness must lead to chaotic futility and despair. The living presence of Christ in heart and life gives true value and purpose to our existence and endeavors.

St. Paul declared: "Christ . . . lives in me." And he prayed for the Christians at Ephesus that "Christ may dwell in your hearts by faith" (Ephesians 3:17). That is not empty sentiment or wishful thinking, but divine reality. "I in them" (John 17:23), in the believers, Christ said in His high-priestly prayer.

Christ in us! This means a moral change and spiritual transformation. A new relationship has been established, and in consequence thereof new attitudes, new desires, and new ideals are produced and activated. Life itself has assumed a new purpose and direction. It now becomes a privileged and cherished opportunity for rendering an exalted service to God and our fellow men.

Christ in us! This means that I now have a strong defender against myself and my persistent sins. Although I am tempted sorely, "He who is in [me] is greater" (1 John 4:4) even than these.

Take ever greater possession of me, O Christ, in heart and life that I may trust in You more fully and live increasingly unto You in response to Your gracious indwelling. Amen.

Christ through Us

And His name—by faith in His name—has made this man strong whom you see and know, and the faith that is through Jesus has given the man this perfect health in the presence of you all. Acts 3:16

A little boy underwent a critical operation. When he was to be discharged from the hospital after a long convalescence, he called the surgeon and said: "Mother will never hear the last of you." If we fully realized what Christ has done for us, we would say to Him: "My friends and acquaintances will never hear the last of You."

When Christ dwells in our hearts by faith, His mercy and grace will find inevitably expression through us. This was true of the apostles and early Christians. Through the word of their testimony, their life and conduct, the light of the Word continued to shine in the sin-darkened world.

Christ uses His church to bring His soul-saving, life-transforming grace to the hearts of men. How strange, therefore, that many who profess to be Christians seem so reluctant to speak about their Savior! Men and women are stumbling through life without the peace and hope of Christ and yet we hesitate to extend a lifting, guiding hand.

The crucified and ever-living Christ brings His Gospel blessings to others through us. He still shines in the darkness of troubled hearts and perishing souls. He continues to build His kingdom for the endless ages to come.

Thank You, O Light of the world, that You shine through people such as me. Amen.

The Dreadful Alternative

*So when they had gathered, Pilate said to them, "Whom do you
want me to release for you: Barabbas, or Jesus who is called
Christ?" Matthew 27:17*

Barabbas was in prison because of robbery and murder.
His crime carried with it the death penalty. His doom was vir-
tually sealed. Then Pilate decided to let the accusers of Jesus
choose between Barabbas and Jesus which of the two should be
released. Should Jesus be crucified, as His accusers demanded,
that would mean freedom for Barabbas. Should Jesus be
released, as Pilate hoped, that would mean for Barabbas continued imprisonment and certain death—a dreadful alternative
for Barabbas! Jesus went to the cross. Barabbas was released.

My situation was similar to that of Barabbas. Before God,
I am a criminal—a sinner. I have deserved everlasting imprisonment. My doom was sealed. God saw one possibility for my
release—if His Son Jesus should suffer and die in my place, that
would save me, but that alone. Without that, I would face eternal damnation—a dreadful alternative for me!

St. Paul declares this same blessed reality to me and to all
people: "For our sake [God] made Him to be sin who knew no
sin, so that in Him we might become the righteousness of God"
(2 Corinthians 5:21).

Thou, ah! Thou, hast taken on Thee
Bonds and stripes, a cruel rod;
Pain and scorn were heaped upon Thee,
O Thou sinless Son of God!
Thus didst Thou my soul deliver
From the bonds of sin forever.
Thousand, thousand thanks shall be,
Dearest Jesus, unto Thee. Amen. (TLH 151:2)

Jesus Alone Makes Us Righteous

Who was delivered up for our trespasses and raised for our justification. Romans 4:25

If there is any doubt as to whether a man can stand before God on the basis of his own efforts, we need only consider with Paul the case of one of the greatest—Abraham. All through Scripture he is held up as a model for all, and the highest praise of God is repeatedly heaped upon this mighty man of God. If anyone at all should have had a good standing before God on the basis of goodness, which he was or did, it surely should have been Abraham.

Abraham had standing before God indeed, but it was the standing of faith. Abraham believed God, and that belief in God was counted to Abraham as the righteousness that God demands. In fact, over against all works-righteousness, Abraham is the strongest possible evidence that can be made for faith. He is the father of those who *believe*. His faith must ever remind us of what faith must always be: a holding to God's promise because it is His promise, even when all the evidence of sight and sense and reason are against it.

Now all the promises of God center in Jesus. He died. Why? Because He was delivered for our offenses. His was the sacrificial death for our sins. That is God's promise in Christ. But Jesus rose from the dead. Why? That we might be justified, that in Him we might be what God wants us to be. Firm faith—bestowed by God—in this atonement of Christ is not staggered by unbelief, overwhelmed by the enormity of sin, conquered by repeated and constant failures. Faith trusts God to regard us as He says He does in Christ Jesus.

Heavenly Father, in Your mercy ever keep my eyes fastened on Jesus only as the Author and Finisher of my faith. Amen.

The Greatest Hour in History

And Jesus answered them, "The hour has come for the Son of Man to be glorified."   *John 12:23*

What does this mean to us? Christ died for us. "Behold the Lamb of God, who takes away the sin of the world!" exclaims John the Baptist (John 1:29). Obviously, we belong to the world, so we are also included. Christ laid down His life *for us*.

But this precious truth is too good to keep for ourselves. Christ died for all. We must share this joy with others, neighbors and friends. And how wonderful! We can go to any man, woman, or child and tell them: *Christ died for you*. No one is excluded. The door of God's mercy is wide open to welcome each and every penitent. Saint and sinner can find healing and help at the cross. So we must plead with all whom we know: Come and behold with us this Jesus who brings forgiveness and peace, hope and salvation to all mankind.

How grateful we ought to be for this hour! That was the most glorious moment in history when Jesus by *dying* gave life and salvation to us all. Dead in sin, we have been raised to a newness of life and stand in God's grace as children of His household. Surely we must come in spirit to Christ's cross during this Lenten season and ponder upon His passion and God's amazing love.

Jesus, You have purchased us with Your own precious blood. Accept us today as we pledge anew to serve You with all our heart. Let no other interest keep us from setting aside time to ponder Your crucifixion and death, whereby we are redeemed and saved, heirs of the eternal glory of heaven. Amen.

Saints in Christ

To all those in Rome who are loved by God and called to be saints: Grace to you and peace from God our Father and the Lord Jesus Christ. Romans 1:7

Because of Christ's death and resurrection, we Christians are called saints, that is, holy ones. As we review our lives and look back into our yesterdays, must we not admit that we have not at all times walked the saintly way? We have not always placed our Lord first nor given to Him all glory with heart, lips, and hands. If God looks at us just as we are, He cannot call us saints.

As saints we must bear witness to Him who died for us that we might be forgiven and set free from the bondage of sin and Satan. We, too, must invite friends and acquaintances to come and hear this soul-saving Gospel.

During Lent we are constrained more than ever to meditate on the suffering and death of Jesus and tell of His redeeming cross to all who will listen. This Lenten season we must rededicate ourselves to this Savior and give our heart and our lives and our love to Him in service and sacrifice that all may know that we belong to Jesus, called saints by the grace of God.

But God looks at us believers through the cross. He completely covers our transgressions with the spotless holiness of Jesus, His Son. Because of Christ's precious blood not one spot remains. No wonder the believers through the ages have devoted themselves during this season to pondering the passion of our Lord.

Gracious Savior, dwell in our hearts and our homes that as children of Your grace we may at all times live as becomes those who dwell in Your household. Amen.

Our Sympathetic High Priest

For we do not have a high priest who is unable to sympathize with our weaknesses, but one who in every respect has been tempted as we are, yet without sin. Hebrews 4:15

When Job's three friends heard of all the evil that had come upon him, they came, each from his own place, to mourn with him and comfort him. When Jesus passed through the agony of Gethsemane, He also craved the sympathy of the inner circle of His disciples. When these slept, an angel came and strengthened Him.

In seasons of distress and grief we all seek the sympathy and comfort of our friends. We are comforted to know that they share our toils and trials, help us bear our burdens and afflictions, and thus enter with us into our joys and sorrows.

If human sympathy can be so soothing and so comforting, how blessed, indeed, must be the pure, exalted, sinless, unselfish sympathy of the Son of God and Son of man! His is a real sympathy, growing out of a true and sinless humanity. He lived and labored in this sinful hospital of the world. He felt the fevered brow and pulse with His own love-laden hands. He marks each sufferer's tears and never turned a deaf ear to their cries. For all their afflictions He was afflicted.

When we are tempted, we remember that He was in all points tempted as we are, yet without sin. When we suffer, we remember that He was the Prince of sufferers. In our sorrow we remember that He was the Man of sorrows. In our affliction we remember that by His stripes we were healed. In the hour of death we remember that He conquered death and made it an avenue of life.

Savior, like a shepherd lead us. Amen.

February

Christian Compulsion

"We must work the works of Him who sent me while it is day; night is coming, when no one can work." John 9:4

The word "must" emphasizes that which is mandatory and obligatory. Our brief text is one of many Gospel passages in which our Savior, by use of this word "must," indicates that our Christian duties are never to be regarded as optional, a matter of choice.

As a lad of twelve He said, "I *must* be in My Father's house" (Luke 2:49). When He was urged to remain in a certain locality, Jesus stated, "I *must* preach the good news of the kingdom of God to the other towns as well" (Luke 4:43). The Good Shepherd told His hearers, "And I have other sheep that are not of this fold. I *must* bring them also, and they will listen to My voice" (John 10:16). Nicodemus was not to marvel that the Master said, "You *must* be born again" (John 3:7). Zacchaeus heard the explicit news from the Lord, "I *must* stay at your house today" (Luke 19:5).

It is indeed good news that Christ felt compelled to finish the work the Father gave Him to do. Therefore, toward the end of His ministry He told the "disciples that He *must* go to Jerusalem" (Matthew 16:21) and that "the Son of Man *must* suffer many things" (Mark 8:31), for only through His substitutionary sacrifice and faith in its atoning merit can we be saved. "As Moses lifted up the serpent in the wilderness, so *must* the Son of Man be lifted up, that whoever believes in Him may have eternal life" (John 3:14).

Heavenly Father, grant us the grace to echo the words of John the Baptist concerning Your glorious Son, "He must increase, but I must decrease" (John 3:30). Amen.

The Power of Faith

"And whatever you ask in prayer, you will receive, if you have faith." Matthew 21:22

"Whatever you ask in prayer, you will receive." Really, *whatever* I ask?

Take note of the rest of the verse: "if you have faith." To have faith means to trust, to have confidence in someone. When we pray, we pray in faith. We trust our Lord.

We have confidence in His wisdom as well as in His power and love. We do not know what to pray for, for we do not know what is good for us. But He knows, and in His wisdom He will grant us just that. That is the reason why the best prayer is always the prayer of our Lord in Gethsemane, "*Your* will be done" (Matthew 26:42).

We can pray that prayer with full confidence that we shall receive *all* things that are best for us. We may not realize what is best for us—but God knows! The Bible says: "And we know that for those who love God all things work together for good" (Romans 8:28).

This Lenten season reminds us that there is one thing we really need, and that is God's forgiveness for our sins. We have this forgiveness through Christ. Scripture says: "He who did not spare His own Son but gave Him up for us all, how will He not also with Him graciously give us all things?" (Romans 8:32). God has given us His dearest and best in Jesus. He will not fail to give us gifts of less value as we need them.

Lord, give us such a faith as this;
And then, whate'er may come,
We'll taste, e'en now the hallowed bliss
Of an eternal home. Amen. (TLH 396:6)

Forsaken of God

My God, my God, why have You forsaken me? Why are You so far from saving me, from the words of my groaning? Psalm 22:1

One of the basic human fears is to be alone. In the middle of the night a little child will awaken from a bad dream and cry, "Daddy, are you there?" Back comes the reassuring voice, "Yes, Daddy is here." Still not sure that the bad dream is not real, the child will say, "Daddy, is your face toward me?" Then when the father assures the tot, "Yes, Daddy's face is toward you," the child will close his eyes and drift off into slumber. This inborn dread of being alone offers a small insight of the forsakenness by God suffered by our Lord on Calvary, where in that supernatural darkness of Good Friday He shouted from His cross, "My God, My God, why have You forsaken Me?" (Matthew 27:46).

This word "forsaken" from our tortured Redeemer presents a baffling mystery. The Son of God is cut off from His Father. Not only has the Father turned His face from His Son, but He has actually forsaken Him. Here is a baffling puzzle. The eternally inseparable Godhead becomes separated in working redemption for the sins of the world.

One day a child, while reciting John 3:16 at confirmation instruction, mistakenly said "forgotten" instead of "begotten." Taking advantage of this slip, the minister said, "Yes, God gave His only *forgotten* Son. God *forgot* His Son on the cross that He might *remember us*."

Despite my sins, Lord, remember me on the Last Day. Amen.

The Silence of the Crucified One

But when He was accused by the chief priests and elders, He gave no answer. Matthew 27:12

During war, military units often observe radio silence as a security measure to conceal their whereabouts. Accused persons sometimes remain silent, likewise as a security measure, lest they admit their guilt by speaking. Sometimes their silence has the opposite effect; refusing to speak makes them appear guilty.

Jesus was silent when accused. Was He afraid to speak lest He appear guilty? Why did He not defend Himself?

It was for my sake that Jesus remained silent. He refused to defend Himself that He might defend me. Jesus remained silent before the courts of man that He might speak in my defense when I stand accused before the court of God. Jesus permitted Himself to be punished in my place that He might now intercede for me and, on the basis of His suffering and death, induce the Judge of heaven and earth to declare me acquitted, forgiven. "Who is to condemn? Christ Jesus in the one who died—more than that, who was raised—who is at the right hand of God, who indeed is interceding for us" (Romans 8:34).

E'er since by faith I saw the stream
Thy flowing wounds supply,
Redeeming love has been my theme
And shall be till I die. Amen. (TLH 157:4)

Sorrow Turned to Joy

"Truly, truly, I say to you, you will weep and lament, but the world will rejoice. You will be sorrowful, but your sorrow will turn into joy." John 16:20

Tears and laughter, sorrow and joy—these are the experiences of people all over the world. Sometimes it seems there are more tears than laughter. Sometimes it seems that others have the laughter and we have the tears.

Life's experiences train the God-fearing. All things work for good to those whom God loves and disciplines as sons. The hard experiences of life are the fires that test and temper Christian character.

The world goes along its carefree way and soon becomes careless. Neglect God, and we shall soon neglect right. Fail to worship God, and we shall worship ourselves. Comes the day of sorrow, grief, bereavement, and misfortune! What then? The world has no one to turn to.

We Christians and the Christian Church regularly face times of difficulty. The world hated Christ; it will also hate us. The day will come, however, when our sorrow will be turned into joy. This joy we do not build on money, health, good material fortune. We build our joy on God and the Savior. God will triumph. God will bless. For a time we Christians may weep and lament, but eventually sorrow shall turn to joy.

Dear Lord, give us that faith that outlasts our sorrows, and let us see our sorrow turn to joy. Amen.

Jesus Asks Questions

"What do you think about the Christ? Whose Son is He?" They said to Him, "The Son of David." Matthew 22:42

The enemies of Jesus had asked Him three questions, hoping to embarrass Him and to discredit Him before the people. They had not succeeded. Now Jesus asked: "What do you think about the Christ? Whose Son is He?" The Pharisees and the Sadducees answered at once, "The Son of David." But Jesus went on: "Right! But how can David, the ancestor of the Christ, call Him Lord?" And Jesus quoted the Scriptures, Psalm 110:1.

This was an embarrassing question for His enemies. In the Jewish law a son could never be the lord over his father or other ancestor. The older man always had higher rank and honor in the family. There was no answer to this question except to admit that the Christ, Jesus, must be both the Son of David according to the flesh and the Son of God according to the Spirit. This they refused to admit, and so they were silent.

Thank God that by His Holy Spirit He has given us the answer. For Jesus, the Christ, is both David's Son and Lord, true man, born of the Virgin Mary, and true God, begotten of the Father from eternity, that He might die for us and redeem us from all our sins. By this redemption we are "His own and live under Him in His kingdom and serve Him" (*Luther's Small Catechism*).

Heavenly Father, we pray You, preserve our faith in Jesus as our God and our Savior. Amen.

March

That We Might Have Hope

For whatever was written in former days was written for our instruction, that through endurance and through the encouragement of the Scriptures we might have hope. Romans 15:4

On each Lord's Day, unless we are detained by sickness or other emergency, we go to the house of God. There we worship our Lord and devoutly direct our attention to the sacred Scriptures, the Word of God.

The Scriptures have a purpose. They are written that we might have hope. Without them we should be as dead souls walking in the darkness of hopelessness and helplessness. We turn to the Bible and find the promise of this text supported by many writers and in many ways.

Of the man who is truly blessed, it is said that "his delight is in the Law of the Lord, and on His Law he meditates day and night" (Psalm 1:2). The Word hidden in the heart is a safeguard against sins. The man who hears the words of Christ and does them is likened to the man who builds his house on a rock. To those who hear and believe is given the crown of everlasting life. "Whoever hears My word and believes Him who sent Me has eternal life" (John 5:24).

All this supplies us with a most precious hope. This Christ-centered hope cheers our hearts, brightens our lives, and directs our faith-filled vision to that indescribable inheritance that our Lord is holding in reserve for us. There our hope will be transformed into joyous experience, the experience of the unchanging presence of God.

Gracious Lord and God, grant that through patience and comfort of Your Word we may embrace and ever hold fast this blessed hope through Christ, our Savior. Amen.

March

Divine Substitution

Surely he has borne our griefs and carried our sorrows; yet we esteemed him stricken, smitten by God, and afflicted. Isaiah 53:4

In France during one of Napoleon's campaigns, a man was drafted into the army but hired a substitute, who went to war and fell in one of the battles. Later this same man was drafted again for the same war. He went to the recruiting office and, producing his papers, proved he had hired and paid for a substitute who had died in battle. Accordingly, the entry was made after His name: "Died in the person of his substitute on the battlefield of Rivoli."

Eleven times in this chapter, Isaiah states in various ways that Jesus was *our* Substitute. As such He bore *our* sins with their grief and sorrows in His own body. With His blood He paid in full the price for *our* guilt. By His suffering He endured the curse of *our* sin. At the cost of His life He purchased *our* redemption. Through His death He reconciled *us* to His heavenly Father. We died in the person of Christ, our Substitute on the battlefield of Golgotha.

Henceforth we need add nothing to His perfect sacrifice. Because He became our Substitute, all things are now ours by God's grace in Christ Jesus.

As our Substitute our Lord assures us of God's abiding love for every need of life. He promises us His providential care, by which even the seeming ills of life become blessings in disguise. He guarantees our final and complete victory over sin, death, and hell.

Thanks be to You for being my Substitute, O Christ. Amen.

The Cup

And going a little farther He fell on His face and prayed, saying, "My Father, if it be possible, let this cup pass from Me; nevertheless, not as I will, but as You will." Matthew 26:39

In the Garden of Gethsemane Jesus spoke of a cup. "My Father, if it be possible, let this cup pass from Me." Jesus was speaking of the dreadful pain and suffering He must endure, the penalty of all of our sins. It was like a cup of bitter medicine.

Jesus was willing to atone, or make good, for our sins; but when it came to actually enduring the pain for us, it seemed more than He could bear in His state of humility. So He prayed that, if there was any other way of delivering the world from sin, He might avoid drinking of this cup.

Thank God, the sacred record reveals that Jesus emptied the cup to its last dregs for us. Having done that, He can now offer us the "cup of salvation" (Psalm 116:13). We may drink of it freely every day, enjoying all the blessings of God because Jesus has taken all our sins upon Himself.

Occasionally we must still suffer, as Jesus prophesied, "You will drink My cup, but to sit at My right hand and at My left is not Mine to grant, but it is for those for whom it has been prepared by My Father" (Matthew 20:23). But even in the midst of tribulation the eternal cup of salvation—filled for us by our Christ—sweetens all our temporary sorrows.

Heavenly Father, give me the cup of salvation and take away my cup of sorrow, according to Your will, for Jesus' sake. Amen.

God Supplies

"And do not seek what you are to eat and what you are to drink, nor be worried." Luke 12:29

Here I am worrying all morning, really worrying. Weekly I confess in worship: "I believe in God the Father Almighty." Do I really believe this?

Little children do. There they lay fast asleep, not once vexed with the thoughts: What shall I eat? Will I get new shoes?

Why does the child rest so peacefully upon her bed? Because she really believes that her mother will provide breakfast and that her daddy will buy new shoes that fit her growing feet. She does not doubt this for a moment.

But her parents are only human. Their ability to help is limited. And we have an almighty Father who is able to do far above all that we ask. He has never failed us. Why, then, be of doubtful mind?

"And my God will supply every need of yours according to His riches in glory in Christ Jesus" (Philippians 4:19), said Paul. Now, Paul's God is also our God. Yes, He is our loving Father in Christ. He spared not His own Son to redeem us. Certainly He will not forsake us in the hour of trouble.

Why, then, doubt? Our God will supply all our needs, for He is the Almighty, who loves us with an everlasting love in Christ Jesus, our risen Lord and living Redeemer.

Gracious Father, teach us, day after day, to bring our worries to You and go from Your presence with a song in our hearts, for Jesus' sake. Amen.

Saved by Substitution

For our sake He made Him to be sin who knew no sin, so that in Him we might become the righteousness of God. 2 Corinthians 5:21

Isaac had a narrow escape. To test the faith and obedience of Abraham, God told him to sacrifice his only son, Isaac. Just in the nick of time, God stopped Abraham from slaying his son. He provided a ram to be sacrificed instead. Isaac was saved by substitution.

The many animals sacrificed by the priests in Old Testament times dramatized the fact that the guilt of the people had been transferred to a substitute that was slain in their place. They were saved by substitution.

The substitutions in Old Testament times were a "shadow of the things to come" (Colossians 2:17), pointing to the cross, for God "made Him to be sin for us who knew no sin that we might be made the righteousness of God." Jesus "knew no sin"—had never committed one. He was made "to be sin for us"—was held accountable and punished for our sins. Now we are "made the righteousness of God"—God treats us as though we were as righteous as Jesus. He forgives our sins completely. We are saved by substitution.

A crown of thorns Thou wearest,
My shame and scorn Thou bearest,
That I might ransomed be.
My Bondsman, ever willing,
My place with patience filling,
From sin and guilt hast made me free. Amen. (TLH 171:7)

Jesus Keeps House

You open Your hand; You satisfy the desire of every living thing.
Psalm 145:16

Many people think that our Lord is concerned only with their spiritual welfare. They do not understand that He also supplies all their bodily needs daily.

One evening Jesus demonstrated His mercy to many people by giving them supper. All day this large crowd had heard Him preach. Now as it was near sundown, Jesus fed them. He took five loaves of bread and two fishes from the basket of a little boy and multiplied the same so that five thousand men, plus the women and children with them, were fed and had enough.

Miracles like this are still taking place. As we eat bread every day, we should think of Him who raised the wheat. The meat we eat now was, months ago, some prize cattle being fattened for this. Our Lord knows we need good clothing. Hence the sheep grazing in the meadows are growing wool on their backs for our warm winter clothing. One cannot pass a beautiful cotton field in the South without seeing how much this product means to our comfort.

Because Christ our Brother has redeemed us by His blood, God the Father is once again *our* Father. He graciously provides His dear children with everything needful, most especially our much-needed salvation. "All this He does only out of fatherly, divine goodness and mercy, without any merit or worthiness in me" (*Luther's Small Catechism*).

Lord, keep us mindful of all the blessings we receive, and help us to be satisfied with them. Receive our humble thanks for Your mercy. Amen.

There Is a Balm in Gilead

That evening they brought to Him many who were oppressed by demons, and He cast out the spirits with a word and healed all who were sick. Matthew 8:16

One Sunday evening, as our Lord went to the home of His disciple Peter, a great multitude followed. People came from the entire city of Capernaum, bringing those who were ill and diseased. It was indeed a picture of human misery and suffering. It moved our Lord to tender compassion. As the evangelist summarizes, He "healed all who were sick."

Not once did the heavenly Physician refuse to help those who needed Him! Not once was He limited in His ability to help, or shocked by the gravity of the illness, or perplexed as to how it should be treated! How graciously He offered Himself as the Helper of the helpless.

God's people can never forget that even today a willing heavenly Physician stands at their side. By stretching out His mighty hand He always helps. He never loses a patient. Either in His mercy He affects a cure through His agents, the physicians, gives the needed strength to go on, or calls our loved ones from all pain and sorrow to permanent health and happiness in heaven by His grace.

Help of the helpless, oh, abide with me. Amen. (LW 490:1)

Blessed Are the Humble

"Blessed are the poor in spirit, for theirs is the kingdom of heaven." Matthew 5:3

For the next few days we will focus on Christ's Sermon on the Mount and, in particular, to the Beatitudes. They give food for good thought during this Lenten season.

Jesus first speaks to us of humility. We are Christians, people of God, heirs of eternity. By the residue of our sinful nature, we naturally are inclined to boast of our goodness. But what reason do we have for pride? We sin miserably! Who are we that we should be so privileged of God? We are His people only because of His grace in Christ Jesus, our Savior.

Humility *is not* attained. Humility comes to us as a divine gift. Humility is to be found and made a part of our lives only when we, by Baptism, become participants in the life and death of our Lord Jesus Christ. There we share in our Lord's humility and meekness. There we see the lengths to which God has gone to redeem us from our unworthiness and to save us for all eternity. There we come into contact with a love that is beyond our human understanding.

We are poor sinners, unworthy of the least of God's mercies. But God loves us. While we were yet sinners, Christ died for us. There is no goodness in ourselves of which we can boast. There can be only divinely created humility. And because of Christ's humility for us, ours is the kingdom of heaven.

Thank You, Lord, that by Your humility You gave me the kingdom of heaven. Amen.

Blessed Are the Sorrowful

"Blessed are those who mourn, for they shall be comforted."
Matthew 5:4

No doubt, when Jesus made the statement above to the people gathered before Him, they were shocked. What blessing can come out of sorrow?

When Jesus spoke these words, He was thinking of something more than the sorrows of our everyday lives. But even here the joy that is born of sorrow is usually greater—more sanctified, more genuine. But Jesus was thinking of a spiritual sorrow: the sorrow one has because of his sins; the sorrow over one's inability to do and to love as God commanded; the sorrow over the lack of spiritual progress in daily living.

As you and I look back on our yesterdays, we are confronted with all our shortcomings. We see how we have failed in measuring up to God's standard of life. We have unnecessarily and harshly criticized our neighbor for doing that of which we ourselves are guilty; we have not always spoken the truth in love; we have lived much for ourselves and little for God. With this realization there comes over our spirits a contrition and sorrow for our sins and lack of spiritual progress. But we seek the forgiving grace of God, who speaks comfort and peace to our sorrowing hearts. Out of our sorrow there is born joy: joy born of God's Spirit through the Word; a joy that springs from the Gospel of Jesus Christ. Christ has fully paid the price for all sins. The joy of the kingdom of heaven is now ours eternally.

O Jesus, create and sustain and preserve in us the joy of Your forgiveness. Amen.

Blessed Are the Meek

"Blessed are the meek, for they shall inherit the earth."
Matthew 5:5

Perhaps the least practiced Christian virtue is that of meekness. To be respected, most people think one must wield the big stick and assert one's power and authority. Jesus speaks in directly the opposite way. He says the meek are the ones who will be blessed, for "they shall inherit the earth."

Who are the meek? Those who realize their utter dependence upon God, without whose help they can do nothing. This meekness is ours when, judged by God's standard of life, we realize how sinful and weak we really are. Then there is neither the desire nor the inclination to assert ourselves, to boast of our own righteousness and ability. It is then that we realize how dependent upon God we really are for all physical and spiritual blessings. Then a spirit of true meekness comes into our lives.

In that meekness there is found unspeakable blessing, for we shall inherit all the good things of the earth. Ours shall be hope and peace, forgiveness through faith in the atoning merits of Christ. With meekness and thanksgiving we shall receive all that a loving God is so willing to bestow. In us there will be the thorough realization that all we have and possess comes to us only by the grace of God. Instead of being lost in our own weakness, we shall be strong in the strength of the atoning Christ for time and for eternity.

O God, grant us this strength through meekness. Amen.

Blessed Are the Righteous

"Blessed are those who hunger and thirst for righteousness, for they shall be satisfied." Matthew 5:6

Sometimes we may become weary of hearing that we are to be good and are to show in our lives the faith that is in our hearts. But when God gives us the gift of faith, He also adds a peace and serenity that goes beyond human understanding. Such serenity of life is ours only when our lives are a continual hungering and thirsting after that righteousness which is found in our Savior, Jesus Christ, who secured it for us on Calvary's cross.

This intense desire for the righteousness of Christ becomes a part of our lives at that very moment when we give God priority over everything else, that is, in conversion. In any situation in life God will then come first, and we shall make a supreme effort to do those things He wants us to do—worship His name, make regular and daily use of His Word and prayer, frequently participate in the blessed Sacrament, and lead godly lives. In such seeking after the righteousness of Christ there are untold blessings, for Jesus says we shall be filled. On another occasion He expressed it in this way: "Seek first the kingdom of God and His righteousness" (Matthew 6:33). To this command an all-encompassing promise is attached: "All these things will be added to you."

O Jesus, cover us with Your righteousness during this Lenten season and always. Amen.

Blessed Are the Merciful

"Blessed are the merciful, for they shall receive mercy."
Matthew 5:7

If ever a word had a Christian connotation, it is "mercy." Only the Christian heart is truly merciful. Only the Christian can show the kind of mercy that God requires of us. Mercy had its beginning in God, who gave His only-begotten Son for the salvation of the world. God looked upon man in his sinful and lost condition and had mercy upon him. In that mercy God decreed that by the death of His Son eternal salvation should be made available to all mankind. Truly God is merciful.

Because of the mercy of God we have peace within our hearts. By the mercy of God we are forgiven all our sins, and we rest in the certain hope of eternal life. God has had mercy on us. We must have mercy on our fellow men. Blessed by mercy, we should with it bless others.

In a world that is cold and hardhearted, it is the Christian who must practice the virtue of mercy. Next to our faith in God, there is no greater joy on earth than to help our fellow man, to let flow into his life something of that love and concern Christ has for us. "Be merciful, even as your Father is merciful" (Luke 6:36). From Christ's mercy toward us—and His mercy alone—springs forth our mercy toward others.

O God, give us a clear vision of Your mercy in Christ that we may obtain and show mercy. Amen.

March

Blessed Are the Pure

See what kind of love the Father has given to us, that we should be called children of God; and so we are. The reason why the world does not know us is that it did not know Him. Beloved, we are God's children now, and what we will be has not yet appeared; but we know that when He appears we shall be like Him, because we shall see Him as He is. And everyone who thus hopes in Him purifies Himself as He is pure. 1 John 3:1–3

In His Sermon on the Mount our Savior made a promise to His believers that if they are pure of heart, they shall see God.

Who can ever be pure of heart? The pure of heart are those who, realizing that by nature they are sinful and unclean find comfort and joy in the blessed truth that "the blood of Jesus His Son cleanses us from all sin" (1 John 1:7). Their hearts having been purified by faith, they think and do those things that are pure in God's sight.

By declaring us pure of heart through the Word, the Holy Spirit enables us to see God in the glory of His grace. We see Him in our preservation from all evil, in our recovery from some serious illness, in the success of our business or profession, in our answered prayers.

But we shall yet see God even more wonderfully when we see Him perfectly in eternity. There "we shall see Him as He is." Thus we confess with the prophet Job, who said: "Yet in my flesh I shall see God, whom I shall see for myself, and my eyes shall behold, and not another" (Job 19:26–27).

O God, grant us purity of heart that we may see You through all eternity. Amen.

Blessed Are the Peacemakers

"Blessed are the peacemakers, for they shall be called sons of God." Matthew 5:9

Christ through His death for our atonement has brought about our reconciliation. He has made peace between man and God, against whom man has so grievously sinned and whose wrath and displeasure he has incurred. By faith in Christ we are at peace with God.

Christ also makes us peacemakers. That is, He now uses us as the vehicles and the mouthpieces of His peace, which we proclaim to the entire world. Opportunities for such peacemaking are to be found in our homes, in family relationships, in business dealings, wherever there may be a difference of opinion. We who know the peace of God are the ones qualified to bring peace to others. Thus we show ourselves to be that which God has already created us to be: the children of God.

O God, give us strength and courage to bring our fellow men to peace with You and with one another. Amen.

The Cross

And when they came to the place that is called The Skull, there they crucified Him, and the criminals, one on His right and one on His left. Luke 23:33

Jesus is the great Uniter of men. God "has made from one man every nation of mankind to live on all the face of the earth" (Acts 17:26). And Jesus has redeemed us to God by His blood so there is neither Jew nor Gentile, Greek nor barbarian, male nor female. All are one in Him. With Him there is no respect of persons.

Jesus is also the great Divider of men. All those who confess Him as Lord and Savior are one. But they are not one with unrepentant, unbelieving sinners. The cross divides all people into two groups.

Two thieves were crucified with Jesus. Both were sinners. The one remained unrepentant. He reviled Jesus. "Save yourself and us!" he said (Luke 23:39). The other confessed his sin and confessed Jesus as his Lord. He believed that Christ was coming into His own kingdom through death. These two men became separated because of Jesus.

The cross forever divides our sinful world into two separate worlds. There are those who are for Christ and those who are against Him. There is no neutral ground. Those who are His know it. "My sheep hear My voice, and I know them, and they follow Me. I give them eternal life, and they will never perish, and no one will snatch them out of My hand" (John 10:27).

In the cross of Christ I glory,
Tow'ring o'er the wrecks of time. Amen. (LW 101:1)

The "I Am"

Jesus said to them, "Truly, truly, I say to you, before Abraham was, I am." John 8:58

In the Gospel according to St. John, our Lord and Savior makes amazing assertions concerning Himself. Not the least is the statement of today's verse: "I am."

We are finite beings; our lives are limited by time and space. We think and act in terms of a beginning and an end. Unlike us, Jesus says He is eternal—He always was and always will be. He lives and reigns to all eternity. While this truth is beyond human understanding, it is a most precious article of our Christian faith.

Our Jesus is the same yesterday, today, and forever. He whose word of power brought the earth into being is the same Savior whose power operates in and directs our lives. He who during His life on earth had mercy and compassion on the sick, the downtrodden, and the sorrowful is the same Jesus who comforts us in all our trials and tribulations. He who was the great Friend of sinners, giving His life on Calvary's cross for the eternal salvation of souls, is the same Jesus whose blood cleanses us from all our sins and washes us whiter than snow. He who made the promise that where He is there shall His servants also be is the same Christ with whom we shall live through all eternity.

O God, grant that we believe in Jesus as the eternal Son of God and our blessed Redeemer. Amen.

March

The Zero Hour

And Jesus answered them, "The hour has come for the Son of Man to be glorified." John 12:23

During Lent, we remember our Lord's trip to Calvary by retracing His steps in order to behold again that His love is divine. Without the suffering and death of Jesus on Golgotha's cross, we would have no hope and heaven would be closed. Our faith would be meaningless, our life despairing. Through Jesus' death we find peace with God, for Jesus *is* the Lamb of God who takes away the sin of the world—*my sin*. Nothing is left undone.

At the cross we find healing for our soul and are restored to grace. We dwell in the presence of Jesus and are living in that faith which saves. The burdens of the day become lighter, the uncertainties are removed, and our ordeals are more readily met because Jesus is our Friend, who sticks closer than a brother.

That hour when Jesus gave Himself for our redemption is the zero hour in history. Although Jesus went down into death and hell, He came forth triumphantly to be proclaimed victor for time and eternity.

Today angels and saints and all Christendom give Him glory and honor as the risen Lord. He has given us peace with God and hope in the darkest hour of the night and guarantees us salvation through His resurrection.

Lord Jesus, continue in me that I may be with You forever. Amen.

The Joy before Him

Out of the anguish of his soul he shall see and be satisfied; by his knowledge shall the righteous one, my servant, make many to be accounted righteous, and he shall bear their iniquities.
Isaiah 53:11

The Ethiopian (Acts 8) was puzzled when he read this chapter on his way back home from Jerusalem. And well he might be. Isaiah had spoken of one whom he calls Immanuel, "God with us" (Matthew 1:23), "Wonderful Counselor, Mighty God, Everlasting Father, Prince of Peace" (Isaiah 9:6). Here he speaks of this same person as being despised, forsaken, pierced, crushed, beaten, and oppressed. He climaxes this tragedy by calling Him "a man of sorrows, and acquainted with grief" (Isaiah 53:3).

The secret of that mysterious union of "Immanuel" with this unmatched suffering is to be found in such expressions as "wounded for *our* transgressions . . . crushed for *our* iniquities" (Isaiah 53:5).

Through all of His vicarious pain and sorrow, therefore, Jesus looks to the outcome, "the joy that was set before Him" (Hebrews 12:2). Before His eyes there rises a kingdom, consisting of all who believe in Him as their personal Savior. It pervades, yet transcends the kingdoms of this world. It will continue to grow until that day when it will merge with that of heaven, where countless redeemed will join the angels' chorus in the theme of eternity: "Worthy is the Lamb who was slain, to receive power and wealth and wisdom and might and honor and glory and blessing" (Revelation 5:12).

Love so amazing, so divine,
Demands my soul, my life, my all! Amen. (LW 114:4)

Lent and Love

*In this is love, not that we have loved God but that He loved us
and sent His Son to be the propitiation for our sins. 1 John 4:10*

Like all of the seasons of the Church year, Lent speaks
God's love to the Church and the world. Christmas proclaims
the love of God the Father, who sent His only Son into the
world. Pentecost celebrates the love of God the Holy Spirit, who
alone makes possible our acceptance of God's love. Lent tells of
the love of God the Son, who died on the cross for the sins of all
mankind. There is joy in the Lenten message, the joy in knowing God's infinite love for us.

There is also sorrow in the Lenten season, sorrow particularly over our lovelessness to God. Every failure in our love to
one another is failure in our love to God. Every sin against
God's Law is failure to love, for "love is the fulfilling of the Law"
(Romans 13:10). Nothing we give or give up, nothing we do or
abstain from doing, can change our persistent lovelessness. But
"where sin increased, grace abounded all the more" (Romans
5:20). "In this is love, not that we have loved God but that He
loved us and sent His Son to be the propitiation [appeasement]
for our sins."

During Lent we make our confession: "I know my transgressions, and my sin is ever before me" (Psalm 51:3). On Good
Friday, God points us to the cross, where Jesus hung for our forgiveness. At Easter, God gives us further answer to our confession by pointing to the empty tomb.

Thanks and praise be to You, O God of love! Amen.

March

God's Goodness—Man's Repentance

Or do you presume on the riches of his kindness and forbearance and patience, not knowing that God's kindness is meant to lead you to repentance? Romans 2:4

The prodigal son had wasted everything in sinful living. His situation was desperate. What would he do? It was then that the memory of his father's goodness urged him to return home. Repentant, he said, "Father, I have sinned against heaven and before you" (Luke 15:18).

The psalmist reminds us that our Father in heaven "daily bears us up" (Psalm 68:19). Out of "the riches of His kindness" God supplies us every day with "all that [we] need to support this body and life" (*Luther's Small Catechism*).

Out of "the riches of His kindness and forbearance and patience" in Jesus Christ, God also "daily and richly forgives all my sins and the sins of all believers" (*Luther's Small Catechism*). "All this He does only out of fatherly, divine goodness and mercy, without any merit or worthiness in me" (*Luther's Small Catechism*).

How ungrateful, if we were to despise the riches of God's goodness! "Bless the LORD, O my soul, and forget not all His benefits" (Psalm 103:2).

Not despising the Lord's goodness, however, also demands daily repentance. Repentance means to confess our sins and to plead for pardon for Jesus' sake. This pardon God has already provided to you in the death and resurrection of His Son!

O God, forgive us our failures to appreciate as we should the riches of Your goodness. Help us also today, wherever we may be, to hallow Your name by bringing forth rich fruits of repentance. Amen.

What Jesus Meant to Peter

And the Lord turned and looked at Peter. And Peter remembered the saying of the Lord, how He had said to him, "Before the rooster crows today, you will deny Me three times." And he went out and wept bitterly. Luke 22:61–62

After our Lord had instituted the Holy Supper, He went to Gethsemane with His disciples. On the way He told them that on that very night they would fall away from Him. Peter replied that he would rather die with Him than deny Him.

It was not very long, however, before the Savior's warning proved to be true. Peter followed Jesus when He was taken to the palace of the high priest. While he was in the courtyard, a woman accused him, "You also were with the Nazarene, Jesus" (Mark 14:67). Peter became frightened and denied knowing Jesus.

For some time Peter's conscience did not seem to bother him very much because of his denial. But then Jesus passed by and looked at him.

Our consciences, too, frequently go to sleep. The minute we look up and see Jesus watching us, however, we begin to realize how terrible our wrongs really are. But the moment we become aware of this fact, something should happen on the inside. Something did happen to Peter. He realized his sin and wept bitterly. In the presence of Jesus we must, like Peter, shed tears of repentance and acknowledge our guilt to God.

If a look from Jesus caused Peter's conscience to become alive, then the love in the Savior's eye also reminded him that Jesus was the Lamb of God that takes away the sins of the world. This love likewise has forgiven you all your sins.

Blessed Lord Jesus, help us, by Your Spirit, to return again and again in true repentance to You for mercy and forgiveness. Amen.

"Where Is the Lamb?"

And Isaac said to his father Abraham, "My father!" And he said, "Here am I, my son." He said, "Behold, the fire and the wood, but where is the lamb for a burnt offering?" Genesis 22:7

If we could penetrate the darkest jungles and the most remote deserts, we would find no savage race without a consciousness of sin, without readiness to attempt to make good for that sin.

No person is saved by his own blood. Not the labor of our hands or ever-flowing tears can atone for sin. "Here is the fire and the wood, but where is the lamb?" asked the innocent lad. And so, with true Christian insight, we may say: "Here are the noble intentions and resolutions, here are the deeds done and the money given. But how useless they all are without the Lamb!"

Christ became the sacrificial Lamb to satisfy the claims of divine justice. It is true—God is love, and because of His love He sent Christ into the world to save us. We must remember, however, that God is also justice. His justice demanded punishment, even the shedding of blood. Therefore Christ shed His blood on the altar of the cross.

There is an ancient Jewish legend that on the night of the Passover a young Jewish maiden was so troubled she could not sleep. "Father," she anxiously inquired, "are you sure the blood is there?" He replied that he had ordered it sprinkled on the lintel, as God commanded. The restless girl was not satisfied until her father carried her to the door to see for herself. Lo! the blood was not there. Hastily the father remedied the omission.

Safely sheltered under the sin-atoning blood of the Lamb of God, we have security and peace.

O Lamb of God, grant me, washed and cleansed in Your precious blood, in heart and life a rich measure of Your peace and joy. Amen.

A Battle Predicted

"I will put enmity between you and the woman, and between your offspring and her offspring; He shall bruise your head, and you shall bruise His heel." Genesis 3:15

Satan was to bruise the heel of the woman's Seed, which was Christ. Satan was to have his hour. But Satan would have his head bruised. A head bruise is worse than a heel bruise.

The devil is the archenemy of God and man. And over two thousand years ago when Christ, the Son of God, came from heaven to champion man's cause, there was a battle, a showdown if you like, for the souls of men. Christ won the war for the liberation of lost mankind.

The old evil foe tried to conquer the Friend of sinners in that wilderness temptation. He tried it in that struggle in the Garden of Gethsemane. He tried it while Christ hung on the cross and evil men chided the suffering Christ, "He saved others; He cannot save Himself" (Matthew 27:42). But our Lord went through with it all, "proclaimed to the spirits in prison" (1 Peter 3:19), and rose from the dead—Satan's conqueror!

"Since therefore the children share in flesh and blood, He Himself likewise partook of the same things, that through death He might destroy the one who has the power of death, that is, the devil" (Hebrews 2:14).

O blessed Savior, we thank You that You conquered for us the prince of darkness. Amen.

The Shepherd's Love

"I am the good shepherd. The good shepherd lays down his life for the sheep." John 10:11

The relationship between shepherd and sheep was that of love. They constituted his all, and he was their lone defense and provider. There was no risk he would not take for his sheep. He had purchased them—they were his, and he was determined to keep them at all cost.

This describes our Good Shepherd, Jesus, and His relationship to us, His sheep. He has purchased us, "not with perishable things such as silver or gold, but with the precious blood of Christ" (1 Peter 1:18–19). We are His property. As long as we remain His sheep, His love surrounds us, protects us, comforts and cheers us. It is a love that spares nothing. It will sacrifice and labor so the needs of the sheep are adequately met. Thus the psalmist says, "The Lord is my Shepherd, I shall not want" (Psalm 23:1).

The knowledge and conviction that the Shepherd loves us so intensely fills us with security and peace despite the evils that lurk in the shadows all eager to devour us. We can go about our daily tasks in the certain knowledge that the love and concern of our heavenly Shepherd attends us.

Moreover, the love of the Shepherd is directed toward the individual sheep as well as the entire flock. Each sheep is made to feel as though it were the favorite of the Shepherd. Jesus would have us feel that we are not just one of many, but that we have been singled out for His loving concern.

Heavenly Shepherd, surround us always with Your love. Amen.

March

The Shepherd's Care

"For the Gentiles seek after all these things, and your heavenly Father knows that you need them all." Matthew 6:32

Good pasture, with ample water and good shelter, is the prime requisite for a flock, and the shepherd will give his all to secure it for his sheep. Although he travels far and leads his sheep through wandering paths, he wants the right kind of pasture.

His care is also demonstrated at eventide when he beds them down. If he wants to have his sheep spend the night in an enclosure, he will straddle the entrance and make each sheep pass through between his legs. As they pass under him, he gives them a thorough check. He notes the bruises, the cuts, the sprains, and whatever else may need attention, and administers the aid required.

All this reflects the relation of the Good Shepherd, Jesus, to each of us. Our physical needs are His concern. "Your heavenly Father knows that you need them all." He will not fail to supply them.

God's Word and Sacrament are designed to supply us with spiritual refreshment. This is the manna that keeps our souls strong and healthy. By this steady diet we build up our spiritual reserves that will stand us in good stead when the evil day descends. His promises of forgiveness assure us of His abiding love. He understands our weaknesses and stands ready to help us conquer them.

Heavenly Father, take away from us all worry and concern, and fill us with trust in Your loving concern. Amen.

The Shepherd's Eyes

The eyes of the LORD are toward the righteous and His ears toward their cry. Psalm 34:15

The eyes of the shepherd are ever scanning the flock. His eyes are quick to discern the dangers and evils that lurk in the thickets or under the rocks. His eyes are quick to note a shadow where there should be no shadow, the unnatural bending of the tall grasses or shrubs that would indicate a dangerous beast lurking there to pounce upon an unwary sheep.

His eyes are quick to note when any one of the flock is missing. The other sheep may be quite unconscious of the missing one, but the shepherd notes it at once and begins his search.

It is a great comfort to know that the heavenly Shepherd, Jesus, has such a watchful eye toward His own. And inasmuch as He is the all-seeing One, no foe can lurk in any shadow; no enemy, however clever at disguise, can make his approach but that He knows it.

The enemies of our souls are many. Satan lays many clever snares, but the Good Shepherd is never fooled. The sinful world also sets alluring things before us, and we are strongly tempted to partake or participate. But the Good Shepherd knows what harm can result and seeks to keep us from following.

Thank God that the eyes of the Shepherd, who seeks to bring us into the fold again, are upon us.

Lord Jesus, forgive our straying, and keep us ever with You. Amen.

The Shepherd's Strength

The salvation of the righteous is from the LORD; *He is their stronghold in the time of trouble. Psalm 37:39*

David tells us that while he served as shepherd to his father's flock, he encountered a lion and a bear and slew them. Here he demonstrated not only his strength, but also his willingness to risk his life for the sheep. The mere hireling is apt to run when the odds are too great against him. The shepherd that actually loves his flock will stand between them and all dangers and shield them with his very life.

So long as we are under the care of the heavenly Shepherd, we need not fear the claw of the bear or the tooth of the lion. We know we have a mighty defender who battles for us and with us against the evil foe, the foe who desires our overthrow. Satan, the aggressive enemy, never lets up. If he is foiled in one approach, he tries another. The evil world also tries its very best to snatch us from the side of the Good Shepherd, promising us richer and better pastures than we have. And our own sinful heart ever prompts us to give in and follow.

Against these temptations we cannot stand alone. Someone stronger than we must fight. And our Shepherd does this. He is more than a match for all our foes. He gained the victory over them by His death and resurrection, and that victory is made ours through Holy Baptism.

Our enemy is put to shame,
His short-lived triumph o'er;
Our God is with us, we exclaim,
We fear our foe no more.
From the hymn, "Welcome, Thou Victor in the Strife," verse 2.

Strengthen us with Your might, O Christ, that we not be overthrown. Amen.

The Shepherd's Faithfulness

Keep your life free from love of money, and be content with what you have, for He has said, "I will never leave you nor forsake you." Hebrews 13:5

The shepherd is always with his flock. In the heat of the summer you do not find him looking up a cool spot under some ledge of rock for an afternoon snooze while his sheep are wandering about in the staggering heat of the day. In the cold of winter you do not find the shepherd crawling into some cave and huddling about a fire while his sheep are left to shift for themselves in the cold and the storm. No, he stays with them. He shares the heat and the cold with them. He is always approachable.

This makes for security. The sheep do not panic when they see that their shepherd is near.

How true of the heavenly Shepherd, Jesus! "I will never leave you nor forsake you." "Behold, I am with you always" (Matthew 28:20).

When the heat of affliction bears down upon us, He stays by our side with His promises of relief and refreshments. The cool of the day follows the heat of the day, and His protective presence helps us immensely.

When the winter of doubt and disappointment and discouragement overtake us, He is right there with His steady encouragement and peace.

We praise You, O Lord, for Your faithfulness to us. Amen.

The Shepherd's Tenderness

He will tend his flock like a shepherd; he will gather the lambs in
his arms; he will carry them in his bosom, and gently lead those
that are with young. Isaiah 40:11

The tenderness of our heavenly Shepherd is an outstanding characteristic. Think of His dealing with some folks during
the time of His earthly ministry.

Remember what He said to Zacchaeus, the man ostra-
cized and hated by all others? "Hurry and come down, for I
must stay at your house today" (Luke 19:5). And we know the
transformation that came over that man.

Remember the woman taken in adultery? How vehe-
mently she was accused by the self-righteous Pharisees? But
Jesus said to them: "Let him who is without sin among you be
the first to throw a stone at her" (John 8:7).

And after the accusers had left, being convicted by their
own consciences, Jesus turned to the woman and said:
"Woman, where are they? Has no one condemned you?" (John
8:10). And when she said: "No one, Lord," Jesus said to her:
"Neither do I condemn you; go, and from now on sin no more"
(John 8:11).

That same tenderness Jesus shows toward us when we
have strayed. No harsh words of criticism and denunciation,
but words of love and welcome and forgiveness. Nor is His control that of the cold bit thrust between the teeth or the sting of
the lash, but: "I will counsel you with My eye upon you" (Psalm
32:8).

Lord Jesus, may each of us be more sensitive to the compulsion of Your
love. Amen.

The Lamb of God Silent

He was oppressed, and he was afflicted, yet he opened not his mouth; like a lamb that is led to the slaughter, and like a sheep that before its shearers is silent, so he opened not his mouth. Isaiah 53:7

A Lamb goes uncomplaining forth, The guilt of all men bearing;
And laden with the sins of earth, None else the burden sharing!
Goes patient on, grows weak and faint, To slaughter led without complaint,
That spotless life to offer; Bears shame, and stripes, and wounds and death,
Anguish and mockery, and saith, "Willing all this I suffer."

This Lamb is Christ, the soul's great Friend, The Lamb of God, our Savior;
Him God the Father chose to send To gain for us His favor.
"Go forth, My Son," the Father saith, "And free men from the fear of death,
From guilt and condemnation. The wrath and stripes are hard to bear,
But by Thy Passion men shall share The fruit of Thy salvation."

From morn till eve my theme shall be Thy mercy's wondrous measure;
To sacrifice myself for Thee Shall be my aim and pleasure.
My stream of life shall ever be A current flowing ceaselessly,
Thy constant praise outpouring. I'll treasure in my memory,
O Lord, all Thou hast done for me, Thy gracious love adoring.
    (TLH 142:1–2, 4)

O silently suffering Lamb, help me likewise to bear my burdens without complaint, but with full trust in You. Amen.

The Upper Room

And He took bread, and when He had given thanks, He broke it and gave it to them, saying, "This is My body, which is given for you. Do this in remembrance of Me." Luke 22:19

Here our blessed Savior celebrated the last Jewish ceremonial Passover before the feast was buried forever in His own eternal sacrifice. Here He gathered His weary, wavering disciples about Himself once more and spoke to them of faith and love and hope and joy, of the sorrow of earth, and of the waiting mansions in heaven. Here He made His last will and testament, instituting the Sacrament of His body and blood.

This holy gift of heavenly food directs us to the great central fact of the Christian faith—it tells us of atonement, of reconciliation with God through Christ's death. This meal is not merely a memorial. Our Lord took bread and wine and with these gave to His disciples His very body and blood. What for? For the remission of sins. It was a seal upon everything He had said, the pledge of everything He had promised.

We cherish this gift that continually expresses our Savior's dying love. We gratefully and obediently remember the urgent words of our Savior: "Do this in remembrance of Me." Penitently, believingly, and frequently we partake of this precious Sacrament for the comfort and peace of our souls, for our greater assurance and certainty, for a strengthened and more intimate fellowship with our God and Savior.

Blessed Savior, who has instituted the Sacrament of Your body and blood as a memorial of Your Passion and a seal and pledge of Your forgiving mercy, grant that we may treasure it and partake of it diligently to our peace and joy, for a strengthened faith and purified life. Amen.

April

God's Guarantee

He who did not spare His own Son but gave Him up for us all,
how will He not also with Him graciously give us all things?
Romans 8:32

The Federal Deposit Insurance Corporation, an agency of the United States Government, guarantees certain bank deposits. This guarantee gives to a depositor a sense of security. The depositor knows that the resources of the corporation are pledged to redeem the promise the bank made to pay whenever he needs his money.

God has likewise given us a guarantee, as it were, that He will redeem every promise He has ever made to provide for all our wants, both of body and soul. That guarantee bond is the gift of His own Son to be our Savior. "He who did not spare His own Son but gave His up for us all, how will He not also with Him graciously give us all things?" The argument is this: If God has done the greater, offering up His only-begotten Son for redemption, then surely it is reasonable to conclude that He, whose Word is truth, will also do the lesser, supply all other needs we may ever have.

Think of the Holy Supper as a special guarantee offered us by our gracious God. The Lord gives us, under the bread and wine in the Sacrament, the Savior's body and blood, to guarantee to each of us personally that the blessings of Christ's sacrificial suffering and death are truly ours.

Lord Jesus, we beseech You that we, too, may find in this Sacrament assurance of full pardon for our sins, increase of our faith, and strength for our Christian life. May every celebration of this Holy Supper remind us of Your saving death and go with us as an abiding benediction on our life and service for You. Amen.

The Lord's Supper

*And He took bread, and when He had given thanks, He broke it
and gave it to them, saying, "This is My body, which is given for
you. Do this in remembrance of Me." Luke 22:19*

Our blessed Lord has provided us with a powerful means
to strengthen our faith and to increase our courage to fight all
our spiritual enemies. In the night before His death after the
Passover meal Jesus took bread and gave thanks and broke it
and gave it to His disciples saying: "This is My body, which is
given for you." Likewise: "This cup that is poured out for you is
the new covenant in My blood" (Luke 22:20).

Every time the Lord's Supper is properly celebrated, the
living Lord is present. When we eat the consecrated bread, He
imparts to us that body which He sacrificed for us on Calvary's
cross. Likewise when we partake of the cup, He in a supernatural manner imparts that blood which was shed for us for the
forgiveness of all our sins.

We rest assured, strengthened in our faith, that we are
completely redeemed, since our Savior "offered for all time a
single sacrifice for sins" (Hebrews 10:12). "By a single offering
He has perfected for all time those who are being sanctified"
(Hebrews 10:14).

Every time we partake of the Lord's Supper, God in His
grace deals with us personally and conveys to us individually
the complete benefit of Christ's redeeming work and merit.

*Glorified Lord and Savior, as we come to Your heavenly feast, replace
our doubts with a strong faith. Remove our guilt, and impart to us
Your righteousness. Fill our hearts with courage and zeal to serve You
and our neighbor in true holiness all the days of our life. Amen.*

His Blood on US

And all the people answered, "His blood be on us and on our children!" Matthew 27:25

How far-reaching these significant words uttered by the people on that day on which they crucified our Lord! Through the ages this utterance has pursued their children's children who cried out: "Away with Him, away with Him!" (John 18:15).

"His blood be on us" is the sneer of the indifferent who reject Christ Jesus as Savior. They are not interested and pass by shrugging their shoulders, saying: "What is that to us?" (Matthew 27:4).

"His blood be on us" is the cry of those terrified by the Law of God. Their consciences have been aroused and awakened. They behold the holiness of God and their own sinfulness. As the finger of guilt points at them they will say to the mountains, "Fall on us" (Luke 23:30). They know that the Law of God condemns them. "The soul who sins shall die" (Ezekiel 18:4).

"His blood be on us." O blessed words to the believer! For the blood of Jesus Christ cleanses us from all sin. As I look up to the cross, I know that Jesus is my substitute, atoning for my sin. He took upon Himself the load of my transgressions and that of the whole world. Now His blood is on us, washing us whiter than snow.

Lord Jesus, Savior of all, give us grace to come to Your cross in this sacred week and find cleansing, healing peace, and life eternal. Amen.

The Precious Christ

So the honor is for you who believe, but for those who do not believe, "The stone that the builders rejected has become the cornerstone." 1 Peter 2:7

Peter wrote the above to the Christians who were scattered throughout the region now known as Turkey. These Christians were suffering persecution. But through it all they had one possession that no one could take from them. This was the precious Christ.

Jesus is not the only gift God gives us. He gives us many beautiful things, our homes, our families, a wonderful, colorful, enchanting world with all the products of His divine artistry and generous goodness. But Jesus is the most precious of God's gifts.

We shall not recognize this fact unless the Spirit of God has first convinced us that we are needy sinners. But once that has been achieved, then the Spirit can go on and teach us to see ever more clearly how precious Jesus really is. Then He helps us see Jesus as the One who has saved us from our sins by His great work of salvation.

Jesus is precious also because He is our Friend. He has shown us through His brief ministry how concerned He is to heal the sick, befriend the poor, comfort the sorrowing, feed the hungry, cleanse the lepers, and so forth.

Jesus is precious because He is our Guide. He lived a sacrificing life of love so we might learn from Him how we are to live.

Jesus is precious because He inspires us to do what we do, not for reasons of selfish gain and reward, but from motives of love.

Jesus is precious because He is our Hope. Through Him alone is it possible for us to look forward with joy and certainty to an eternal happiness.

Gracious God, we thank You for the gift of the precious Christ. Amen.

A Confident Expectancy

"Yet a little while and the world will see Me no more, but you will see Me. Because I live, you also will live." John 14:19

We have from God a glorious promise that we live not merely for a time, but for eternity. Death will bring life's little day to a close, but death is merely a brief interruption of our physical existence. In the light of the invincible Easter truth, we have an absolute certainty regarding our future existence. Christ arose and lives; therefore we, too, shall arise and live.

The captain of a transatlantic liner related that years ago one of his passengers was Jenny Lind, the Christian young lady who had dedicated her beautiful voice to the Lord. One morning she arose early and, standing on the bridge, saw the sun rise out of the trackless ocean. That radiance of daybreak awoke within her heart thoughts of eternity, and she began to sing from Handel's *Messiah* the unforgettable aria beginning: "I know that my Redeemer liveth" and ending: "I, too, shall live."

If from the heights of our Christian faith we greet each new day with the song of Easter triumph: "I know that my Redeemer liveth," we can end all of life's days with the Christ-centered confidence: "I, too, shall live."

Yes, the best is still to come. Since Christ has conquered sin and death and lives forever as our King victorious, we, and all who sleep in Him, are assured of life and blessedness unending. When the trumpet sounds on the last great Easter morn at the end of time, we shall come forth from our sleeping chambers, clothed with light and immortality.

This confident expectancy cheers and sustains our hearts in life's trials and troubles. It deepens our longing to be forever with our Lord.

I know that My Redeemer lives! Amen.

"All Power Is Given unto Me"

And Jesus came and said to them, "All authority in heaven and on earth has been given to Me." Matthew 28:18

The disciples, obedient to Jesus' command, assembled on a mountainside in Galilee. There He appeared to them to awe them with His presence and to uplift them with His words. And strong, majestic words they were! "All authority in heaven and on earth has been given to Me." Only God's Son could make such a claim. Only He has universal power. Creation hearkens to no other voice. "At the name of Jesus," cries St. Paul, "every knee should bow, in heaven and on earth and under the earth" (Philippians 2:10).

Jesus has power to *rule*. All nations bow to His command. His mighty hand is seen in nature, in history, and in every human life. He indeed is "King of kings and Lord of lords" (1 Timothy 6:15).

Jesus has power to *judge*. Everyone must stand before His throne. There He will discern every thought, probe every conscience, search every heart. He will separate His friends from His foes. On the Last Day He will say either "Well done!" or "Depart!"

Jesus has the power to *save*. He came to seek and to save that which was lost. On Good Friday His mission was accomplished, and on Easter His victory appeared. His prophecy came true: "And I, when I am lifted up from the earth, will draw all people to Myself" (John 12:32). His power forgives our sins, sustains our life, defeats our foes, and will bring us to heaven at last.

Thank You, dear Jesus, that You exert Your power for my benefit. Amen.

April

Still the Wonderful Christ

Jesus Christ is the same yesterday and today and forever.
Hebrews 13:8

"His name shall be called Wonderful" (Isaiah 9:6), exclaims the ancient prophet Isaiah. The historian H. G. Wells names six men as history's greatest, but then he adds that the absolute greatest, in a class all by Himself, is Jesus. No one else is like Him. And we Christians know this as we confess that Jesus is "God of very God."

He is wonderful in His birth, for in Him was no sin. The child born of the Virgin Mary was the Son of God made flesh by the miraculous operation of the Holy Spirit.

He is wonderful as prophet. None ever spoke as He did. The kindest word ever to fall from lips of humans was uttered by Jesus. "Come to Me, all who labor and are heavy laden, and I will give you rest. Take My yoke upon you, and learn from Me, for I am gentle and lowly in heart, and you will find rest for your souls" (Matthew 11:28–29). "For God so loved the world, that He gave His only Son, that whoever believes in Him should not perish but have eternal life" (John 3:16).

He is wonderful as the Lamb of God, sacrificed for our sins and making complete satisfaction for our many transgressions. This Jesus, dead and placed into the tomb, rose the third day to live eternally.

Divine Savior, beneath Your cross we take our stand to be washed and healed today and to the end of days to see You in glory. Amen.

Only a Risen Christ

And if Christ has not been raised, your faith is futile and you are still in your sins. 1 Corinthians 15:17

When the keystone drops out of an arch, the arch will surely fall. So also, when the keystone of our faith falls, which is Christ's resurrection, then Christianity as a whole will fall. Redemption falls to ruin and leaves us still in our sins. The only Christ who has power to atone for sin is the risen Christ, who became sins for us that we might become the righteousness of God in Him.

The apostle presents this issue in clear and telling language. If there is no resurrection, as the Sadducees and others in His day believed, then is Christ not raised? Accept that as your creed, and you may as well close the door that leads to pardon, peace, and life. Then our religion is a monstrous illusion.

Only the risen Christ can explain Calvary and the healing streams of mercy and love that flow from there. Only a risen Christ can explain the events of the resurrection morning and of the succeeding days until a cloud received Him out of sight. Only a risen Christ can explain the day of Pentecost and the onward course of Christianity through twenty centuries of history and achievement. And let us be certain—only a risen Christ can save us from our sin. The resurrection of Christ is the final seal of assurance of our own resurrection from the dead.

So strengthen our faith, divine Lord and Savior, by Your resurrection, that in every circumstance of life we may never doubt Your faithfulness and truth. Amen.

My Shepherd

The LORD is my shepherd; I shall not want. Psalm 23:1

Here David, once a shepherd boy, is essentially saying: "All that I ever was to my sheep, that the Lord is to me. He knows me even better than I could know the individual sheep of my flock. He cares for me, provides for me, guides me, and protects me. Great God that He is, yet He is just such a shepherd to me!"

The divine gift of faith enabled David to say that. David had been not only a great king and a great psalmist but also a great sinner! How, then, could he claim the Lord as his Shepherd? Because he believed that this Lord was also the promised Messiah who would come and redeem sinners, even sinners like himself.

He did come. And when Jesus said: "I am the Good Shepherd. The Good Shepherd lays down His life for the sheep" (John 10:11), He declared that David, for as great sinner that he was, could still call the Messiah "my Shepherd."

When we read this Psalm and make its words our own and dare to call the great God our Shepherd, we, too, believe Him to be our Savior who laid down His life for us, who fought the wolves of sin and death and hell, and saved us from the fangs of Satan.

We, the sheep of His flock, stand at His empty tomb and sing: "For You were slain, and by Your blood You ransomed people for God" (Revelation 5:9). Therefore, "I shall not want," and "I will fear no evil" (Psalm 23:4), not even sin, death, and hell—the greatest of all evils!

Lord, I fear no foe with thee a hand to bless. Amen. (LW 490:4).

Social Security

The LORD is my shepherd; I shall not want. Psalm 23:1

David knew that our spiritual requirements are our greatest needs. In Psalm 32 he sings: "Blessed is the one whose transgression is forgiven, whose sin is covered" (Psalm 32:1). David also knew that as long as we live in this world, our bodies, too, would have needs and that we must have food and clothing and shelter.

From personal experience David also knew the fears and worries associated with these bodily wants. During his boyhood days, when he worked as a shepherd; later, when he was persecuted by King Saul; and still later, when he was a king, but forced to flee before the conspiracy of his own son Absalom, he had known danger and want and privation. On more than one occasion he had seen death itself staring him in the face.

Yet, even in all these trying circumstances, the Lord had provided for all his needs and had not permitted his enemies to do him any harm.

People today are very much concerned about their future physical and material welfare. But nothing can ever compare with what we have right *now*: our Good Shepherd, the God from whom all blessings flow and who enables those who believe in Him to say: "I shall not want."

Lord, keep me from all fear and worry! Amen.

Rest

He makes me lie down in green pastures. He leads me beside still waters. Psalm 23:2

At first thought it might appear that the Shepherd doesn't know much about His job because the first thing He does is to put His sheep to rest. Surely, we think, the first job of a shepherd ought to be to put them to work—to find pasturage and let them feed!

But I remember seeing cattle drives from farmyards to stockyards for shipment to market: the cattle were constantly milling, frothing, sweating. One of the big problems was to keep them calm and to make them rest periodically.

Those cattle drives illustrate life in this bewildered, nervous world: people scrambling, scratching for a living, rushing, hustling, anxious and concerned—disturbed without by the tensions of the times, and worried within by the guilt of conscience.

In the midst of this cacophony, listen to the voice, the Good Shepherd: "Take your rest here with Me! Stop worrying! Quit your scrambling! I have atoned for all of your sins! I have defeated all your enemies! I have won for you forgiveness and a Father's never-failing love! Peace! Be still!"

Jesus, still lead on
Till our rest be won. Amen. (LW 386:1)

April

Right Paths

He restores my soul. He leads me in paths of righteousness for His name's sake. Psalm 23:3

David did not permit his sheep to remain at rest in the glades, basking quietly and at ease in the green pastures and by still waters. After they had been refreshed, he called them forth again and took them out to clamber over the steep hillsides of Judea. That was a necessary part of their development, to grow into strong and sturdy sheep.

So the Christian life is not always "resting" in church, feeding upon the bread and water of life. The Christian life is active. Motivated by the Gospel, Christians work with Christ, and, if need be, suffer with Him.

As we make our way through the world, Christ in His Word leads us. We walk, first of all, "in paths of righteousness," i.e., in the right paths that the Good Shepherd has marked out for us, and we should walk in these right paths "for His name's sake."

Lord, lead me in Your righteousness. Amen.

Through the Shadow

Even though I walk through the valley of the shadow of death, I will fear no evil, for You are with me; Your rod and Your staff, they comfort me. Psalm 23:4

Having reviewed all of his experiences with the Good Shepherd through the years and finding that He had provided for all his need and kept his enemies from doing him any harm, David now looks toward the approaching end of his life, and he asks, Will He be my Good Shepherd even then? And he answers: "Even though I walk through the valley of the shadow of death, I will fear no evil."

David's faith is not just stoic courage in the face of something inevitable. Two phrases in particular indicate that. Note first that he says he will walk not "into" the valley, but "through" the valley of death. He believes that he will not remain in death's dark valley, but that he will pass through it to the other side, to the life beyond, where he will "dwell in the house of the LORD forever" (Psalm 23:6).

Note also that he calls it "the shadow of death." For him death has lost its reality; it is but a shadow of its former terrifying self. David believed that the Good Shepherd would "[abolish] death and [bring] life and immortality to light" (2 Timothy 1:10). Through faith in the coming Redeemer, death lost its sting and the grave its victory.

We have the same glorious Gospel of our Good Shepherd's redeeming death and triumphant resurrection. The living Lord also says to us: "Because I live, you also will live" (John 14:19), and: "I am the resurrection and the life. Whoever believes in Me, though he die, yet shall he live, and everyone who lives and believes in Me shall never die" (John 11:25–26).

Lord, take my hand, and lead me. Amen. (LW 512:1)

Two Sticks

Even though I walk through the valley of the shadow of death, I will fear no evil, for You are with me; Your rod and Your staff, they comfort me. Psalm 23:4

Here is a rather strange statement. It must sound very peculiar, especially to little boys. For what is a rod? And what is a staff? Someone may answer: Sticks! A rod and a staff, two sticks, they comfort me. Well, I did not get much comfort from sticks as a boy, either at home or at school. Boys nowadays may not know much about that, but in my boyhood days, sticks were a source of considerable discomfort!

How, then, can a rod and a staff be a comfort to me? The rod is nothing other than the symbol of authority. For example, Pharaoh feared when he saw Moses' rod, and the waters of the Red Sea parted when Moses stretched forth his rod by God's authority!

At my Baptism, Christ called me by my name and said with divine authority, "You are Mine. I bought you with the price of My holy, precious blood! I am your Lord, your Shepherd. No man shall pluck you out of My hand."

The staff is a symbol of protection. It is the shepherd's crook. With it the shepherd guides the sheep and lifts them back to safety when they fall, or he throws it with unerring aim at the wolf or wild dog that threatens the sheep.

So God takes care of me with His rod and staff, and that comforts me! I'm not dependent upon my own strength and resources.

Lord Jesus, help us to find our defense in You. Amen.

Christian Sorrow

"Truly, truly, I say to you, you will weep and lament, but the world will rejoice. You will be sorrowful, but your sorrow will turn into joy." John 16:20

Here grief is foretold: "You will be sorrowful." The prophet described Christ as "a man of sorrows, and acquainted with grief" (Isaiah 53:3). The chosen disciples wept and lamented for their Lord and for themselves. They loved Him dearly, and His suffering and pain could not fail to produce suffering and pain in them. They realized with deepest pain and grief their own sinfulness, and how they had increased His sorrow through their selfish disloyalty and unfaithfulness.

Is not this our own experience? Being acquainted with Christ, we are acquainted also with grief, above all, with the one great cause of all grief—sin. We weep for our sins and the sins of those about us. We mourn by reason of all our sufferings and afflictions. We mourn in sympathy with the sufferings and afflictions of others.

"But your sorrow will turn into joy" (John 16:20). Therefore we sorrow not as they who have no hope. Instead of bearing our sorrow with stoic resignation, we rather rejoice and glory in it, confidently expecting it to be turned into endless joy sooner or later.

Light of lights, shine through the gloom, and turn our tears to gladness. Amen.

Seeing Jesus

"A little while, and you will see Me no longer; and again a little while, and you will see Me." John 16:16

To the disciple who loves his Lord, it is not the cares and grief of this present time that really oppress him. Nor is it the burden of this life's tasks and duties. It is rather the Savior's withdrawal of His visible presence from His people.

"You will not see Me" (Matthew 23:39). The bereavement and sorrow of the disciples was caused by their not seeing Him. The Lord had removed Himself, not from their presence but from their view. They did not see Him. How terribly long those three short days, from Good Friday to Easter, must have seemed to them; yet they were such "a little while"! When they saw Him again, all the sorrows of those three days were swallowed up in the breathless joy of that blessed moment. "Then the disciples were glad when they saw the Lord" (John 20:20).

At His ascension our Lord was taken up, and a cloud received Him out of sight. "Men of Galilee, why do you stand looking into heaven?" (Acts 1:11). He shall come again, visibly. "Every eye will see Him, even those who pierced Him" (Revelation 1:7). His coming will bring everlasting joy to His people, joy in the sight of the Lord, when they will see Him face to face as He is.

Lord, open my eyes, that I may behold Your face. Amen.

The Easter Sunrise

And very early on the first day of the week, when the sun had risen, they went to the tomb. Mark 16:2

The rising sun of Easter revealed the empty tomb of the risen Lord. Before long Mary Magdalene, Johanna, Salome, and other women saw the living Jesus. The same day, at evening, disciples, hidden behind closed doors, saw Jesus again, who identified Himself by His pierced hands and feet. Historically it is proved that the grave was empty and Jesus was seen alive on that first day.

The risen sun of Easter dispels the gloomy shadows of sin and death. By reason of our sinful nature the guilt of transgressing against the will of God hangs over us and fills the soul with fear of the judgment to come. The risen Lord promises peace and forgiveness. God is reconciled through the cross of Calvary. Jesus' resurrection proclaims to sinful man that the risen Lord has defeated the powers of hell and set us free. Therefore death holds no terror for us believers. We pass through its shadows into the presence of God. The risen Jesus says: "Because I live, you also will live" (John 14:19).

Risen Lord, dwell with me now and forever. Amen.

April

No More Tears

"He will wipe away every tear from their eyes, and death shall be no more, neither shall there be mourning nor crying nor pain anymore, for the former things have passed away." Revelation 21:4

In vain mother Eve held the head of her son Abel on her knees and caressed his cheeks and tenderly called his name. There was no response. His eyes were closed in death's long slumber, his lips were sealed, and his heart had ceased to beat.

"We must all die; we are like water spilled on the ground, which cannot be gathered up again" (2 Samuel 14:14). Jesus Himself wept at the grave of Lazarus, His friend. On Good Friday, Mary stood beneath the cross with a sorrow too great for tears. Luther called this life in which we live a "vale of tears." If we have not yet found it so, the hour of bereavement may be at hand.

What heavenly comfort for us to know that there will be no bereavement, nor trials of any kind, in the world to come! God, our loving Father, will wipe away all tears from our eyes; that one glimpse of heaven will compensate us for all tears ever shed!

The tears that welled up in the Savior's eyes as He looked down upon apostate Jerusalem were more than tears of sympathy, more than pearls in the sight of God; they were a part of the price He paid that our tears might be forever dried.

Be still, my soul, though dearest friends depart
And all is darkened in the vale of tears;
Then you will better know his love, his heart,
Who comes to soothe your sorrows and your fears. Amen. (LW 510:3)

Sorrow into Joy

"Truly, truly, I say to you, you will weep and lament, but the world will rejoice. You will be sorrowful, but your sorrow will turn into joy." John 16:20

Here is the promise of grief assuaged. Like the joy of the hypocrite, so the sorrow of the Christian is but for a moment. "Those who sow in tears shall reap with shouts of joy" (Psalm 126:5).

It was so with the disciples. All the sorrows of Good Friday were swallowed up in the high and holy joy of Easter. Christ's resurrection was life from the dead for them, and their sorrow for Christ's sufferings was turned into such joy that it could not be dampened and embittered by any sufferings of their own.

This is exactly what our Lord also promises us. He went through His own grief "for the joy that was set before Him" (Hebrews 12:2), and in His Word He reveals three things to us concerning this joy and our participation in it.

First there is the joy of reunion. "I will see you again" (John 16:22). Separation is but for a little while. This same Jesus will surely come again. All doubt will be cleared away, interrupted communion revived, and joy restored.

Then there is the rejoicing that will result from Christ's victory. "Your hearts will rejoice" (John 16:22). Yes, indeed, in His presence is fullness of joy that no tongue can tell, no heart conceive!

Third and best of all: "No one will take your joy from you" (John 16:22). God will wipe away all tears from our eyes, for the former things are passed away. Grief is swallowed up in everlasting joy.

Dear Jesus, restore to me the joy of Your salvation. Amen.

The Cure of Care

Cast your burden on the LORD, and He will sustain you; He will never permit the righteous to be moved. Psalm 55:22

The person who carries a heavy load cannot do much of anything else. The person who is weighted down with worry is too busy with his self-imposed burden to find time and energy for his real tasks.

Man would be justified in worrying if he were his own god, if he had to face a dangerous, competitive, and largely predatory world alone with his own feeble power.

Worry directly contrasts with our oft-repeated creed: "I believe in God the Father Almighty." It shows distrust in the many reassuring promises of God, who is faithful.

How can we worry if, with the apostle St. Paul, we stand under the cross of our Savior and draw the same conclusion: "He who did not spare His own Son but gave Him up for us all, how will He not also with Him graciously give us *all things*?" (Romans 8:32, emphasis added).

The psalmist therefore urges: "Cast your burden on the LORD." No matter how large or small, no matter what its nature, drop all of it from your shoulders, and lay it at the feet of God, of whom we read: "He cares for you" (1 Peter 5:7). The apostle Paul takes up the strain and states it in unforgettable words: "Do not be anxious about anything, but in everything by prayer and supplication with thanksgiving let your requests be made known to God" (Philippians 4:6).

In Thee I place my trust, On Thee I calmly rest. Amen. (TLH 435:2)

We Cannot Come Down

And I sent messengers to them, saying, "I am doing a great work and I cannot come down. Why should the work stop while I leave it and come down to you?" Nehemiah 6:3

When Nehemiah returned from the captivity of Judah, he and his followers immediately began rebuilding their ruined city—"the walls of Jerusalem that were broken down and its gates that had been destroyed by fire" (Nehemiah 2:13). Shortly after the work of restoration had begun, the enemies of God's people attempted to halt the rebuilding of Jerusalem by ridicule, by force, and finally by trickery. When any attempt was made to lure Nehemiah from the walls of the ruined city, his stock answer was: "I am doing a great work, and cannot come down." And those words were said not in pride, not in vanity, but in a divinely revealed realization that he was doing the Lord's work.

What an example for us! The forces of evil constantly beset us. In the home, on the farm, in the factory, at school, in play, or at work we face temptation. It is comforting to know that the same God who enabled Nehemiah to resist the onslaughts of his enemies stands at our side, giving us strength through Christ to remain on the heights on which He would have us walk. Looking to Him for the power to resist evil, we, too, have the strength to repel our tempters with Nehemiah's watchwords: I am doing a great work, and cannot come down.

Lord Jesus, give me Your Holy Spirit, that I may do the things that are befitting the mercy You have shown to me. Amen.

From Darkness to Light

Out of the depths I cry to you, O LORD! Psalm 130:1

Two of the outstanding hymns that flowed from the heart and the pen of Dr. Martin Luther were "A Mighty Fortress Is Our God" and "From Depths of Woe I Cry to Thee." The melody of one was in the major key and the other in the minor key.

The 130th Psalm, which inspired the latter hymn, is the nearest approach in the Old Testament to chapter 8 of the Epistle to the Romans. This psalm offers an exact picture of what took place in the soul of Luther. He was led out of indescribable depths of distress to see the plenteous redemption in Jesus, our Savior. He was as one who waited in the night and then saw the beautiful sunrise at Calvary.

Luther wrote the hymn in 1523. Several months later, a poor old weaver sang it in the streets of Magdeburg and offered it for sale at a price that would help him put food on the table. He was cast into prison by the burgomaster, but 200 citizens marched to the town hall and would not leave until he was freed.

When Luther, during the Augsburg Diet, was at the Castle of Coburg and suffered much from inner conflict, he invited his friends to sing, in defiance of the devil, such hymns to extol and praise God.

The psalm is an inexhaustible treasury of comfort that speaks of the great comfort God gives to us in His resurrected Son, Jesus, who died to overcome every adversary.

Lord, we thank You for Your unfailing mercy. Amen.

The Head of the Church

For the husband is the head of the wife even as Christ is the head of the church, His body, and is Himself its Savior.
Ephesians 5:23

The body of Christ on earth is the Christian Church. Christ's love for the church was so great that He was willing to leave His Father's home and come down to earth to win her for His bride. It cost Him His mortal life, but even this He was willing to pay in order to claim His bride. His love for her is an everlasting love. There is nothing He will not do for her, if it is for her welfare. He is her Provider, her Defender, and her Director in all matters. As a loving husband is the head of the wife, so Christ is the head of His church.

If Christ is the head of the church, then she should hearken to His voice in all things. The world at times seeks to charm her with its ways. Oftentimes the devil seeks to worm his way into her affections. Sometimes even men seek to usurp the place of the true head of the church. No man or council of men dare ever come between her and her true head. If she is the bride of Christ, she will hearken only to His voice and seek only to serve Him.

As a wife leans upon her husband, so the church leans upon Christ. He says, "I will never leave you nor forsake you" (Hebrews 13:5). His knowledge, His power, His love, are all at her disposal. He assures His bride that no real harm will ever come nigh her if she is faithful to Him. He rules the whole world for her well-being. We can look quietly upon all the perplexities and fear no evil.

Lord Jesus, come daily with healing love into our hearts. Amen.

Joy in Heaven

"Just so, I tell you, there is joy before the angels of God over one sinner who repents." Luke 15:10

The occasion for this statement was the parable of the lost sheep. The shepherds of the Middle East knew and loved their sheep. If one of them strayed from the fold, there was an immediate, anxious, and diligent search. When it was found, the shepherd laid it on his shoulders, rejoiced, and shared his joy with his friends.

> *None of the ransomed ever knew*
> *How deep were the waters crossed.*
> *Nor how dark was the night the Lord passed through,*
> *Ere He found His sheep that was lost,*
> *When all through the mountain thunder-riven,*
> *And up from the rocky steep,*
> *There arose a glad cry to the gates of heaven:*
> *"Rejoice, I have found my sheep!"*

From the hymn, "Ninety and Nine," verse 3.

In this same chapter of Luke's Gospel follows the story of the prodigal son. How his father's heart melted with compassion when he saw him coming home, changed and penitent! How he kissed him and pressed him to his bosom! Calling for new clothing and the fatted calf, he said: "Let us eat and celebrate. For this my son was dead, and is alive again; he was lost, and is found" (Luke 15:23–24). In the same way, the Lord Jesus rejoices over each of us, whom He has redeemed with His precious blood.

Thank You, dear Lord, that there is rejoicing in heaven that You found me. Amen.

Heirs of God

For the mind that is set on the flesh is hostile to God, for it does not submit to God's law; indeed, it cannot. Romans 8:7

A hard-working father had never been able to get out of the tenement section of the city. Where he lived, there was no patch of sunshine; there were no lawns, no shrubs, no flowers, only narrow, noisy, crowded streets and untidy gutters. One day he fell heir to a lovely home on the west side of town, where the air was pure and the skies were blue. The children went racing through the house and through the garden, shouting: "Is this ours, Father, is this ours?" "Yes," he said, with a new light in his face, "it is ours!" It belonged to the children as joint heirs, because it belonged to the father.

It is not what a child does that makes it the heir of its father, but the parentage. We are children of God on two counts: "God sent forth His Son, born of a woman, born under the Law, to redeem those who were under the Law, so that we might receive the adoption as sons" (Galatians 4:4); and, "To all who did receive Him, who believed in His name, He gave the right to become children of God" (John 1:12).

I am now Your child, O Lord, not by my choice or decision but by Your loving action and Yours alone. Amen.

Christians Live in Hope

Blessed be the God and Father of our Lord Jesus Christ!
According to His great mercy, He has caused us to be born again
to a living hope through the resurrection of Jesus Christ from the
dead. 1 Peter 1:3

During the last world war people in many countries lived in constant fear. The roaring of enemy bombers, the bursting of shells, and the shrieks of pain and death kept the people dazed and afraid.

Many heroic stories are still told about the calmness of long-suffering Christians who lived through all those hours of terror without losing hope. They felt confident that the almighty Maker of heaven and earth was still watching over His world and able to keep the souls of His elect safe in His protecting arms of love.

Peter points to the foundation of the Christian's hope. God the Father through His abundant mercy has brought about the Christian's spiritual rebirth through the resurrection of Jesus Christ from the dead.

Christ, too, fell in the terrible war between God and Satan, predicted in the Garden of Eden. But He gave up His life freely for the salvation of mankind. He had power to lay down His life, and He had power to raise it up. His resurrection is the foundation of our hope.

Every Christian lives in the assurance that God keeps all His promises. He believes that "for those who love God all things work together for good" (Romans 8:28). It makes no difference what the trouble is. "In all these things we are more than conquerors through Him who loved us" (Romans 8:37).

Dear Jesus, grant me faith to believe in You always as my Savior. And let me live constantly in the hope of life eternal. Amen.

Heralds of Peace

Behold, upon the mountains, the feet of him who brings good news, who publishes peace! Keep your feasts, O Judah; fulfill your vows, for never again shall the worthless pass through you; he is utterly cut off. Nahum 1:15

A mighty army is encamped around Jerusalem. The chosen people seem hopelessly outnumbered. Yet the prophet speaks of Sennacherib and his hosts as already destroyed. A herald appears upon the mountaintop with flares announcing peace to a troubled nation.

Next Sunday Christian pastors will ascend their pulpits. They will speak to people who are surrounded by enemies of their souls. They will speak of victory to such as they deeply feel the attacks made upon their faith. They will speak of peace to the Christian church at a time when she seems to be fighting for her very existence.

They are not dreaming. They are not indulging in wishful thinking. They know whereof they speak. The written Word of God is their authority.

The victory is in the past. Jesus crushed the head of Satan and his allies through His atoning death on the cross. The full fruits of the victory, however, are in the future. Jesus will reign supreme. Peace, eternal peace, will come to His own.

Oh, let them spread Thy name,
Their mission fully prove,
Thy universal grace proclaim,
Thine all-redeeming love! Amen. (TLH 488:4)

There Shall Be No More Death

And which now has been manifested through the appearing of our Savior Christ Jesus, who abolished death and brought life and immortality to light through the Gospel. 2 Timothy 1:10

If all the lovely flowers of spring withered and ended with the end of the Easter celebration, what a poor springtime it would be! Likewise, if all the joy and hope of the Easter resurrection ended and faded with that day, we should be left comfortless. As it is, our life is like a fairy tale written by God's fingers, a tapestry deftly woven by unseen hands, prepared for another, better world, where there shall be no more death.

"God did not send His Son into the world to condemn the world, but in order that the world might be saved through Him" (John 3:17). Now every breath we breathe, every step we take, every mile we travel is but in the direction of the grave. "The last enemy to be destroyed is death" (1 Corinthians 15:26).

A man who had long defied God and religion stood helpless at the coffin of his daughter. Overcome with grief, he managed to say: "Good-bye, little girl, forever," and turned away. Then the mother was wheeled in. She had been an invalid since the deceased girl was born. "God has been good to us to let us have these twelve years," she said tenderly. "It is not good-bye; a little while, and we shall see each other again!"

What a wondrous prospect! What a picture of heaven! No more death, and no more fear of death! Trusting our Redeemer, we rejoice that we shall not die, but live and declare the works of the Lord!

Thank You, dear Jesus, that Your forgiveness is so great that not even death can hold me. Amen.

The Glory That Is to Be

Beloved, we are God's children now, and what we will be has not yet appeared; but we know that when He appears we shall be like Him, because we shall see Him as He is. 1 John 3:2

We are children of God though faith in Christ Jesus. This is the highest honor that can come to man. With this privilege we have received a new heart through the regenerating power of the Holy Spirit.

Like the apostle Paul we, time and again, sigh: "I see in my members another law waging war against the law of my mind and making me captive to the law of sin that dwells in my members. Wretched man that I am! Who will deliver me from this body of death?" (Romans 7:23–24). We are sometimes frightened by what emerges from our hearts. We wonder whether after all we are new creatures in Christ, being led by the Spirit of Christ.

We have God's own promise, however, that this struggle will not continue forever. One day it will appear that we are children of God. We shall be like Him. The grandeur of His image will be completely restored in us. We shall be a part of the perfection of heaven.

With this goal in view, we, with the power of the Holy Spirit, continue our struggle faithfully and valiantly. We confidently say with the battle-scarred veteran of the cross, St. Paul: "Not that I have already obtained this or am already perfect, but I press on to make it my own, because Christ Jesus has made me His own" (Philippians 3:12).

They see the triumph from afar
With faith's discerning eye. Amen. (TLH 445:5)

Spiritual Bodies

It is sown a natural body; it is raised a spiritual body. If there is a natural body, there is also a spiritual body. 1 Corinthians 15:44

Our whole being, body, mind and soul, is spotted and defiled by sin. From infancy to old age, we are subject to injury, disease, infirmity, and death. And finally this frame of clay is laid away to await an amazing change and a glorious resurrection, which is our heritage in Christ Jesus.

See the lumbering caterpillar, how laboriously he propels himself along the ground! His body shall not last for long! Presently he weaves himself into his little silken shroud, to all appearances dead to the world. Then one day the little coffin opens, and he comes forth, the same living organism, yet different, wondrously transformed. He is no longer ugly, handicapped, crawling on the ground, but a new being, with a new life, sustained by gorgeously colored wings, able to flit about in the sunshine from flower to flower and tree to tree.

In that wondrous world of light and love we shall bear the image of the heavenly. We shall have the same bodies, as Job certifies, but they will be changed, perfected, beautified, incorruptible, and clothed with immortality, bodies fashioned like our Savior's glorious body. Raised in power, we shall be no longer subject to time and space, neither hunger anymore nor thirst anymore.

Remember me when You return in glory, dear Jesus, and raise my body to eternal joys. Amen.

No Irksome Toil

No longer will there be anything accursed, but the throne of God and of the Lamb will be in it, and His servants will worship Him. Revelation 22:3

Work is as truly God's ordinance as prayer. Honest toil, as a rule, has its own reward, promoting health, independence, satisfaction, and stewardship. But how easily our tasks become a drudgery and a burden, whether we work to live or live to work! In the United States one man in every eight is a supervisor, or boss, set to see that others perform their duties faithfully.

Since the days of Adam and Eve, when the curse came on the ground because of sin and God said, "By the sweat of your face you shall eat bread, till you return to the ground" (Genesis 3:19), man has had to fight for his existence and survival. He has had to battle every inch of the way against thorns and thistles, roaring beasts, insect pests, floods, droughts, frosts, hot winds, tornadoes, hail, disease, and barrenness.

The Bible paints the picture of heaven by describing what will *not* be there: No more curse, no more irksome toil, no more death. No, heaven shall not be a vacuum. But it shall be the absence of everything caused by our sin. Because Jesus so profoundly paid the price for *every* sin, no result of sin shall remain for us in eternity. "His servants will worship Him," but it will be a joyful service of the Lord, described as having charge over cities, judging the world (1 Corinthians 6:2), sitting with Him on His throne, reigning forever!

Lord, by Your grace enable me to endure what remains of this sorrowful life, and bring me at last to the resurrection life that is to come. Amen.

United with God

*Remember that you were at that time separated from Christ,
alienated from the commonwealth of Israel and strangers to the
covenants of promise, having no hope and without God in the
world. But now in Christ Jesus you who once were far off have
been brought near by the blood of Christ. . . . For through Him
we both have access in one Spirit to the Father. Ephesians
2:12–13,18*

Paul, in chapter two of his letter to the Ephesians, writes
of various blessings that have come to us through Christ, our
risen Lord. In the words here quoted, he reminds us that
through Christ we have peace with God.

The Christians at Ephesus to whom Paul first wrote this
letter had grown up as pagans in a pagan world. When the story
of Jesus came to the Ephesians, they first of all found the true
God revealed in Christ. They found in Christ the One who had
taken their sins away so there was no further barrier to keep
them from God.

What Jesus did for the Ephesian Christians He also
achieves in us. As we, like the Ephesian Christians, place our
faith and trust in Jesus, we too will be firmly united with God.
This is God's plan for us. He loves us and does not want us to
go through life without His protecting love and concern.

This is a wonderful thing for us to know. Life can at times
become very rugged. If we were without God in this world, then
we would be truly in a bad way.

But, thank God, that is not how it is. We have a Savior, and
through Him we are united with God. With Him we can face up
to the most bitter realities of life. "If God is for us, who can be
against us?" (Roman 8:31).

*Precious Savior, we thank You that You have provided the way for our
reunion with the true God. Be pleased by Your Spirit to work faith in
our hearts and to keep us with God. Amen.*

Hope

Remember that you were at that time separated from Christ, alienated from the commonwealth of Israel and strangers to the covenants of promise, having no hope and without God in the world. But now in Christ Jesus you who once were far off have been brought near by the blood of Christ. Ephesians 2:12–13

Paul, who reminded the Christians at Ephesus that they had become reunited with God through the risen Christ, here recalls for them that through Christ they also have found hope.

The Ephesians before their conversion were without hope, as are great masses of people in our own day. To see how true this is, we need but look at the many in our own country who pin their hope for a happy tomorrow on material things. So many are counting on the support they hope to get out of pension funds, insurance annuities, Social Security funds, investments, and the like. Most assuredly we are not to suppose that such provisions for old age are wrong or displeasing to God, but we are to remember that all of these matters do not provide a solid basis for hope.

But even that is not the whole story. The plain fact is that we don't even know whether we shall live long enough to qualify for pensions and annuities. And if we do, we still have eternity to reckon with.

What we need is a foundation for our hope more solid than the Rock of Gibraltar, and one that reaches beyond the span of this life. Such a hope can be found only in the Rock of Ages, only in Christ, in Him who overcame death, in Him who promised: "Behold, I am with you always" (Matthew 28:20). "Come to Me, all who labor and are heavy laden, and I will give you rest" (Matthew 11:28). "Where I am, there will my servant be" (John 12:26). Only He can provide us firm, safe anchorage for our ultimate hope.

We thank You, O God, that You have filled our fearful and uncertain hearts with a blessed hope through Christ, our risen Savior. Amen.

A Threefold Blessing

*The LORD bless you and keep you; the LORD make His face to shine upon you and be gracious to you; the LORD lift up His countenance upon you and give you peace. "So shall they put My name upon the people of Israel, and I will bless them."
Numbers 6:24–27*

More than three thousand years ago, the Lord command-ed Aaron, the high priest, to use these words to bless the children of Israel. These words are among the most familiar of the entire Bible. In many churches they are spoken every Sunday at the close of the service, assuring the worshipers of God's continuous and abiding blessing.

In the first part of the benediction the Lord God promis-es us all the blessings we need for this life—the wants of the body. "The LORD bless you and keep you." What a wonderful promise! It assures us of God's gracious provision, help, and guidance.

Next we are assured of the blessing of divine grace. When the Lord's face shines upon us, we enjoy His forgiving love and mercy. "The Lord . . . be gracious to you." There is no finer promise. There is no greater blessing.

"And give you peace." Peace—what a priceless blessing! God at peace with us! O wonder of wonders!

Daily we take these precious words into our hearts and lives: the assurance of the threefold blessing of the Lord—the blessing of bodily needs, the blessing of divine grace, and the blessing of heavenly peace.

The very God of peace sanctify us wholly, and the grace of our Lord Jesus be with us. Amen.

A Blessed Walk

For at one time you were darkness, but now you are light in the Lord. Walk as children of light. Ephesians 5:8

About 750 years before the birth of Christ, Isaiah said in prophecy: "The people who walked in darkness have seen a great light; those who dwelt in a land of deep darkness, on them has light shined" (Isaiah 9:2). In the fullness of time this prophecy was fulfilled. He was born who later said of Himself: "I am the light of the world. Whoever follows Me will not walk in darkness, but will have the light of life" (John 8:12).

The members of the Ephesian congregation had at one time been "people who walked in darkness." They could not answer such questions as: Who is the true God? What is God's will for me? How shall I be saved?

Then the great apostle Paul came to them bearing the Light of the world. He told them of Christ and His cross. He explained how Jesus gave His life in payment for the world's sins. Thus they were spiritually enlightened. Now they knew that the true God is the Triune God, Father, Son, and Holy Ghost; that faith in Christ saves; and that God wants His children to glorify Him in their lives.

Could these Christians, then, with this wonderful thing having happened to them, still walk the old paths they had followed in their days of spiritual darkness? No, that was unthinkable. Now they must walk as children of light, as enlightened children of God.

Having been enlightened, may we let our light shine, O God. Amen.

Kyrie

But the tax collector, standing far off, would not even lift up his eyes to heaven, but beat his breast, saying, "God, be merciful to me, a sinner!" Luke 18:13

Like a single strand of scarlet in a cloth of gold, the penitent cry, "God, be merciful to me, a sinner," is threaded through Christian worship. What is the Christian's chief reason for worship but that God forgives sinners? What should waken praise and thanksgiving and service if not that God "does not deal with us according to our sins, nor repay us according to our iniquities" (Psalm 103:10)?

Two thoughts, therefore, occur over and over in every Christian's worship of God. One is the thought of our own sinfulness. It is crushing to human pride to be confronted with the terrible truth that there is no soundness in us, that we are sick unto death, and that there is no one to make us whole again. Least of all can we, already gripped with fear and trembling, heal ourselves. Pitifully and plaintively the cry goes up from our despair, "Lord, have mercy!"

Out of such loss of confidence in ourselves and trust in the compassion of God alone there arises the second recurring theme of Christian worship, "The blood of Jesus His Son cleanses us from all sin" (1 John 1:7). Here is the rebirth of hope, not in us, but in God; the blood of Jesus Christ, His Son, cleanses us from all sin. Here is the end of despair, not because we have saved ourselves, but because God in Christ has saved us from sin, death, and the devil.

Lord, have mercy upon us. Christ, have mercy upon us. Lord, have mercy upon us, and give us Your peace. Amen.

Purposeful Suffering

And the people stood by, watching, but the rulers scoffed at him, saying, "He saved others; let Him save Himself, if He is the Christ of God, His Chosen One!" Luke 23:35

"And the people stood by, watching." They saw Jesus crucified with the malefactors, one on the right hand and the other on the left. Under the cross they saw the soldiers cast lots to divide His garments. They saw fulfilled what Isaiah had prophesied of the Man of Sorrows, that He was numbered with the transgressors.

In Caesarea Philippi His disciples had confessed: "You are the Christ, the Son of the living God" (Matthew 16:16). At His Baptism and later at the transfiguration, God the Father declared: "This is My beloved Son, with whom I am well pleased" (Matthew 3:17). "The rulers scoffed at Him, saying, 'He saved others; let Him save Himself, if He is the Christ of God, His Chosen One.'"

Jesus did save others. He came from the throne of God not merely to comfort the distressed, heal the sick, and raise the dead, but He came to seek and to save that which was lost. He came to do the will of His Father and to drink the cup of His suffering to the bitter dregs. He came to suffer in order to deliver us from eternal suffering.

Because of this, saints and angels sing in eternity: "For You were slain, and by Your blood You ransomed people for God from every tribe and language and people and nation" (Revelation 5:9). In Him "we have redemption through His blood, the forgiveness of our trespasses" (Ephesians 1:7).

Lord Jesus, Lamb of God, daily cleanse us and keep us in Your grace. Amen.

God-pleasing Tears

"You are those who have stayed with Me in My trials." Luke 22:28

A great multitude of people followed Jesus on the way to Golgotha for the crucifixion. When some of the women saw Jesus and realized He was to die innocently on the cross under whose load He had just collapsed, they gave way to their emotions and bewailed and lamented Him.

Jesus, turning to them, said: "Daughters of Jerusalem, do not weep for Me" (Luke 23:28). Their Lord was saying, in other words, "I delight to do My Father's will, that I suffer and die to atone for the sins of the world. But weep for yourselves and for your children, for the ungodly and impenitent, who want My blood to come upon them and their children."

Here we have a most solemn warning from the lips of our Savior. We have reason to weep for ourselves. If we look into our own heart and see the brood of evil thoughts and lusts, if we look into our lives and remember our many neglects and ugly sins, we have reason to weep for ourselves.

But let this weeping not be a mere emotional outburst of sorrow, but one of sincere repentance. "For godly grief produces a repentance" (2 Corinthians 7:10). Godly sorrow—that is, sorrow created by God through His Law—causes us to know our sin so we might throw ourselves into the arms of a loving Savior, whose blood cleanses us from all sin.

Thou alone, my God and Lord,
Art my Glory and Reward.
Thou hast bled for me and died;
In Thy wounds I safely hide. Amen. (TLH 356:5)

Jesus Gives Us Peace

On the evening of that day, the first day of the week, the doors being locked where the disciples were for fear of the Jews, Jesus came and stood among them and said to them, "Peace be with you." John 20:19

It was Sunday evening in the city of Jerusalem some 2000 years ago. Jesus had risen from the dead early that morning but only a few of the disciples had seen Him, and they were still confused because of the events of the last few days. They gathered behind closed doors because they were afraid. Their leader had been crucified. They were not sure He was alive. All of their hopes seemed shattered. There was nothing to do but hide.

Jesus knew what they needed. He came to them. He spoke to them, "Peace be with you." This was what they needed more than anything else, the presence of Jesus and the peace He alone could give.

Today we hide from many things. Sometimes there is a fear of growing old, a fear of the future, a fear of ourselves, a fear of life itself. We need the ongoing proclamation of the peace of God. It is not a peace that will be announced from the capitals of nations. But it comes from the proclamation of the Gospel of the crucified and risen Savior. His peace is ours.

Luther once said that we should live as if Christ had died yesterday, had risen today, and were coming tomorrow to bring us His peace. This was the message of Jesus on that Sunday evening so many years ago. This is still the message of the church.

Heavenly Father, remove fear from our hearts, and speak words of peace to our souls. Amen.

Jesus Gives the Holy Spirit

And when He had said this, He breathed on them and said to them, "Receive the Holy Spirit." John 20:22

When Jesus rose from the dead, He appeared to His disciples. He gave them peace and joy and sent them forth with heavenly power. He gave them the Holy Spirit. This was the gift that would give power to their words. This power would convince men of their sin and change their hearts and lives.

Sunday after Sunday all over the world and in many different languages, millions of Christians speak these simple but majestic words: "I believe in the Holy Spirit, the holy Christian church, the communion of saints, the forgiveness of sins, the resurrection of the body, and the life everlasting" (*Luther's Small Catechism*).

It may seem odd to confess "the forgiveness of sins" in the Third Article, under the work of the Holy Spirit. Jesus earned it, accomplishing this divine work by His suffering and death on the cross. But the Holy Spirit now brings it to us in God's Word and in the Holy Sacraments. That is the connection.

Forgiveness of sins is for all people. The treasure-house is full. This treasure must be brought to men or men brought to this Gospel in order to receive its benefits. This is the work that the Holy Spirit does. The church is a group of believers gathered in faith by the Holy Spirit, who uses Word and Sacraments to connect us to Jesus' death and resurrection for the forgiveness of our sins.

Heavenly Father, grant us Your Holy Spirit. Amen.

A Lesson in Geography

"I am the good shepherd. The good shepherd lays down his life for the sheep." John 10:11

We are all familiar with Psalm 23, but have we ever noticed its "geography" in the Bible? When we speak of geography, we usually think of countries and territories, not psalms.

Now, what about the "geography" of Psalm 23? It is "bounded" on one side by Psalm 22 and on the other by Psalm 24. Psalm 22 is Mount Calvary: "My God, My God, why have You forsaken Me? . . . They have pierced my hands and feet" (Psalm 22:1,16). This is the suffering Christ—redemption—the source of our faith—the beginning of the Christian life. And Psalm 24 is Mount Zion: "Lift up your heads, O gates! And be lifted up, O ancient doors, that the King of glory may come in!" (Psalm 24:7). This is the reigning Christ—heaven—the end of our Christian faith and life!

Thus, between the beginning of the Christian life (Mount Calvary) and its end and consummation (Mount Zion), lies the long, deep valley of life in this world. And in this valley, so filled with dangers and fears and the problems of life, we find the Good Shepherd with His sheep, caring for them, leading them, guiding them, protecting them.

We must know and believe Psalm 22 before we can appreciate Psalm 23. We must see the Christ of the cross, the sword raised against the Shepherd, and know the value and meaning of the blood shed on Mount Calvary, before we can ever know the sweetness of the Shepherd's care or the final rest on Mount Zion with the King of glory!

We thank You, Good Shepherd, for giving Your life for us. Amen.

The Spirit's Revelation

These things God has revealed to us through the Spirit. For the Spirit searches everything, even the depths of God. 1 Corinthians 2:10

The instruments of the scientist have laid bare many of the secrets of nature. In ages past, men had no knowledge of the tiny creatures of God that we can now see with a microscope. The telescope lets men see into distant spaces the eye could never reach. But the secret of salvation man cannot discover. It lies hidden in the heart of God. The Bible calls it the hidden wisdom, which was kept secret since the world began. The Old Testament speaks of the darkness that covers the earth and, through sin, hides the way of salvation from the eyes of men.

But God did not leave the world in this darkness. The things we did not know and could never discover by human wisdom God has revealed to us by His Spirit. It was the Spirit of God who spoke to the Old Testament prophets and told them of the Savior who was to come. It was the same Spirit of God who spoke to the apostles and evangelists of the New Testament and told them what all the things they had seen in Jesus of Nazareth really meant. Men could know by themselves that Jesus died, but it was only by the revelation of God that they could know He died to pay for the sins of all the world. By nature we knew nothing of the truth of God. But by the revelation of the Holy Ghost we know that Jesus loves us, that He has taken away our sins, and that by His grace we are saved.

Holy Spirit, we thank You for having made the Way, the Truth, and the Life known to us. Amen.

The Lord Went Up

So then the Lord Jesus, after He had spoken to them, was taken up into heaven and sat down at the right hand of God. Mark 16:19

In the forty days between His resurrection and His ascension, Jesus had appeared about ten times to approximately 550 people. The disciples were being prepared for a new relationship, different from that which had existed before Jesus' crucifixion.

The ascension of Jesus has important meaning for us. It marked the completion of His earthly ministry. For 33 years He had lived and walked among men. For three years of His public ministry He had taught concerning Himself, the kingdom of God and eternal life. This was now accomplished.

The ascension of Jesus made provision for His universal presence at all times in all places. While He was here on earth, He limited Himself as to time and space. Now He gave the promises: "Behold, I am with you always, to the end of the age" (Matthew 28:20); "For where two or three are gathered in My name, there I am among them" (Matthew 18:20).

The ascension of Jesus provided for the establishment of the Christian Church throughout the world. While He was here on earth, Jesus taught and chose His disciples. Now He gave them the promises of the Comforter, the Holy Spirit, who would lead them into all truth. Then Jesus was received up into heaven, to the right hand of God, the place of honor, majesty, power, and glory. He ascended that He might be with us always.

Heavenly Father, grant that, as Jesus ascended into heaven, we too, may be received by You. Amen.

The Lord Works with Us

And they went out and preached everywhere, while the Lord worked with them and confirmed the message by accompanying signs. Mark 16:20

The ascension of Jesus marked a turning point in the lives of the disciples. Before this they had been fearful, timid, and uncertain. Now they became fearless, bold, and sure of what they had to do.

They went forth. They could not return to their previous way of living and their former occupations. They were chosen men, and they went where they were sent.

They no longer confined their teaching and their activities to their own people or their own locality. They went and preached everywhere. Jesus had told them they were to be His witnesses in both Jerusalem and in all Judea, in Samaria, and unto the uttermost parts of the earth.

This they did with amazing power and tremendous results. They did not walk alone. The Lord was walking with them.

In the same way, the all-powerful Gospel goes forth into the world through the preaching of the Church, and through our participation in the proclamation of the Gospel. And we know that our labor is not in vain in the Lord. He is working in us and through us. He will never leave us nor forsake us. He accomplishes that which we can never achieve—the salvation of the lost.

Heavenly Father, grant us Your presence, and continue to work with us and through us. Amen.

The Lord Is with Us

"Teaching them to observe all that I have commanded you. And behold, I am with you always, to the end of the age." Matthew 28:20

Just before Jesus ascended into heaven, He gave His disciples directions for carrying on His work after His physical presence would be removed from the earth.

Jesus told His disciples to go and make disciples of all nations. We must go forth. It makes no difference whether it is next door, across the street, in the next city, in another state, or across the ocean.

Jesus said we must baptize in the name of the true God—the Father, the Son, and the Holy Ghost. Baptism is not to be the end, but the beginning of the Christian life.

Jesus said that we must teach all men of all nations to observe all things He has commanded. We must likewise regularly hear the preaching God's Word ourselves, returning continually to the life-giving promises of His Gospel.

Although we are given the great command, "Make disciples," we never walk alone. We have the promise of His presence: "Behold, I am with you always," "I will never leave you nor forsake you" (Hebrews 13:5).

Lord Jesus, live in us, according to Your promise, that we may be certain of being with You now and sure of being with You forever in heaven. Amen.

Ascension Blessings

"In My Father's house are many rooms. If it were not so, would I have told you that I go to prepare a place for you?" John 14:2

The Christian world today stands with the disciples and reverently looks up as Jesus leaves the world in which He has spent thirty-three momentous years and returns to His Father.

The departure of Jesus from a world torn with conflict and groaning with pain appears to be an irreplaceable loss. In reality, however, it is another step in the divine plan for redeemed man.

Jesus is not lost to us. While on earth, He was visibly available to comparatively few. Now He, in His mercy, is available to all who will come to Him.

At the same time He is active on our behalf at the right hand of God. "Far above all rule and authority and power and dominion" (Ephesians 1:21), He rules the world for the benefit of His church. He, the righteous, as our advocate pleads our cause.

He, the forerunner, is preparing a place for us in the Father's house of many rooms. Therefore, when we leave this life, we shall not be homeless wanderers. Like the penitent thief, we shall be with Jesus in paradise. The place is now ready for us.

The ascension of our Savior, therefore, is an event that thrills us and gives us new courage for life's journey. Home, eternal home, is at the end of the road.

Draw us to Thee
Unceasingly,
Into Thy kingdom take us;
Let us fore'er
Thy glory share,
Thy saints and joint heirs make us. Amen. (TLH 215:5)

What God Forgets

"And no longer shall each one teach his neighbor and each his brother, saying, 'Know the LORD,' for they shall all know Me, from the least of them to the greatest, declares the LORD. For I will forgive their iniquity, and I will remember their sin no more." Jeremiah 31:34

"Forgive and forget" is an expression combining two noble virtues. We find them hard to master individually, let alone together. While the circumstances of sin against us will cling to our memory, we know we should forget the resentment and rancor that accompany it. We may try hard, but as in everything else, only God can do this to perfection.

David prays, "Remember not the sins of my youth or my transgressions" (Psalm 25:7). Another psalmist pleads, "Do not remember against us our former iniquities" (Psalm 79:8). All of us can make these prayers our own. We remember sins we have committed, but we want God to forget them.

God's promise comes in the gracious and merciful words, "I will remember their sin no more." This forgetting is not easy. It took the death of His Son to cancel the debt caused by our sin, but once it had been done, the handwriting of the Law against us was blotted out as well.

If a person still owes a bill, the creditor sends statement after statement. When the bill is paid, the creditor forgets the debt. No more statements are sent. God has marked "Paid" the account against us, and He remembers our sin no more.

Oh, from our sins hide not your face;
Absolve us through your boundless grace!
Be with us in our anguish still!
Free us at last from ev'ry ill! Amen. (LW 428:5)

The Needle's Eye

"Again I tell you, it is easier for a camel to go through the eye of a needle than for a rich person to enter the kingdom of God."
Matthew 19:24

The English unbeliever David Hume once said that if anyone really believes the Bible, it is a miracle. He was ridiculing the Christian faith, yet his words are true. When a man realizes he is a lost sinner, who has deserved only the wrath of God, and that the only hope for him lies in Jesus Christ, who came and did for him what he could never do for himself, then a blind man has been made to see. His darkened eyes have been enlightened by the Holy Ghost. The Bible actually speaks of such a man as having been raised from the dead.

And when the Savior says it is easier for a camel to go through the eye of a needle than for a rich man to enter the kingdom, He shows us how great a miracle is performed when an unbeliever becomes a believer. It is evident that this work of making a Christian out of a natural man is a work man can never do himself. The Lord Himself says this is impossible with men. But God can do all things. He can make a camel go through a needle's eye. Rich men have been saved. But in any case, whether they are rich or poor, if they are saved, something has been done that only God can do.

Through Baptism and the Word, the Holy Ghost has made us Christians. For that great work, God be praised forever.

Holy Spirit, we thank You that You have brought us to know and to believe with certainly that Jesus loves us and saves. Amen.

Forgotten Sins

"And no longer shall each one teach his neighbor and each his brother, saying, 'Know the LORD,' for they shall all know Me, from the least of them to the greatest, declares the LORD. For I will forgive their iniquity, and I will remember their sin no more." Jeremiah 31:34

God gives man the gift of memory. And a truly precious gift it is. We find much joy in reliving some of the pleasures of the past, and we treasure the things that keep those memories alive.

Yet memory can become a source of distressing pain and of much sorrow. "The devil stands in all memories," said Henrik Ibsen as he remembered the sins of his youth. He puts these words into the mouth of a character in one of his plays: "Me, who to remember dare not and who never can forget." Surely it is true of all of us that too often the sins of the distant past come back to torment us and to make us feel once more the bitterness of a troubled conscience.

Although we may remember, God promises to forget. "I will remember their sin no more" (Jeremiah 31:34), He says. We may not understand how the all-knowing God, to whom the past, the present, and the future are an open book, can forget our sins, but this is what He has promised to do. This is one of the great miracles of our good Lord, that He, who cannot forget anything, will not remember our sins.

"I will remember their sin no more." What a wonderful way to show us how completely our sins have vanished from His sight! They have been washed away by the blood of His Son, Jesus. Whenever the devil reminds us of our sins, we quickly remember that for Jesus' sake God has forgotten them.

Lord Jesus, remember not our many transgressions. Amen.

The Holy Ghost

"And I will ask the Father, and He will give you another Helper, to be with you forever, even the Spirit of truth, whom the world cannot receive, because it neither sees Him nor knows Him. You know Him, for He dwells with you and will be in you." John 14:16–17

"Come, Holy Ghost, God and Lord, / With all your graces now outpoured / On each believer's mind and heart" (*LW* 154:1). This is the ardent prayer of each Christian. We address the Third Person of the Godhead: "Creator Spirit, by whose aid / The world's foundations first were laid, / Come, visit ev'ry humble mind" (*LW* 167:1). Why?

Without the work of the Holy Spirit in our hearts, Christ would have died in vain. By Word and Sacrament the Holy Spirit works faith in our hearts and keeps us in the saving faith to the end. Without the work of the Holy Ghost there would be no faith in Christ, no Church, no heaven for us.

At Jerusalem, ten days after Christ's ascension, 120 timid disciples were gathered together. Suddenly there was a sound from heaven like a rushing mighty wind. Before the day was over, 3,000 souls were baptized, converted, and added to the Church. The Holy Ghost had worked miracles of His grace by the Word, which He had put into the mouth of the apostles.

St. Paul assures us: "Do you not know that you are God's temple and that God's spirit dwells in you?" (1 Corinthians 3:16). "The Spirit Himself bears witness with our spirit that we are children of God" (Romans 8:16).

Holy Spirit, all divine,
Dwell within this self of mine;
I your temple pure would be
Now and for eternity. Amen. (LW 166:6)

When Fear Vanishes

When I saw Him, I fell at His feet as though dead. But He laid His right hand on me, saying, "Fear not, I am the first and the last, and the living one. I died, and behold I am alive forevermore, and I have the keys of Death and Hades." Revelation 1:17–18

Fear of the future has laid a paralyzing hand upon many. Upon such people Jesus lays His friendly right hand and says: "Fear not, I am the First and the Last." None has been before Him; He is from everlasting. None will be after Him; He is to everlasting. There came a day when it seemed as if others would outlive Him. A lifeless body was all that seemed to be left of Him when He died on the cross. But on Easter Sunday, He returned to life with a glorified body. He now lives forever.

With the same love with which He died for us He now lives for us. At this time of year we marvel at God's unmeasured activity as He, through the forces of nature, provides food for the body and beauty for the soul. More wonderful, however, is the care of the risen Savior for those who believe in Him. To each of us He says: "Fear not, for I have redeemed you; I have called you by name, you are Mine" (Isaiah 43:1). There is not an experience or a task in which He is not at our side. He guides. He protects. He provides. He strengthens. In all of human history, He has not once failed a person who trusted in Him.

With the shepherd king we therefore confidently look into the future and say: "I shall not want" (Psalm 23:1).

In suff'ring be your love my peace,
In weakness be your love my pow'r. Amen. (LW 280:4)

I Am with You—in Suffering

For I consider that the sufferings of this present time are not worth comparing with the glory that is to be revealed to us.
Romans 8:18

The pain resulting from a surgical operation can sometimes be intense and agonizing. For a short while, it may even increase and become far greater after the operation than it was before. But in time the pain disappears, and the patient then appreciates absence of pain as never before.

In a far greater sense, the glory that Christ Jesus won for us, and that will be ours through faith in Him, far outweighs any suffering we may for a little while endure upon this earth. He tasted of pain to its utmost degree to win for us the ultimate, promised absence of pain and the joy of heaven for all eternity.

And yet, when we do suffer, especially if our pain is agonizing and prolonged, we inevitably wonder why. At such a time a child of God in Christ knows that even pain must work for his good—that God has a specific purpose and design in letting this occur in the paths upon which He leads us. Moreover, God promised to sustain us and help us to bear it through His abiding presence. In the greatest of our sufferings, He ever bids us look upward to the glory, which shall be revealed in us.

Lord Jesus, help us to endure the hurts and pains of this life until we partake of the glory You have won for us. Amen.

You Are Mine

But now thus says the LORD, He who created you, O Jacob, He who formed you, O Israel: "Fear not, for I have redeemed you; I have called you by name, you are Mine." Isaiah 43:1

This verse is addressed to believers. It tells them that they have nothing to fear. Yet still we fear so many things—sickness, death, helpless childhood, defenseless old age. We fear nature's upheavals, wars, and tumults. We fear nearly everything.

When a strong father tells his son, "Take courage; I am with you," fears are allayed. Our God is the greatest Father, loving, almighty, and all-wise.

One great reason why I need not fear is that He has redeemed me. Not even sin and Satan can overthrow me. Through the death of Jesus, God's Son, a price was paid for my soul, and I was redeemed from every power of evil that could conquer me.

Besides, I was given a name. God knows me personally and calls me by name as a shepherd calls his sheep. Jesus, God's Son, prayed for me and gave me a place in the covenant of God's family.

To remove all doubt and fear, God tells me, "You are Mine." God has claimed me; I belong to Him. I am God's child. Let no one dare touch me. As long as I am His, His I will remain. No worldly power will take me from Him.

Heavenly Father, You have sought and found me, and I belong to You. May the assurance of my redemption be ever present with me to drive away all fear and doubt through Jesus Christ, my Savior. Amen.

MEMORIAL DAY, MAY 30   READ ISAIAH 31

Freedom from Fear

Fear not, for I am with you; be not dismayed, for I am your
God; I will strengthen you, I will help you, I will uphold you
with My righteous right hand. Isaiah 41:10

On Memorial Day we remember the sacrifice of those
who have suffered the loss of life and limb in the defense of our
nation. Their blood and pain is the price that has been paid for
our freedom. As long as our country endures, we shall owe to
those people a debt of gratitude.

But our expression of thanks to these people should not
become idolatrous. It is above all to God that thanks are due for
the freedom we enjoy in our country. It is He who has granted
success to our arms and victory in our battles. The greatness of
our country is due not to our superior might, but only to the
blessing of Him who gave Gideon and his three hundred the
victory over the countless soldiers of Midian.

As we look to the future in this restless world of wars and
rumors of wars, we can fearlessly face the things that come as
long as we have the assurance that our good Lord is with us and
that our blessed Savior is at our side. Military victory and political freedom may not always be ours, but as long as we know
that He loves us and will never leave us, we know also that all
things, no matter what they may be, will work together for our
good. Only in His promises, telling us He will forgive us our
sins for Jesus' sake, God will be with us to help us and to
strengthen us. Only in these promises shall we find true freedom from fear.

Lord, grant our land perpetual victory over its enemies. Amen.

May

A Visual Reminder of the Greatest Work

*And He took bread, and when He had given thanks, He broke it
and gave it to them, saying, "This is My body, which is given for
you. Do this in remembrance of Me." Luke 22:19*

Some of us wear a watch that belonged to our father or a
necklace handed down from our mother. When we wear them,
we are reminded of those we love. A better reminder is a pho-
tograph. We can hardly escape remembering people as we see
their photo. But the best reminder is a monument to the life's
work of an individual; it calls to mind not only who he was but
also what he was.

Our Lord left such a memorial in the Sacrament of the
Altar. Earthly elements, carrying in them divine power and life,
describe who He is—God incarnate, the Word made flesh, Son
of God and Son of man.

Not only do we remember who He is but also what He
came to do. We remember Good Friday and Easter. This meal
brings us His body and blood for the remission of our sins.
What greater mark of love can there be!

Your holy body into death was given,
Life to win for us in heaven.
No greater love than this to you could bind us;
May this feast that remind us! O Lord, have mercy!
Lord, your kindness so much did move you
That your blood now moves us to love you.
All our debt you have paid;
Peace with God once more is made. O Lord, have mercy! Amen. (LW
238:2)

A Majestic God

Who has measured the waters in the hollow of His hand and marked off the heavens with a span, enclosed the dust of the earth in a measure and weighed the mountains in scales and the hills in a balance? Isaiah 40:12

God measures the waters in the hollow of His hand. The prophet here speaks of the waters that cover more than half the surface of the earth. He has in mind all the rivers and the lakes and the oceans of the whole world. And of all these waters, he says that God can hold them in the hollow of His hand.

Every day the City of Chicago pumps about one billion gallons of water out of Lake Michigan. Yet one cannot notice any difference in the level of the lake. We can scarcely imagine how much water this lake must contain. But if we look at a map, we would see that Lake Michigan is a drop in the bucket compared with the Pacific Ocean. And just as we begin to understand how great this ocean is, the prophet comes and says the Lord can measure not only the waters of this one ocean, but all the waters on the face of the earth in the hollow of His hand.

What a marvelous picture we have here of the glorious majesty of God! And this God is our God. This is the same God who has forgiven us our sins for Jesus' sake. This is the God who loves us, the God who has promised: "I am your shield" (Genesis 15:1). And if this God is our Fortress and our Defender, of what shall we be afraid? The dangers that threaten us may be great, but He is always greater.

Dear Lord, defend us from all danger, and protect us from all evil, for Jesus' sake. Amen.

'Tis Done

*When Jesus had received the sour wine, He said, "It is finished,"
and He bowed His head and gave up His spirit. John 19:30*

What a glorious cry, "It is finished!" All the world can
rejoice, for this victory brings salvation to every human soul.
Christ has redeemed us all.

Many battles have been fought and won. They have been
far-reaching in their importance; but none of such consequence
as this victory of Christ on the cross. He has completed our salvation. We are redeemed from the power of Satan. The sting of
death is removed. Sin has no hold on us.

As Jesus entered upon His great passion, He prayed:
"Father, the hour has come" (John 17:1). He came to redeem
the lost. Did He accomplish His work? Confidently He cried
out on the cross: "It is finished!"

All the world has been reconciled. All sins, great and
small, have been paid for with His blood. None need say that his
sins are too many and too great for Jesus to bear. He died for the
ungodly. He died for all. And He says that whosoever believes in
Him shall not perish. He does not promise that we shall never
hunger because He finished salvation. He does not say that we
shall never die because He has died on the cross; never suffer
because He shed His blood. We shall not perish, but have everlasting life.

So there is hope for all. Salvation is there for every human
being. None need perish. What more can we ask? Is there any
Gospel like this Good Friday Gospel?

Now to be thine, yea, thine alone,
O Lamb of God, I come, I come. Amen. (LW 359:6)

A Wonder-working God

"Who is like You, O LORD, among the gods? Who is like You, majestic in holiness, awesome in glorious deeds, doing wonders?"
Exodus 15:11

Moses spoke these words as he stood with the children of Israel on the shores of the Red Sea and praised God for the miracle He had done in parting the waters to deliver them from the armies of Egypt. To them that miracle was proof that their God was far greater than all the man-made idols of the heathen.

Today men often find fault with the miracles and say they cannot believe them. The real truth is that they do not want a God who is too great. They are afraid of a God who does wonders and works miracles. They are proud of a science that can make two bushels of corn grow where only one grew before, but they are ashamed of a God who can feed five thousand men with five loaves and two fishes. They are astonished at a science that can, after years of research, destroy a few particles of matter, but they reject the God who can create a whole universe in six days. They are happy over a research program that can develop a vaccine for polio, but they want nothing to do with a God who can cure leprosy with a touch. Isaiah ridiculed the gods of the heathen because they could do so little. Modern man ridicules the true God because He can do so much.

But this God, who stands above all things, glorious in holiness, fearful in praises, doing wonders, is our God and our Savior, and the greatest wonder that He ever did was that He loved us and let men nail Him to a cross for our salvation.

Lord, be our God, and let us be Your people always. Amen.

Show Your Faith by Your Works

What good is it, my brothers, if someone says he has faith but does not have works? Can that faith save him? James 2:14

St. Paul says in Romans 3:28: "For we hold that one is justified by faith apart from works of the law." St James asks: "What good is it, my brothers, if someone says he has faith but does not have works? Can that faith save him?" At first glance it may seem that St. James and St. Paul contradict each other. But James is speaking to people who excuse their lack of good works by claiming the saving faith inevitably results in good works. He does not say faith is ineffective or faith does not save, but that faith without works is not really faith. "Faith apart from works is useless" (James 2:20).

St. Paul, on the other hand, emphasizes saving faith as the only way to heaven to people who think of getting there without faith by their works. Also St. Paul admonishes his hearers to a "faith working through love" (Galatians 5:6). And his Epistles are filled with admonitions to good works and to a life in accordance with God's Law. The difference between Paul and James is not a difference in doctrine, but a difference in emphasis. Paul speaks of justification by faith; James of the fruits of faith. Both are God's gifts to you in Christ.

Lord, increase our faith, and give us also a rich measure of good works, for Jesus' sake. Amen.

The Holy Trinity

The grace of the Lord Jesus Christ and the love of God and the fellowship of the Holy Spirit be with you all. 2 Corinthians 13:14

The Bible teaches that God the Father, God the Son, and God the Holy Ghost are three persons in one Godhead. This is a mystery we cannot understand. It is a mystery we cannot even define.

The Bible makes no attempt to explain the Trinity. We Christians confess this revelation of God although we cannot define it, explain it, or understand it. We identify ourselves by it by calling ourselves Trinitarians.

Today's verse is often used in worship as a benediction. These words have been given such a high place of honor because they express in a brief way the entire blessing of the Christian religion.

The word "grace," which occurs in the New Testament more than ninety times, has been defined as the free, loving, unmerited favor of God.

The "love of God." God loves us, even despite our lovelessness. We would not know about the love of God if it were not for the grace of our Lord Jesus Christ.

The "communion of the Holy Ghost." This means that the Spirit of the living Lord goes with us always. By the Spirit we have fellowship with God and we have the assurance of His abiding presence at all times.

Eternal Lord, we pray upon ourselves the grace of our Lord Jesus, Your wondrous love, and the indwelling of Your Holy Spirit. Amen.

Life's Little Day

Yet you do not know what tomorrow will bring. What is your life? For you are a mist that appears for a little time and then vanishes. James 4:14

As we walk through life, we are always face to face with the three parts of our little day on earth—the past, the present, and the future. It is always good for us to consider our attitude about the time God has given us. Sometimes we are ashamed of our past. Sometimes we look upon the present merely as a time to live through and spend it only to look forward to a day that may never come. Often we face the future with no joy and no hope. Tomorrow will be like today, dull and drab, and all we can do is to try to get out of it as much as we can, hoping that somehow things will turn out all right.

Our Savior is the Lord of all life and all time. Having redeemed us and set our feet on the road to eternity, He has now given us the power to see life's little day as He would have us see it. The past is His because He has forgiven it. Tomorrow is His because it comes from Him. Only today is ours, a gift from His hand, to be used according to His gracious will and purpose. He has taken also our time on earth into His nail-torn hands, redeemed it with His blood, and now sanctifies it daily by His Holy Spirit. All change and decay serve only to bring us nearer to Him and His heaven, where there is no time. Life's little day will ebb out into the sea of eternity.

Grant us, O Lord, to live life's little day in gladness and peace. Help us to reach life's eventide victorious over sin by Your power, eternal God, world without end. For Jesus' sake. Amen.

Man Proposes, God Disposes

Instead you ought to say, "If the Lord wills, we will live and do this or that." James 4:15

A foolish rich man had laid up money and goods that he thought would last a lifetime. Feeling secure, he said boastfully, "Soul, you have ample goods laid up for many years; relax, eat, drink, be merry" (Luke 12:19). He did not give thanks to God for his blessings, and he had no thought of ordering his life according to God's wishes. He felt he had earned what he had and he could do as he pleased. That night he died. Man proposes, but God disposes.

This verse not only reminds us that God orders our lives, but it also admonishes us to *speak* as if He does. Many Christians in the past had the custom of saying. "If the Lord wills, we will go here or there, we will do this or that." This good custom deserves to be revived. But the attitude of the heart is more important than use of the words. Our hearts are to be grateful and humble, and they are to respond to the will of God in all things.

James does not, of course, discourage planning and careful forethought. Scripture nowhere condemns planning as such, but only planning that does not take God into account. God gave us intelligence that we might plan with care. But all our plans should be made in view of the uncertainty of life, in view of our dependence on God for life and health, and in view of our need for His guidance and blessing. "My times are in Your hand" (Psalm 31:15), David said in acknowledging his dependence on God.

Lord, help us to acknowledge Your rule and to commit our lives to You. In Jesus' name. Amen.

A Defiant Faith

What then shall we say to these things? If God is for us, who can be against us? Romans 8:31

Here is the declaration of a triumphant and defiant faith—defiant against everything that would lead into temptation and sin. The holy apostle is sure that God is for him; therefore he knew that it matters not who might be arrayed against him.

Possibly the apostle was thinking about what was written in Psalm 56. There the psalmist pours out his soul to God: "My enemies trample on me all day long, for many attack me proudly. When I am afraid, I put my trust in You. In God, whose word I praise, in God I trust; I shall not be afraid. What can flesh do to me?" (Psalm 56:2–4).

St. Paul had been through many conflicts. He had been persecuted by Jews and Gentiles because He preached Christ crucified. He bore on his body the marks of the Lord Jesus. He knew that the sufferings of this present time could not separate him from the love of God in Christ Jesus. He knew that although he went down to apparent defeat, the final victory belonged to Christ, and he would share it. "We are more than conquerors through Him who loved us" (Romans 8:37).

This faith and these words of divine assurance have heartened the ministers and the missionaries of the cross and their consecrated lay coworkers throughout the Christian era. God is faithful. He has already won the battle for us!

Dear Lord Jesus, enable us also to fight the good fight of faith and to lay hold on eternal life. Amen.

Righteousness by Faith

And he believed the LORD, and he counted it to Him as righteousness. Genesis 15:6

Abraham believed the promises of God although they ran counter to his human reasoning. That he would have a son and that from this son he would have many, many children of faith did not seem likely, humanly speaking. He had no son, and he was advanced in years. His wife, Sarah, was barren.

But nevertheless Abraham believed the promises. He looked to the heavens. He saw the stars, and he knew God had promised him descendants as many as their number. So he went on trusting God.

When the Bible declares Abraham righteous, not one single good work is mentioned, although Abraham had many to his credit. Instead he is declared righteous because he took God at His word. This faith accepted the promised Christ, the Savior of man.

Thousands of years later, when Paul argues for the righteousness of the sinner on the basis of faith in Jesus Christ, he used Abraham as his classic example. Paul says, "Christ is the end of the Law for righteousness to everyone who believes" (Romans 10:4). Jesus also uses Abraham as an example. Of him He said: "Abraham rejoiced that he would see My day. He saw it and was glad" (John 8:56).

O Lord, give us a sanctified faith as Abraham's, that we, too, may be declared righteous through the blood of Your dear Son, in whose name we ask it. Amen.

Salvation by Faith

And Hagar bore Abram a son, and Abram called the name of his son, whom Hagar bore, Ishmael. Genesis 16:15

Abraham had two sons, the one, Ishmael, by a slave woman; the other Isaac, by a free-woman. Ishmael's tragic life is not passed over in silence by the Bible. He was a slave, while his brother Isaac was free. Ishmael was cast out of the family, while Isaac remained. He owned nothing, but his brother was the heir and son of the promise that in him all the nations of the earth would be blessed. Ishmael got nothing.

Paul says this story of the two sons has a spiritual lesson. He explains this in his Epistle to the Galatians. There are but two beliefs. Ishmael's corresponds to the religion of the Law, a religion represented by a slave. All who practice this religion look to God as one who said nothing more than: "Do right and live; do wrong and perish." But the other religion looks up to God and, while it teaches that the Law condemns, it also reveals that the Gospel frees. The Law keeps us at a distance from God, while the Gospel tells of Christ, the Savior, and brings the sinner close to God. The Law excludes us from the family of God because of our sins, while the Gospel draws us by the promise of forgiveness and salvation into the household of God. The former is the religion of Ishmael; the latter, the religion of Isaac, sets us free because another, Christ, has paid our fine.

Lord, preserve to us the religion of faith that we might accept Your salvation through Jesus Christ. Amen.

June

The Changed Name

No longer shall your name be called Abram, but your name shall be Abraham, for I have made you the father of a multitude of nations. Genesis 17:5

God often changed a person's name as a way of speaking assurance and faith to that person. Thus Sarai was changed to Sarah, Jacob to Israel, Oshea to Joshua. Here Abram becomes Abraham, meaning "father of a multitude." That was done to strengthen Abraham's faith and to remind him that he was the father of all Israel, of the Messiah, and of all believers in Christ Jesus.

Paul calls Abraham, "The father of all who believe without being circumcised, so that righteousness would be counted to them as well" (Romans 4:11). Thus Abraham's changed name designates him as the father of the faithful.

Jesus once told a parable of a son who left his home and lost his father's good name. The story of the prodigal son is tragic until the son at last returned to his father's house, repentant and pleading for mercy. The whole family of God likewise once went astray in the beginning of time. But now God has been reconciled with His children, and Christ has reconciled the children with their Father.

We derive our name—Christian—from Christ. God, our heavenly Father, gives us this name when He brings us into His family of faith through the waters and Word of Holy Baptism.

O Christ, may we bear Your name in faith and show that we are Yours with a life that corresponds to our profession. Amen.

The Justice of God

"Far be it from you to do such a thing, to put the righteous to death with the wicked, so that the righteous fare as the wicked! Far be that from you! Shall not the Judge of all the earth do what is just?" Genesis 18:25

The prayer life of the patriarch Abraham is rich in his repeated pleading for Sodom and his nephew Lot. He prays that even if only ten are righteous within the city, it be not destroyed. His prayer shows sympathy, charity, humility, fervent persistence, and solid faith. The final argument for this sparing of Sodom is God's justice.

God mercifully consents to the request of Abraham. Abraham is assured that if there are only ten righteous in the city, Sodom will remain. But not even ten are found, so it is destroyed—but Lot and his family are spared.

Abraham possessed a strong sense of God's justice. The judge must do right, and his decision must go unquestioned. It was this same sense of God's justice that brought Jesus as a man into the world. Human flesh had to suffer for human sin; therefore the one who was to suffer had to take human flesh, His body and blood, from the human race. For this reason Abraham's great descendant was born of the Virgin Mary.

Our faith in Jesus, the Son of God and the Son of Abraham, is founded on the same foundation as was Abraham's: on the justice of God. God has shown mercy to sinners, fulfilling the promise He spoke to Abraham. He has done so in Jesus of Nazareth, Abraham's Lord, yet Abraham's Son.

Lord, open our hearts that we may accept the great mystery of godliness, the fulfillment of Your justice, God manifest in the flesh through Jesus Christ, our Lord. Amen.

Our Unseen Allies

He said, "Do not be afraid, for those who are with us are more than those who are with them." 2 Kings 6:16

The Syrians had waged war against the King of Israel. Several clever military snares had been set to entrap the army of Israel, but somehow every secret device of the enemy had reached the king's ears, and Benhadad the Syrian was baffled and angry. Was there an informant, he wondered? "None, my lord, O king; but Elisha, the prophet who is in Israel, tells the king of Israel the words that you speak in your bedroom" (2 Kings 6:12). "Go and see where he is, that I may send and seize him" (2 Kings 6:13). To Dothan marched the Syrian army and they laid siege to the city.

In the morning the prophet and his servant were the first to discover that the plain around the city bristled with Syrian spears. The servant of Elisha whispered though white lips, "Alas! My master, what shall we do?" (2 Kings 6:15). The untroubled prophet said, "Do not be afraid, for those who are with us are more than those who are with them." Then Elisha prayed and said, "O Lord, please open his eyes" (2 Kings 6:16–17). At once the physical veil was lifted from the servant's vision. "And he saw, and behold, the mountain was full of horses and chariots of fire" (2 Kings 6:17).

Lord God, let Thy holy angel be with me, that the wicked foe may have no power over me! Amen.

Rest in the Lord

*Be still before the LORD and wait patiently for Him; fret not
yourself over the one who prospers in his way, over the man who
carries out evil devices! Psalm 37:7*

There are times when all of us need rest. During a long,
hard day of work we look forward to the promise of rest in the
evening. After many months of labor we welcome the quiet of
vacation days. Such rest makes us ready once more to face the
heat and burden of life.

For us Christians there is, however, another and a better
rest. Long ago David said; "Be still before the LORD and wait
patiently for Him." A child of this world may stop working, but
there is no true rest for him. Even if he tries to forget the problems of the day, the problem of sin always remains. Sin never
lets anybody rest.

Only we Christians can really rest. We also sin, but we can
take our sins to our Savior and find forgiveness for them. The
harsh words we have spoken today, the anger in our hearts, the
sinful worry in our lives, all these we bring to God and ask Him to
forgive them. And God never fails to forgive. He remembers our
Savior's death and, for His sake and because of His merit, blots
out all our sins. He gives us the most precious rest in the world,
the rest from sin. Countless Christians who have gone before us
have tasted this rest. In Him our hearts can rest forever.

*Yet your sinless death has brought us
Life eternal, peace, and rest;
Only what your grace has taught us
Calms the sinner's deep distress.*

*Jesus, may our hearts be burning
With more fervent love for you;
May our eyes be ever turning
To behold your cross anew. Amen. (LW 90:2–3)*

Jehovah-Jireh

So Abraham called the name of that place, "The LORD will pro-vide"; as it is said to this day, "On the mount of the LORD it shall be provided." Genesis 22:14

Many place names in the Bible reveal the meaning of famous events. Thus Eden recalls the delight of the first human family, and Babel, the tower of pride and confusion, reminds us of how God confused the languages of arrogant men. When Abraham met the supreme test of his faith and obeyed God by taking his beloved son Isaac to the mount of sacrifice, he called the place where he sacrificed the ram in the stead of his son, Jehovah-Jireh: "God will provide" (Genesis 22:8).

The name expresses a resolute confidence that as God has created and given life, man's needs will never exceed the Lord's ability to provide.

When man is in dire straits, God can always supply his want. His is the power that can! Particularly was this true when God spared not His own Son, but delivered Him up for us all. That mount has become the evidence of God's utmost preservation. There He has for all time provided for the sinner's greatest need—forgiveness. At Joseph's tomb, from which Jesus rose on the third day, God lifted all despair of death and provided the hope of the resurrection of the body. From Olivet, Jesus as the ascending Lord prepared a place for us. Thus God through Christ has provided us with everlasting life.

So the believer has always a Jehovah-Jireh: "The Lord will provide."

O Lord, who did provide for us the Lamb that takes away the sins of the world (John 1:29), give us at all times enough faith to know You will provide. Through Jesus Christ. Amen.

What God Remembers

He remembers His covenant forever, the word that He commanded, for a thousand generations. Psalm 105:8

"You can depend on him. He keeps his promises." When someone says this about another, we agree it is an excellent recommendation. You can depend on God! He keeps His promises! He remembers the covenant He made with mankind and keeps it.

The covenant goes back to the promise to Adam that the Seed of a woman would conquer the seed of Satan. This was restated to Abraham and his children: it was renewed throughout the history of the Israelite people. We sometimes forget promises in a matter of days, but in thousands of years God did not forget. He sent His Son, made of a woman, made under the Law, to redeem them that were under the Law, that we might be brothers and sisters of Christ.

When the thief hung on the cross, he was concerned about one thing only—that his Savior would remember him. "Jesus, remember me when You come into Your kingdom" (Luke 23:42). The Savior promised He would, and it was as good as done.

God still remembers His covenant. Through the work of His Spirit, people are continually claimed to be His children, made heirs of salvation and joint heirs with Christ, and given the inheritance of everlasting life. Our God remembers His covenant forever; He forgets us never. We can depend on Him! He keeps His promises.

Never permit me, O God, to mistrust the covenant that You have established with me through Christ. Amen.

June

Grow in Grace and Knowledge

But grow in the grace and knowledge of our Lord and Savior Jesus Christ. To Him be the glory both now and to the day of eternity. Amen. 2 Peter 3:18

Divine wisdom is inexhaustible. The full depth of the riches of the Word of God can never be reached by sinful men, but we all can grow. It is God's will that we grow in faith and in good works as long as we live.

The day of the Lord is near, and we are to be prepared for it. False prophets seek to undermine God's Word and the faith of the believers in that Word. We should be able to recognize false prophets for what they are and avoid them. The temptations of the world are subtle and many, and as Christians we should ask for God's grace to be able to judge right and wrong. Our own hearts tempt us to spiritual indifference, to sin, and to a denial of God and His work. We must ask God to help us overcome the sinfulness of our flesh. This God does through faith.

We believe that Jesus Christ died for us and that we are God's own. We are His children, and we are safe in His loving arms. These assurances come to us through the Word, and we grasp them by God's gift of faith. As we faithfully continue to hear and study God's Word, God shall faithfully cause us to grow in grace and in the knowledge of our Lord and Savior Jesus Christ, and this for our continued blessing.

Lord, increase our love for Your Word, and help us to grow thereby. Amen.

The Sentinel before Our Hearts

And the peace of God, which surpasses all understanding, will guard your hearts and your minds in Christ Jesus. Philippians 4:7

This is a very familiar passage, for it is used almost every Sunday in the pulpit immediately after the sermon. It has been referred to as "the benediction after the sermon," assuring the believing worshipers that the peace of God in Christ Jesus, offered and bestowed in the preached Word, will keep their hearts and minds in true faith unto everlasting life.

One of the key words in this benediction is the word "guard." It is taken from military life and was used to describe the task of a soldier who marched back and forth before a tent or a room in which was quartered a very important person. The soldier was guarding that person.

So the peace of God "guards" our minds and hearts. An ever alert sentinel, it marches back and forth, up and down, before the door of our minds and hearts. Not only does it prevent the entrance of harmful thoughts into our minds, but it also shuts out agonizing fears from our hearts.

Behind that impregnable guard sits the Christian, unmolested and unafraid. The troubles, misfortunes, and fears that strike others down, cannot hurt him; they cannot penetrate into his heart and mind to disturb him. The peace of God, the knowledge of sins forgiven, and the promise of the heavenly Father's benign providence act as a safe and secure garrison.

Blessed Savior, grant such peace to keep our minds and hearts. Amen.

The Greatest Prayer Ever Uttered

"I am praying for them. I am not praying for the world but for those whom You have given Me, for they are Yours." John 17:9

The greatest prayer ever uttered unquestionably is the high-priestly prayer of our Lord, preserved for us by St. John. The opening verse reads: "When Jesus had spoken these words, He lifted up His eyes to heaven, and said, 'Father, the hour has come; glorify Your Son that the Son may glorify You'" (John 17:1). As we watch our Christ at prayer as He pours out His heart to His heavenly Father, we are, indeed, on holy ground.

The high-priestly prayer of our Lord has three distinct divisions. In the first eight verses the Lord Jesus is speaking to His heavenly Father about Himself. The Father and the Son are in sweet communion, and the Son is talking to the Father about His own life and work.

Then, in the ninth verse there is a distinct change in the prayer and from this verse to the end of verse nineteen, Jesus is interceding at the throne of the Father on behalf of His disciples. The burden of that part of the prayer is: "I am praying for them. I am not praying for the world but for those whom You have given me, for they are Yours."

At the twentieth verse we reach the third division. From this verse to the end of the chapter the Lord is interceding for all believers. He addresses the Father, saying: "I do not ask for these only [His disciples], but also for those who will believe in Me through their word" (John 17:20). Our Lord looked down the corridor of time and had us in mind who would hear the Gospel and through faith in Him would be made part of His body, the Church.

Thank You, Jesus, that You remembered me even before I was born. Amen.

The Promise

I will multiply your offspring as the stars of heaven and will give
to your offspring all these lands. And in your offspring all the
nations of the earth shall be blessed. Genesis 26:4

To Isaac was given this promise, which was first offered to
Abraham. It is the promise that all the world would be blessed
in the Messiah, who was first promised to Adam and Eve after
their sin in the Garden of Eden. Now that Isaac was deeply conscious of his own sins and the sins of his household, he was to
find comfort, assurance, and salvation in this promise.

As Abraham believed, so Isaac believed the promises and
this faith was accounted to him for righteousness.

Abram's promised great reward, Zion's helper, Jacob's Lord—
Him of twofold race behold—Truly came, as long foretold.
(LW 33:3)

To this Old Testament sinner and saint, Christ is clearly
revealed as his blessing and the blessing of a great multitude
that no one could number. "When the fullness of time had
come, God sent forth His Son, born of woman, born under the
law, to redeem those who were under the law, so that we might
receive adoption as sons" (Galatians 4:4–5). As "by faith Isaac
invoked future blessing on Jacob and Esau" (Hebrews 11:20), so
today we are blessed in all that the Christ has accomplished for
us: forgiveness, new life here, and everlasting life yet to come.
We can stand before our judge with garments washed in the
blood of this Lamb that takes away the sins of the world.

Now my conscience is at peace,
From the Law I stand acquitted;
Christ hath purchased my release
And my every sin remitted.
Naught remains my soul to grieve—
Jesus sinners doth receive. Amen. (TLH 324:7)

Gathered to His People

*And Isaac breathed his last, and he died and was gathered to his
people, old and full of days. And his sons Esau and Jacob buried
him. Genesis 35:29*

Hebron is one of the oldest cities in the world. Near this
venerable city is the cave of Machpelah, the burial place
Abraham purchased for Sarah. There Ishmael and Isaac carried
the body of their father and laid him beside Sarah. At
Abraham's burial the Bible writes his epitaph: "[He] was gathered to his people." Hebrews 11 adds that he died in the hope of
a better country.

Again, years later two other sons, divided by sin, united by
death, would carry their old father, Isaac, to his last resting
place. Isaac beheld the goodness and mercy of the Lord. The
covenant of a promised Savior to come had been continued
through him. At death God took him to his people, the family
in heaven. Isaac gave up his spirit into better hands, the hands
of God. "For there is a future for the man of peace" (Psalm
37:37), for he obtained pardon from the hand of the Lord and
in the promise that he himself was a party to. Jacob and Esau,
the chief mourners, could say, "For my father and my mother
have forsaken me, but the LORD will take me in" (Psalm 27:10).

How it comforts us, too, to know that when death comes,
God gathers His people into the eternal mansions. How it soft-
ens the blow to hear from Jesus' lips when death comes to our
household: "Where I am, there will my servant be also" (John
12:26).

*Almighty and most merciful God, as Your Son commended into Your
hands His Spirit at the hour of death, by Your Holy Spirit support us
in our hour of departure, that we, too, may be gathered to Your people.
Through Jesus Christ, our Lord. Amen.*

Stop Worrying!

"Therefore do not be anxious about tomorrow, for tomorrow will be anxious for itself. Sufficient for the day is its own trouble." Matthew 6:34

"Do not be anxious." What Jesus said in the words prior to this verse gives the main reason why we should not worry at all. Our lives are in God's hands; our heavenly Father knows our needs. The further reason why we should not worry about the future is that also the future is in God's hands, and not in ours. God gives us one day at a time: "Give us this day our *daily* bread" (Matthew 6:11). And He has promised strength for *one* day at a time: "Your bars shall be iron and bronze, and as your days, so shall your strength be" (Deuteronomy 33:25).

These words of Jesus contain not only instruction, but also warning and comfort. The warning is: "Stop worrying!" When we worry, we fail to exercise the faith God has so graciously given and we dishonor God. Our worrying is a sin against God and against ourselves. The comfort Jesus speaks is this: God knows, He loves, He cares. For Jesus' sake our heavenly Father will deal with us in mercy and give us loving care.

I trust, O Christ, in you alone;
No earthly hope avails me.
You will not see me overthrown
When Satan's host assails me.
No human strength, no earthly pow'r
Can see me through the evil hour,
For you alone my strength renew. I cry to you!
I trust, O Lord, your promise true. Amen. (LW 357:1)
Used by permission of Concordia Publishing House.

We Need Forgiveness from God

"And no longer shall each one teach his neighbor and each his brother, saying, 'Know the LORD,' for they shall all know Me, from the least of them to the greatest, declares the LORD. For I will forgive their iniquity, and I will remember their sin no more." Jeremiah 31:34

Why should I need forgiveness from God? I can see a need for forgiveness between people who are angry with each other, but I have no quarrel with God. Forgiveness from Him? Why?

We get a hint why we need God's forgiveness when we see how forgiveness operates on the human level. For, to heal a breach forgiveness is essential. Before a man admits his need for *God's* forgiveness, he must understand that his relationship with God is broken. Although God made us for Himself, our natural tendency is to act as if we own ourselves. This is what "sin" is.

This is why David, when he had sinned against a human being, nevertheless confessed to God: "Against You, You only, have I sinned" (Psalm 51:4). When we hurt others, we hurt God, who has made them.

In Luke 15:11–32, the story of the prodigal (which means "wasteful") son shows how God, who is the father in that parable, wants us, the prodigals, to come back to Him. The only way we can be sure He will accept us again as sons is to hear Him say: "For I will forgive their iniquity, and I will remember their sin no more."

We thank You, Jesus, that through Your perfect life and suffering God forgives us and calls us "sons" and "daughters." Amen.

Be Still!

For thus said the Lord GOD, the Holy One of Israel, "In return-ing and rest you shall be saved; in quietness and in trust shall be your strength." But you were unwilling. Isaiah 30:15

Here is a verse that should be marked in every Christian's Bible. The direction given is as applicable today, to any people or any individual, as it was to Israel in the days of Isaiah. When the hand of God was heavy upon Israel because they had for-saken their Lord, the princes and the people hurried to and fro, excitedly seeking help and strength in human devices and in alliances with heathen kings. Thus they made matters worse. What they needed was to be still, to think upon God and the evil of their ways, and then humbly and penitently to return to the Lord. They needed to get right with God in order to find peace with Him and strength in Him. "Trust in the LORD forev-er, for the LORD GOD is an everlasting rock" (Isaiah 26:4).

Jesus, God's own Son, as He faced satanic opposition, taught us the benefit of quietness: "But Jesus rebuked him, say-ing, 'Be silent, and come out of him!'" (Mark 1:25). When we are in distress of soul, when we realize our sinful weakness and helplessness, let us hear and meditate upon God's faith-creating Word; let us receive the Sacrament of the Lord's body and blood. Then we, too, shall find rest unto our souls.

Blessed Jesus, in our weakness and our woes we came to You. Strengthen us; keep us in Your grace. Amen.

Ready Disciples

I will also speak of Your testimonies before kings and shall not be put to shame. Psalm 119:46

On this afternoon several hundred years ago seven noblemen and the representatives of two cities presented an explanation and defense of their Christian faith to a Diet, or convention, of the Holy Roman Empire and its head, Charles V. That was the Augsburg Confession, the first official statement of what Lutherans believe—what the historian Philip Schaff called "one of the noblest monuments of faith."

The leaders of the Reformation had been summoned to Augsburg to explain why they should not be compelled to return to the teaching of the Church of Rome. This Confession was their reply: God's Holy Word, the Bible, is the only authority for consciences. It teaches and convinces us that no man can gain God's forgiveness and everlasting life by his good works. We are saved only and entirely by God's grace—His Son's redeeming work for us—held and enjoyed through the faith the Holy Spirit gives us by means of the Gospel and the Sacraments.

The signers of the Confession were laymen. When it was suggested that they might endanger their lives if they signed, the Elector of Saxony responded for all: "I desire to confess the Lord. My electoral hat and ermine are not so precious to me as the cross of Jesus Christ." Those men were "ready always to give an answer to every man" concerning their Christian faith, to testify of their Savior and His Word "also before kings." Our Lord Jesus calls for such loyalty to Holy Scripture in every disciple.

Dear Savior, keep us steadfast in Your Word! Amen.

Abide with Me

*But they urged Him strongly, saying, "Stay with us, for it is
toward evening and the day is now far spent." So He went in to
stay with them. Luke 24:29*

*Abide with me, fast falls the eventide.
The darkness deepens; Lord, with me abide.
When other helpers fail and comforts flee,
Help of the helpless, oh, abide with me. (LW 490:1)*

This familiar evening hymn has become one of the best-
loved hymns in the Christian world. Although we sing it most
often as night falls and the shadows lengthen, it is really timeless. It expresses the constant need of our hearts.

As we sing this hymn of prayer, we remember the golden
afternoon in Galilee when our Lord answered it for all time to
come: "Behold, I am with you always, to the end of the age"
(Matthew 28:20). Although a cloud took Him away from our
mortal eyes, no cloud can ever hide Him from the eyes of our
faith.

We may travel far from home and friends, but we remember that He left His home in heaven for us. We may be lonely
among the crowds of a great city, but we remember that He
moved among crowds where no friendly face was seen. We may
think we walk alone, but in the darkness we hear the footsteps
of Him who went to the cross alone—for our sake. Even in the
loneliness of death we shall not be alone; for He has tasted
death for us.

*Lord Jesus, give us the strength to pray in sure confidence that You will
hear: "Abide with us." For Your name's sake. Amen.*

The Nobility of Service

"And whoever would be first among you must be your slave, even as the Son of Man came not to be served but to serve, and to give His life as a ransom for many." Matthew 20:27–28

With these words Christ has instituted the Order of Nobility in His kingdom—the Nobility of Service. If we desire to belong to the Savior's Order of Nobility, we must be ready and willing to serve; and the deeper we sink in loving, self-forgetting service, the higher we shall mount in the scale of greatness—not as the world counts her great, but as Christ reckons them.

Such service comes not by merely following the example of our Christ, but by the life-giving power of His living Word, through which He speaks faith to us and makes us His own. Because our Lord humbled Himself and became obedient unto death, even the death on the cross, we, too, are included in His kingdom. Because "God has highly exalted Him and bestowed on Him the name that is above every name" (Philippians 2:9), we, too, have a participation in that name; we, too, shall rise; we, too, shall live bodily with Jesus in eternity!

Lord, help us more and more to give ourselves in humble service to You and our fellow men. Grant us more and more to recognize that such a life is the only life worth living. Amen.

I Fear No Foe

Even though I walk through the valley of the shadow of death, I will fear no evil, for You are with me; Your rod and Your staff, they comfort me. Psalm 23:4

Our Christian faith is a triumphant faith. There is no foe in the world and no enemy on earth who was not conquered by our Savior's triumph on the cross. Sin, sorrow, temptation, death, all were overcome by Him. His suffering and death removed every enemy who stood between us and our almighty Father in heaven.

Faith in this eternal triumph of our mighty Savior must make our life on earth a conquering life. We are children of the King. We are mighty because He was the mightiest. We are one with Him whom God has given a name above every name, that at the name of Jesus every knee should bow and every tongue confess that He is the Lord, to the glory of God the Father.

By Baptism, God has given us the right to claim our share in His triumph. No enemy can harm us. Sin cannot destroy, sorrow cannot kill, death cannot sting. All our enemies are His enemies, and He has overcome them long ago.

We need this blessed vision of our mighty Savior. We look into all the ages past and see that He has never forsaken His own. We look into the future and know that our cause belongs to Him who has the keys of hell and death.

Then help us, Lord! Now hear our prayer.
Defend your people ev'rywhere
For your own name's sake. Amen.
Then with a mighty hymn of praise
Your Church in earth and heav'n will raise
Their songs of triumph. Amen. (LW 300:4)

Used by permission of Concordia Publishing House.

Precious in God's Sight

Precious in the sight of the LORD is the death of His saints.
Psalm 116:15

Jesus tells us that not even a sparrow falls to the ground without our heavenly Father knowing it; and He adds: "You are of more value than many sparrows" (Luke 12:7). Accordingly God takes note of the death of every human being. When men die in large numbers in famine and plague, in a war or in other tragedies, it is not without meaning to Him, nor should it be to us. The Father of mercies grieves over such loss of human life.

However, the Lord regards as most precious the death of His saints, that is, His Christians. He has entered their names in the Book of Life, and He watches over them all the days of their life, in health and in sickness. He is at their deathbed, be that at home or in a hospital. He speaks to them with the consolation of His Holy Spirit. He wards off the final attacks of Satan and lifts the spirits of His dying saints above the mists of doubt and fear. Into their ears He whispers: "Fear not, for I have redeemed you; I have called you by name, you are Mine" (Isaiah 43:1). The dying saint responds with St. Simeon: "Lord, now You are letting Your servant depart in peace, according to Your word" (Luke 2:29). And after their departure from earth, their death remains precious in God's sight because through death they have entered into heavenly glory.

Dear Savior, prepare us that our death may be precious in Your sight. Amen.

"Hold Thou Thy Cross"

And he said, "Behold, I see the heavens opened, and the Son of Man standing at the right hand of God." Acts 7:56

Once every 24 hours darkness falls over the earth, and the sunlight is shut out. Year after year this march of days and nights goes on. There is constant change—brightness and gloom, sun and shadow, light and darkness. Here on earth nothing ever remains the same.

But one thing remains. Before the eyes of our faith, at morning and at night, in sunshine and in darkness, towers the cross of Christ, the eternal symbol of the love of God for our sin-torn souls. It never changes. Always and forever it brings its blessed message of peace and forgiveness, of comfort and joy. We may lose everything else in life, but clinging to our Savior, we can never lose the cross and all it has meant and still means for our life and death, for time and eternity.

"Hold thou thy cross before my closing eyes" (*LW* 490:5). The cares of the long day steal away, and as we go to rest, only the cross remains. Once it lifted us from the night of sin. Tonight it will carry us safely through the hours of darkness. Once it brought us peace with God. Tonight it will bring us peace from all the noise and heat of the day. And when our last night comes, it will still be here, shining and sure, to carry us up into the final dawn of heaven's eternal day.

Lord Jesus, hold Your cross before our eyes all the days of our life, that we may truly serve and trustingly follow You to the end. Amen.

An Accounting Demanded

So then each of us will give an account of himself to God.
Romans 14:12

Whether or not men like the prospect of it, everyone must appear before God to give an account of himself. In the courts of men, wealth and influence may sometimes succeed in gaining repeated postponements; false testimony may even prevent justice from being done. But when God summons men to give account, a false accounting in the presence of the omniscient Lord will be impossible.

An honest examination of our lives in the mirror of God's commandments will reveal that we have often been guilty of transgressing God's holy Law. Indeed, "who can discern his errors?" (Psalm 19:12). In the judgment scene He pictured for us, Jesus mentions even the failure to do good as sufficient grounds for everlasting punishment. He said: "'Truly, I say to you, as you did not do it to one of the least of these, you did not do it to Me.' And these will go away into eternal punishment, but the righteous into eternal life" (Matthew 25:45–46).

But God's people shall not point to themselves when they are called to account. They shall point to the resurrected Christ, who bore all their sins and penalties. "If anyone does sin, we have an advocate with the Father, Jesus Christ the righteous. He is the propitiation for our sins, and not for ours only but also for the sins of the whole world" (1 John 2:1–2).

O gracious God, have mercy upon us on the Day of Judgment, for Jesus' sake. Amen.

Our Unseen Companions

Are they not all ministering spirits sent out to serve for the sake of those who are to inherit salvation? Hebrews 1:14

On the Lord's Day many Christian congregations assemble for divine worship. In countless groups, large and small, throughout Christendom, the heirs of salvation have fellowship with Christ and with one another.

Also present at worship are those "ministering spirits," the angels of God who gaze with delight upon the proclamations of the Gospel of atonement through Christ Jesus. They hover over the baptismal font every time a Baptism is performed and gather around us as we bow our heads in reverence at the Lord's Table.

"Ministering spirits" the angels are called. Their ministries are manifold. The heavenly Father assigns them to us—the heirs of salvation—as our unseen companions, vigilant and intelligent bodyguards. That accounts for so many deliverances from accidents, the greater part of which are unseen, from perils from the elements, from wicked men, and from Satan and his hosts.

These ministrations continue until the hour of death. Poor Lazarus, the Savior tells us, "was carried by the angels to Abraham's side" (Luke 16:22). So also shall they gather each Christian on the Last Day and be our companions in eternity.

Heavenly Father, let Your holy angels have charge of us to guard us in all our ways. Amen.

Christis Stands By

At my first defense no one came to stand by me, but all deserted me. May it not be charged against them! But the Lord stood by me and strengthened me, so that through me the message might be fully proclaimed and all the Gentiles might hear it. So I was rescued from the lion's mouth. 2 Timothy 4:16–17

In this verse, the apostle Paul refers to his first trial in Rome. He had been cast into prison for preaching the Gospel, for declaring to Jews and Gentiles that Jesus was the Son of God and the *only* Savior of men. Now he sadly reports to his young associate Timothy, who was laboring elsewhere for Christ, that in his trial he stood alone; all others who had shown some interest in him personally, and in the Gospel he preached, had deserted him. Yet he prays, "May it not be charged against them." Then he adds, "But the Lord stood by me." After all, he was not alone in court. Jesus, who Himself had stood in the court of Pilate, now truly, although invisible, stood alongside Paul, "and strengthened me." Yes, the presence of Christ gave His apostle courage and comfort.

Since Paul's time, many other witnesses for Christ have had to stand alone against the foes of Christ and His Gospel. Yet such confessors never were left all alone. Foes might oppose and friends might desert them, but Christ stood by them.

Come what may in our own lives, even when we feel deserted and find ourselves alone, Christ is by our side to strengthen us. He will not fail us.

Dear Jesus, since You are faithful, give us grace to serve You faithfully and to trust You boldly. Amen.

Two Kingdoms

Jesus answered him, "You would have no authority over Me at all unless it had been given you from above. Therefore he who delivered Me over to you has the greater sin." John 19:11

God has given two kingdoms to this world: the Kingdom of the Church and the Kingdom of the State (civil government). Both of these divine kingdoms deal with the problem of human sin, but in radically different ways.

God has established the Kingdom of the State for the control of evil and for the punishment of evildoers, not for mercy. He calls governmental leaders to pursue lawbreakers and evildoers, and "to punish those who do evil" (1 Peter 2:14). St. Paul writes, "Whoever resists the authorities resists what God has appointed, and those who resist will incur judgment. For rulers are not a terror to good conduct, but to bad" (Romans 13:2–3).

In the Kingdom of the Church, however, sinners find peace with God through the forgiveness of their sins solely because of Jesus' death upon the cross for all people (1 John 2:2). The Church holds the responsibility to teach the faith, to judge doctrine as pure or impure, to forgive the repentant, and to withhold forgiveness from the unrepentant. "If you forgive the sins of anyone, they are forgiven; if you withhold forgiveness from anyone, it is withheld" (John 20:23). In this kingdom, you have the forgiveness of sins that will enable you to live and serve faithfully as a citizen in the other kingdom.

Thank You, Lord, for placing me in two kingdoms. Make me faithful, that I may serve both according to Your will. Amen.

God Our Refuge

God is our refuge and strength, a very present help in trouble.
Psalm 46:1

The psalmist wrote this statement both by revelation and out of his own experience. He had repeatedly been hard-pressed; men either could not or would not help him. Forsaken by friends, opposed by enemies, he was helpless and near despair. He threw himself altogether upon the Lord, and He helped in a marvelous way. He found God to be his own personal refuge and source of strength. So he looks hopefully into the future and declares confidently: "Therefore we will not fear" (Psalm 46:2).

Likewise Luther. When he was battling for truth and righteousness and the battle seemed to be going against him; when his soul was in deep distress, he found relief and strength in the divine assurances of this glorious psalm. So he wrote his thoughts into this mighty battle hymn, "A Mighty Fortress Is Our God," a hymn that has cheered the Church through five centuries.

Again the world is in turmoil. Again there is distress among nations. Again the awful destruction caused by the hatred of men strikes terror in the hearts of many. But the believers, at peace with God through faith in Christ, may confidently sing: "God is our refuge and strength, a very present help in trouble. Therefore we will not fear."

Lord, grant us Your peace, and bring courage to our hearts, through Christ. Amen.

The Lord Will Provide

And my God will supply every need of yours according to His riches in glory in Christ Jesus. Philippians 4:19

"Therefore do not be anxious about tomorrow" (Matthew 6:34), Jesus said in the Sermon on the Mount. He meant: don't worry. Likewise St. Paul writes to the Philippians: "Do not be anxious about anything" (Philippians 4:6); that is, be not full of care; don't be anxious or troubled about anything.

It is part of our sinful and fallen human nature to worry. How shall we overcome this tendency to worry? By keeping in mind the goodness and the riches of our heavenly Father and by relying on His gracious promises. We are assured that "For the LORD God is a sun and shield; the LORD bestows favor and honor" (Psalm 84:11). With confidence each of us may say: "The LORD is my Shepherd; I shall not want" (Psalm 23:1).

It is in this context that St. Paul here thanks the Christians at Philippi for the various gifts of love they had sent to supply his need while he was imprisoned at Rome. He assures them that they will be no poorer for what they had given to him. On the contrary, he says that his God and their God will supply all their needs and will do so according to His riches in glory, by or through Jesus Christ. How shall God provide for us today? In exactly the same way—according to His mercy in Christ Jesus!

Lord, our bountiful Father, teach us to trust You fully and to abound in love and good works. Amen.

No Death!

And which now has been manifested through the appearing of our Savior Christ Jesus, who abolished death and brought life and immortality to light through the gospel. 2 Timothy 1:10

The countryside is dotted with cemeteries, and we regularly meet funeral processions on the streets and highways. Does this contradict the statement of St. Paul that Christ "abolished death"? Not at all!

Sin brought with it the curse of death. But Christ atoned for all sins on the cross. Our sins were nailed to His cross; He died our death; and He rose again from the dead, leaving our sins and death forever buried. He changed death for the believers from a curse that seals men in eternal death to a blessing that translates God's children into eternal life. It is, therefore, not death for the Christian to die; it is the entrance into full and perfect life.

In the frontier days on the North American prairies, one of the greatest enemies was the grass fire, which swept along at a fast pace and destroyed everything in its path. When such a fire approached, settlers lit another fire. Standing in the place where their fire had burned, they were safe, for there was nothing more to burn.

Christ did the same thing for us. The fires of God's anger over our sins burned out on Him, and we live because no sins remain to damn us. "The last enemy to be destroyed is death" (1 Corinthians 15:26). Now, when a Christian passes away, others may refer to him with the beautiful phrase, "He is with our Lord." God's children never die.

O Holy Spirit, enable us to live the life resurrected from the power of sin and to obtain everlasting life through Christ. Amen.

Angels All Around

When the servant of the man of God rose early in the morning and went out, behold, an army with horses and chariots was all around the city. And the servant said, "Alas, my master! What shall we do?" He said, "Do not be afraid, for those who are with us are more than those who are with them." 2 Kings 6:15–16

"You have multiplied, O LORD my God, Your wondrous deeds and Your thoughts toward us" (Psalm 40:5), sang David. We join him in praising God's goodness as we think upon His desire for our redemption, His Son's work for our salvation, and all His rich provisions for our daily needs. Not least among those gifts of His love are the ministering spirits, His holy angels, created to protect and strengthen us in this life.

By informing the king of Israel of the things God revealed to him, the prophet Elijah foiled repeated plots of the Syrian king to conquer Israel by surprise attacks. At last, Israel's enemies learned that Elijah was in the town of Dothan. Under cover of night, an army detachment encircled the village. Early the next morning, Elisha's servant discovered the threatening host. "Alas, my master! What shall we do?" Then came this confident reply of the man of God. He knew his Lord's power and His provisions to safeguard His servants. Elisha's confidence was not mistaken. The angelic hosts rendered the Syrian army powerless; indeed, delivered it into the hands of Elisha.

The Lord's might and His messengers are with us still. The pledge holds true even today: "The angel of the LORD encamps around those who fear Him, and delivers them" (Psalm 34:7).

Jesus, Brightness of the Father,
Life and Strength of all who live,
For creating guardian angels
Glory to Thy name we give
And Thy wondrous praise rehearse. Amen. (TLH 257:1)

Jesus, the Open Door

"I am the door. If anyone enters by Me, he will be saved and will go in and out and find pasture." John 10:9

Jesus is the open door to heaven. As the sheep need a door to enter the safe enclosure of the sheepfold, so we also need Jesus the only door to the security of the eternal sheepfold above.

Sin once closed and locked the door to heaven. When Jesus came to earth, saving us from our sins, He unlocked and opened heaven's door again! By His perfect fulfillment of the divine Law and by His all-sufficient substitutionary death on Calvary He has truly become the open door to heaven.

Once a little bird flew into a church during divine worship. Confused and frightened, it fluttered back and forth and up under the ceiling, bruising itself badly against the window panes—and all the while the church door stood open.

At last the little wings became exhausted from their futile efforts, and the bird sank nearer and nearer to the floor until it caught sight of the open door and suddenly disappeared through it.

Like those of the fluttering bird, all our struggles to gain the light and freedom of heaven are futile. Having vainly exhausted every effort to save ourselves, God's Word and Sacraments give us faith in Jesus, the only door to salvation. Through Him alone we will find eternal rest, peace, and happiness.

Grant us grace, blessed Savior, at the last through You to enter life eternal. Amen.

The Heart of the Bible

I have been crucified with Christ. It is no longer I who live, but Christ who lives in me. And the life I now live in the flesh I live by faith in the Son of God, who loved me and gave Himself for me. Galatians 2:20

In the above Scripture verse the great work of redemption is condensed into one sentence of only a few short words.

"The Son of God, who loved me." That the Son of God loved His Father in heaven does not seem strange to us at all. How could He, who is perfectly holy, do otherwise than love a person who is equally holy, yes, who is of the very same essence with Him?

That the Son of God should love the holy angels does not surprise us either. How could He do otherwise than love those perfect beings who serve Him so willingly and so cheerfully?

But when the Son of God loves those who are so far below Him, when His heart goes out in compassion to those who sin daily and grievously—then we stand amazed and exclaim with the apostle St. John: "See what kind of love the Father has given to us!" (1 John 3:1).

The greatest demonstration of this love was given on Calvary when Jesus offered Himself voluntarily upon the cross. St. Paul refers to this act of love when he says: "The Son of God, who loved me and gave Himself for me."

But there is another thought that needs to be emphasized to render this amazing statement personally effective, and that is the thought the little pronoun "me" expresses. It was for *me* that Jesus came to suffer; it was for *me* He died upon the tree. There you have concentrated and summarized everything the Holy Bible reveals to us. And he who believes this truth is a child of God and an heir of heaven.

Thank You, Jesus, that You suffered even for me. Amen.

Alone—Yet Not Alone

"And behold, I am with you always, to the end of the age."
Matthew 28:20

Never before in human history has there been so much loneliness as today. Perhaps this is because of the many aged people who alone remain of their generation, or because of the masses of people concentrated in cities, or because of the number who have left home and family for work or military service. Be that as it may, loneliness is a curse of modern life.

But the Christian need never feel lonely. Regardless of where he goes, he has as his constant companion the invisible ascended Savior, who said: "Behold, I am with you always."

Friends may forsake us; we may be misunderstood by our associates; we may have trouble in our home; we may be confined to a hospital bed or be an inmate of an institution; we may have lost a loved one through death—yet we need not be alone. Everywhere, and at all times, Jesus promises to be that Friend "who sticks closer than a brother" (Proverbs 18:24). He experienced the pangs of loneliness to an infinite degree when as our substitute on the cross He cried out, "My God, My God, why have You forsaken Me?" (Matthew 27:46). True, we can drive Him from us by a life of willful sin, but whenever we come with a repentant heart, He "will never leave [us] nor forsake [us]" (Hebrews 13:5). Alone among men, we are not alone—with Christ.

When we are lonely and miserable, dear Lord, abide with us according to Your promise. Amen.

God's Greatest Blessing

*Three times I pleaded with the Lord about this, that it should
leave me. But He said to me, "My grace is sufficient for you, for
My power is made perfect in weakness." Therefore I will boast all
the more gladly of my weaknesses, so that the power of Christ
may rest upon me. 2 Corinthians 12:8–9*

The apostle Paul was afflicted with a deep-rooted and lingering bodily pain. He referred to it as a thorn in the flesh that
was, "a messenger of Satan to harass [him]." Three times he
asked the Lord to remove the affliction, and he received the
answer: "My grace is sufficient for you, for My power is made
perfect in weakness." Was St. Paul's prayer answered? Indeed, it
was; just as each prayer of every child of God is answered—
always, according to the good and gracious will of God.

St. Paul was given the assurance of God's grace. Although
a smaller blessing was withheld, a greater blessing was assured.

The grace of God in Christ Jesus, the forgiveness of all our
sins, that is God's greatest gift to us. All else, health, honor,
wealth, are as nothing compared with the forgiveness of our
sins. What good would our health, wealth, and honor be if, in
the end, we would perish because of our unforgiven sins? On
the other hand, when we have the grace of God in Christ, all the
misery of the present time becomes light and momentary, not
worth comparing with the glory that is to be revealed to us
(Romans 8:17).

*Lord, increase our faith and trust in You. And although You do not
always comply with our request as we desire, we ask You to help us, in
the midst of trouble and sorrow, to rejoice in Your blessed assurance
that Your grace is more than sufficient for me. Amen.*

Staff of Life

"Our fathers ate the manna in the wilderness; as it is written, 'He gave them bread from heaven to eat.'" John 6:31

Jesus used the story of manna in the wilderness to teach the Jews about a greater manna that God has—a manna from heaven that is for the life of the entire world. "Truly, truly I say to you, it was not Moses who gave you the bread from heaven, but My Father gives you the true bread from heaven. For the bread of God is He who comes down from heaven and gives life to the world" (John 6:32–33).

Just as those who heard these words hungered for this manna of which Jesus spoke, so also do we need this manna for our eternal life. This manna is nothing other than the Son of God, who came down from heaven and offered Himself in sacrifice for us, so we would not die in our sins, but live eternally with Him. This is a manna of which we shall not grow tired. Rather, let us give thanks to God that He continually provides us with this heavenly manna in His Word and in His Sacraments so we may eat, drink, and live.

Thank You, Father, for the heavenly and life-giving manna You gave to us in Jesus. Amen.

Redeemed by Grace

For by grace you have been saved through faith. And this is not your own doing; it is the gift of God. Ephesians 2:8

Can it really be possible that God loves *me*? So often I have failed Him! So often I have sinned! Is it possible that God could consider *me* a saint, poor, miserable sinner that I am?

There is a story of a poor apprentice who made a cathedral window entirely out of the pieces of glass his master had thrown away. When the window was completed, it won the acclaim of all who saw it. His master's boasted work, made of exquisite panels of beautiful glass, was rejected; but the window made of condemned materials by the hand of the unknown artist was given a place of honor in the great cathedral.

Our Savior's kingdom is likewise made up of "rejected materials." From the lowly and rejected He has taken the fallen sons of men and has set them, like diamonds, to sparkle forever in the diadem of His glory. "God chose what is low and despised in the world, even things that are not, to bring to nothing things that are" (1 Corinthians 1:28).

The base things of the world—that means *me*—are what God has chosen, and by His unsearchable mercy in Christ He has drawn me into the company of those whom He will gather "in the day when I make up My treasured possession" (Malachi 3:17). Yes, I can be sure God loves me. And, loving me through Jesus Christ, my Savior, He will guide, protect, and keep me even to the end.

O Lord, I thank You for Your boundless love in Jesus Christ, my Savior. Amen.

The Glory of God

Moses said, "Please show me Your glory." Exodus 33:18

Moses had been granted a greater privilege than any other person since Adam. On Mount Sinai he had seen a reflection of the invisible glory of God.

But he pleaded for more. He felt he would be more satisfied and better equipped for leadership of his people if he were given a clearer and fuller revelation of God's glory. God responded by warning him that no sinful man can survive the sight of the overpowering grandeur and holiness of God. But He promises to pass by him and permit him to behold as much of His glory as he can bear.

Centuries later Philip, a disciple of Jesus, repeated the request of Moses. "Lord, show us the Father" (John 14:8), he pleads. Jesus answers: "Whoever has seen Me has seen the Father" (John 14:9).

In Jesus we have the clearest revelation of God's glory this side of heaven, a revelation adequate to sustain and inspire our faith. If we are to know the glory of the heart of God, let us look toward another mountain, one just outside of Jerusalem. On it is a cross. Upon that a cross hangs the Son of God. As we fix our gaze upon it, a glory radiates from it, a glory expressed in the immortal words: "For God so loved the world that He gave His only Son" (John 3:16).

Jesus, be Thou our Glory now And through eternity. Amen. (TLH 350:5)

"O Lord!"

But for You, O LORD, do I wait; it is You, O LORD my God, who will answer. Psalm 38:15

King David was a good man and a righteous ruler. He feared and loved God. He personally lived and officially ruled according to God's Law. He sang the Lord's praises in psalms written for temple worship. God loved and honored him. And many people esteemed him highly and loved him. But he also had many personal enemies. They hated him because he would not join in their political schemes and unfair practices. His sense of justice and his righteous conduct were a standing rebuke to their wickedness. And so they were envious and hated him.

One day David fell. He sinned grievously against God and men. The good people grieved, but his enemies rejoiced. Now they had something on him. Even David's relatives and friends stood far off; they had no words of charity or of pity. David was broken in spirit and seriously sick in his body. In agony of soul he called upon God: "Do not forsake me, O LORD! O my God, be not far from me! Make haste to help me, O LORD, my salvation" (Psalm 38:21–22). God, in His mercy, heard him.

This story speaks both warning and comfort. Sin brings grief and distress. If we fall, many will rejoice and point the finger of scorn at us. All our past goodness is forgotten and the evil is magnified. Yet God's Spirit enables us to call out "O Lord!" in the certainty that He will be merciful and forgiving to us for Jesus' sake.

Be rich with Your mercy, O Lord, and never let me forget Your benefits. Amen.

Grace Sufficient

But He said to me, "My grace is sufficient for you, for My power is made perfect in weakness." Therefore I will boast all the more gladly of my weaknesses, so that the power of Christ may rest upon me. 2 Corinthians 12:9

St. Paul was blessed with God-given talents. Compared to his fellow apostles, he could truthfully write: "I worked harder than any of them" (1 Corinthians 15:10). But in that very fact also hides the danger of sinful pride and self-satisfaction. Accordingly, the Lord in His wisdom let Paul suffer under an affliction he called "a thorn [that] was given me in the flesh" (2 Corinthians 12:7). Whatever it was, Paul prayed most earnestly to be delivered of this "thorn." But instead of removing this affliction from His beloved apostle, the Lord gave him grace to bear it. God's grace was sufficient for Paul. It enabled him to carry on courageously and to declare: "For the sake of Christ, then, I am content with weaknesses, insults, hardships, persecutions, and calamities. For when I am weak, then am I strong" (2 Corinthians 12:10).

All this is written for our learning and our comfort. To each of us He has given some talents; from each of us He expects some service. But it is only as we realize that we are weak in ourselves can we be strong in the Lord. And so in His wisdom and goodness, the Lord of our life gives us a "thorn," some cross to bear, so we may learn to know the richness, the sweetness, the sufficiency of His grace in Christ Jesus. "God is faithful" (1 Corinthians 1:9). He will never fail us.

Lord of all strength and grace, in all our trials do You sustain us with the sufficiency of Your grace, through Christ. Amen.

Clean Hands

Draw near to God, and He will draw near to you. Cleanse your hands, you sinners, and purify your hearts, you double-minded.
James 4:8

"Go wash your hands," the mother says to her boy as he comes in for supper. He hurriedly splashes water over his hands and wipes the dirt in the clean towel. Then she scolds him for not washing his hands better. How often this scene is repeated in the average home!

God, too, has something to say about us washing our hands. No one can come into His presence, approach Him in prayer, or come to Christ's Supper with filthy hands. Our hands have become filthy through our unrighteousness and by our iniquities. We do that which is forbidden and neglect that which is commanded. We have soiled our hands; all of us have. Therefore the psalmist asks, "Who shall ascend the hill of the Lord?" (Psalm 24:3). "He who has clean hands and a pure heart" (Psalm 24:4) is the answer.

Sin-soiled hands are to be cleansed, and the only cleansing agency is the blood of Christ. His blood was shed to make our hands, our hearts, and our entire lives clean and beautiful. There is no other cleansing power able to make us worthy to come into the presence of our God.

Lord and Savior, Jesus Christ, we thank You for cleansing us from the filth of our sin through Your body and blood. Amen.

Confession—Good for the Soul

Whoever conceals his transgressions will not prosper, but he who confesses and forsakes them will obtain mercy. Proverbs 28:13

When you and I have done something wrong, we can do no better than to tell it all to God. If we do, He is ready for us. He has already offered His Son, our Lord Jesus Christ, for our redemption. As John the Baptist proclaimed, Jesus is "the Lamb of God, who takes away the sin of the world" (John 1:29).

It is not enough, however, that we confess our sins. We must also be ready to forsake our sins. "Whoever conceals his transgressions will not prosper, but he who confesses and forsakes them will obtain mercy." Confession calls for correction. It calls for the amendment of life. It calls us to take heed of Jesus' word to the sinful woman and to all sinners, "From now on sin no more" (John 8:11).

Yet even this command is one we cannot keep apart from Christ. But when the love of Christ comes into our hearts, He gives us a new power and a new desire to resist evil and to fight against sin. Although we may fail, God is quick to forgive time and time again. So it is good both for the life that now is and for the life that is to come that we should bare our souls to God and to make sincere confession of all our transgressions. Praise be to God! Because of Jesus' death and resurrection, we may say along with King David, "And you forgave the iniquity of my sin" (Psalm 32:5).

Dear God, by Your Holy Spirit please grant us the ability to make sincere confession to You that we may know inner peace and find strength for a new and godly life; for the sake of Christ. Amen.

A Great Difference

Looking to Jesus, the founder and perfecter of our faith, who for the joy that was set before Him endured the cross, despising the shame, and is seated at the right hand of the throne of God. Hebrews 12:2

It has been said that the distinction between Christianity and all other systems of religion consists largely in this: that in the others, men are found seeking after God, while Christianity is God seeking after men.

In Christ we behold "God seeking after man." Christ Himself has declared: "The Son of Man came to seek and to save the lost" (Luke 19:10).

A Chinese convert is said to have expressed that truth this way: "A man fell into a deep pit, miry and slippery. As he lay injured at the bottom, Confucius looked in and said: 'My friend, I am sorry for you; if you ever get out of that place, take care that you never fall in again.'

"Then a Buddhist priest came along and said: 'I grieve to see your plight. If you can manage to climb up two thirds of the way, or even half, I might help you up the rest.' Unable to arise, such advice was mockery.

"Then Christ came by. Descending into the pit, He lifted man to safety. 'That,' said the convert, 'is the difference between Christ and others.'"

I am trusting you, Lord Jesus;
Never let me fall.
I am trusting you forever
And for all. Amen. (LW 408:6)

A Faith of Great Value

To those who through the righteousness of our God and Savior
Jesus Christ have received a faith as precious as ours. 2 Peter 1:1
NIV

This is a very important Bible passage for all Christians to
read and memorize. The first thing to notice about this verse is
the very same thing we frequently hear from the Scriptures and
ought to never tire of hearing—that is, that faith does not come
from within you; it comes as God's gift to you. St. Peter writes
to those who "have *received* a faith."

As if that were not amazing enough, the apostle goes on
to say that your faith is as precious and as valuable before God
as his faith. You have "received a faith as precious as ours," writes
the great apostle. That is to say, the faith God gave to you carries all the same privileges and gifts and confidences as the faith
that God gave to Peter himself. At the baptismal font, Jesus said
to you, "Follow Me!" These words carry the same life-giving,
faith-creating power as the "Follow Me!" He spoke to Peter and
Andrew on the seashore in Galilee (Matthew 4:19) and to Philip
in the region of the Jordan River (John 1:48) and to Matthew at
his tax collector's table (Luke 5:27–28).

For all the apostles' greatness, the Lord Jesus proclaims to
you in today's Gospel that you "have received a faith as precious" as the apostles' faith, one of equal value to theirs in its
saving power as it trusts in Jesus alone for salvation.

Thank You, Lord, for Your great gift of faith. Amen.

My Guide

"I am the Way, and the Truth, and the Life. No one comes to the Father except through Me." John 14:6

Life is a journey. Says the Apostle: "Here we have no lasting city, but we seek the city that is to come" (Hebrews 13:14). As Christians we are passing through this world on our way to the heavenly homeland.

Frequently the remark is heard: "We are all going to the same place. We are just taking different roads." As if all roads in life lead to heaven! This is fatal delusion. There are many roads leading to eternity, but only one leads to the Father's house in heaven.

Jesus startled the people of His day by telling them that He was the only way to the Father. The way back to God is blocked by sin. Christ removed that roadblock. It cost Him His life. He shed His precious blood to remove it. He has opened a new way to the Father: it is by faith in Him and His atoning merits.

Christ has given us the road signs to follow in His Word. All ways that men seek to open to God are dead-end roads. Says Jesus: "No one comes to the Father except through Me."

The road back to God through Jesus is not an easy way. We enter it through the "strait" gate of repentance and faith. It is a narrow road. Few take it. But it is the way to life—life eternal.

Blessed Redeemer, help us to ever trust for salvation in You alone. Amen.

A Race that is Already Won

Every athlete exercises self-control in all things. They do it to receive a perishable wreath, but we an imperishable. 1 Corinthians 9:25

Not everyone can qualify for the Olympic games, for a college football team, or for placement in the United States military. Those who are accepted, however, enter into rigorous training, deny themselves rich foods and other indulgences, and focus their attentions solely on the contest in which they are about to participate.

St. Paul compares earthly athletes, who compete for a perishable prize, to Christians who compete (so to speak) for an imperishable prize. By this, St. Paul does not intend to say that we must earn our place in heaven or that some Christians are better "athletes" than others. Rather, he simply underscores for us the great seriousness of this life-and-death struggle in which we daily live. The old man in us would surely like to see us deny Christ, curse God, and die. But the new man daily emerges in the remembrance of Baptism, and this new man lives in righteousness and purity before God. Because of this new man, created for us in Christ Jesus, we shall not fall short of the prize— the imperishable wreath of eternal life!

Guide me ever, dear Lord Jesus, that I may not be disqualified but may receive the prize that You earned for me in Your death and resurrection. Amen.

You Satisfy the Desire of Every Living Thing

They shall speak of the might of Your awesome deeds, and I will declare Your greatness. Psalm 145:6

Martin Luther once made this pointed observation:

If our heavenly Father were not so liberal in the distribution of His gifts, we would be more thankful to Him. If, for instance, He would let all men be born with one leg, and later on, in their seventh year, would give them another leg, and in the fourteenth year would give them one hand, and the other at the age of twenty, then we would appreciate God's gifts and benefits more highly; and we would be more thankful if for a while we were deprived of them and had to do without them. But now God showers His gifts upon us all at once. Just now He has given us a whole ocean of His Word.

The daily reception of our daily bread—whether it comes in large amounts or small—underscores for us all of the great gifts God has for His children. The daily repentance that comes through Baptism calls us to turn away from our disregard for our Lord's constant provision and to receive all good things with thanksgiving. For He who has laid the bread upon my table has also fed me with the Bread of Life—Jesus the crucified and risen Lord—so I will never hunger but shall live eternally.

Dear heavenly Father, give me Your Holy Spirit, that I may be ever mindful of Your great gifts. Amen.

The Chief Sinner

The saying is trustworthy and deserving of full acceptance, that Christ Jesus came into the world to save sinners, of whom I am the foremost. 1 Timothy 1:15

All men are sinners, but St. Paul saw himself as the chief and greatest sinner. As he reviewed his life and recalled how he had once been a frightful blasphemer of Jesus, a bitter persecutor of the early Christian Church, and a proud Pharisee who thought he had pleased God by his actions, the great apostle felt crushed by the weight of his sins. The enormity of his former guilt caused him to confess that he—he, and no other—surely was the greatest sinner in all of human history.

Yet St. Paul also believed with all his heart that God's Son had come into the world to save sinners, and that he, too, was included in this salvation. In fact, the enormity of St. Paul's guilt caused him to praise God all the more because God's grace in Christ had done a mighty work in him. Not only was he forgiven; not only was he restored to a right relationship with God; but now he became God's mouthpiece, called to speak the wonders of salvation to those who had not yet heard.

I can take comfort from St. Paul's example, for God has forgiven me in Christ as surely as he forgave St. Paul. St. Paul may indeed be the chief of all sinners, but I am not very far behind. Praise God for His rich forgiveness and grace!

Chief of sinners or least of sinners—Christ, You died for me. Thank You, Lord, for Your great gift of salvation. Amen.

Sufficient Grace

I thank my God in all my remembrance of you, always in every prayer of mine for you all making my prayer with joy, because of your partnership in the gospel from the first day until now.
Philippians 1:3–5

When Jesus in the Garden of Gethsemane faced the crisis of the cross, He prayed fervently to His Father in heaven, but, being human as well as divine, He also looked to His disciples for sympathetic wakefulness. We sense deep disappointment in His question to them: "So, could you not watch with Me one hour?" (Matthew 26:40).

When Paul wrote the Epistle to the Philippians, he was in prison, but he did not suffer the same sort of abandonment by his friends that Jesus suffered. An uncertain future, possibly death, awaited him. Through it all he had the promise of God, "My grace is sufficient for you" (2 Corinthians 12:9). But Paul was also sustained by the comforting knowledge that many Christians had a deep affection for him and wholeheartedly worked with him in proclaiming the Gospel to the world.

In every hour of the Christian life, there will be times when we feel the great joy of Christian friends all around, who love us and share with us in the kingdom. There will also be times when we feel alone and abandoned, as did Jesus in the garden. But because of what He suffered there and later on the cross, we shall never be abandoned! God has come to us in Christ, He has forgiven us all our sins, and we have His promise that we shall live in His presence forever.

Sustain me in my trials and struggles, O Lord, through the remembrance of what You suffered for my sake. Amen.

July

On-Going Miracles

To those who have obtained a faith of equal standing with ours by the righteousness of our God and Savior Jesus Christ.
2 Peter 1:1

When Luther's followers were invited to the Diet of Augsburg in 1530 to confess and explain what they believed concerning the Scriptures, they boldly confessed what they believed concerning the Church: "It is taught among us that one holy Christian church will be and remain forever. This is the assembly of all believers among whom the Gospel is preached in its purity and the holy sacraments are administered according to the Gospel" (Augsburg Confession, VII, 1).

In writing these words, the Lutherans tapped into the very essence of this gospel. One of the simplest definitions of the Church is that it is the flock of God (1 Peter 5:2). You don't try to locate the flock by trying to find out where its borders are; you locate the flock by finding those things that the flock gathers around, namely, its Good Shepherd and His voice and the things He provides to care for the flock. The Lutherans confessed that the Church is "the assembly of all believers among whom the Gospel is preached in its purity" because Jesus says, "My sheep hear My voice . . . and they follow Me" (John 10:27). The Lutherans could confess that in the Church, "the holy sacraments are administered according to the Gospel" because Jesus says, "The works I do in My Father's name bear witness about Me" (John 10:25).

When you have the Word faithfully preached in your midst, you have the voice of Jesus. When you have the holy Sacraments of Baptism and Communion faithfully administered among you according to the Gospel, you have Jesus' miracles, which speak of Him.

Thank You, Lord, for Your ongoing miracles. Amen.

Mount Sinai and God's Law

And He said to him, "You shall love the Lord your God with all your heart and with all your soul and with all your mind."
Matthew 22:37

While Moses was in the thick darkness that covered the presence of the Lord on the top of Mount Sinai, God spoke to him and gave him the Law. Later, God's finger wrote the Law on tablets of stone. The Holy Spirit inspired Moses, so he wrote God's Law in his books that we now have in the Holy Scriptures. God's Law, the Ten Commandments, which are also written in men's hearts, serves as the basis of all legislation, which may govern all men in their relationship to God and in their relationships among themselves.

The devil, our society, and ever our own inward selves often tempt us to believe wrongly and to think that God did not expect sinful people to keep these laws. God is sometimes pictured as a kind, old grandpa who will close an eye on sin. Human reason foolishly muses that, if we try hard enough, our attempt will justify us. If we fail, Hey! No one is perfect!

Nothing could be farther from the truth than such thoughts. "You therefore must be perfect" (Matthew 5:48) is Jesus' pronouncement, rewording God's demand: "You shall love the Lord your God with all your heart." In this we have failed, every one of us.

But "Christ is the end of the Law" (Romans 10:4). He is our perfection, like us in every way except without sin. And He kept the Law in our place. Making a divine trade with us, He took up all of our sins and bore them in His own flesh. Through Him, in turn, we are declared righteous.

Thank You, Lord, for Your righteousness that You have willingly given to me. Teach me to regard myself in the same way the heavenly Father now regards me for Your sake, regarding me as holy and sinless in His sight. Amen.

The Way to Salvation

Then he brought them out and said, "Sirs, what must I do to be saved?" Acts 16:30

Paul and Silas were in prison because of their preaching. They had been beaten cruelly, yet in the middle of the night they sang praises to God. The Lord shook the prison walls, opened the doors, and by a miracle the chains fell off their hands and feet so they were free. The keeper of the prison would have killed himself if Paul had not stopped him, for he thought the prisoners had fled. When Paul restrained him, he asked, trembling in fear: "Sirs, what must I do to be saved?" Paul answered: "Believe in the Lord Jesus Christ, and you will be saved, you and your household" (Acts 16:30–31). Similarly Jesus was asked one day while at Capernaum: "What must we do, to be doing the works of God?" (John 6:28). And He had answered: "This is the work of God, that you believe in Him whom He has sent" (John 6:29).

Natural man is not always ready to accept so simple a way to salvation. Even we Christians at times ask: "What must I do to inherit eternal life?" (Luke 18:18). We want to earn our own way. Our pride is comforted and abetted when we feel we have done something to merit God's favor. But we are wrong in wanting to earn salvation, for God says: "Believe in the Lord Jesus, and you will be saved."

What is more, God's Holy Spirit works saving faith in our hearts so even our faith becomes a work of God and not something we do. If God does everything for our salvation, we can be sure that nothing is overlooked and nothing can separate us from His love.

Gracious Father in heaven, send Your Holy Spirit into our hearts and into the hearts of men everywhere that we may believe and be saved. Keep the strong, strengthen the weak, and convert the unbelievers, for Jesus' sake. Amen.

If Our Heart Condemn Us

*They show that the work of the Law is written on their hearts,
while their conscience also bears witness, and their conflicting
thoughts accuse or even excuse them. Romans 2:15*

There come moments, even in the life of a Christian,
when the voice of conscience strikes terror into our soul. In the
midst of a busy day or in the quiet hours of the night, our heart
is suddenly pierced by the sharp memory of sin—ugly sin, personal sin, *our* sin—and we experience the pain and agony of
guilt, which drove the apostle to exclaim: "Wretched man that I
am!" (Romans 7:24).

David, the great sinner and great saint, knew the terrors of
an accusing conscience: "When I kept silent, my bones wasted
away. . . . Your hand was heavy upon me" (Psalm 32:3–4). The
burden of sin was greater than he could bear.

But we Christians need bear no burden of sin. "For when-
ever our heart condemns us, God is greater than our heart, and
He knows everything" (1 John 3:20). God looks at us through
Christ. He knows we are sinners, but He also knows that in
Christ our guilt has been atoned, our sins have been forgiven,
our accusing conscience has been silenced!

Afraid of your conscience? "Who shall bring any charge
against God's elect? It is God who justifies. Who is to condemn?
Christ Jesus is the one who died—more than that, who was
raised—who is at the right hand of God, who indeed is interceding for us" (Romans 8:33–34).

*O Lord, restore to me the joy of Your salvation, and take not Your Holy
Spirit from me. Amen.*

Patient Trust in God

But they who wait for the LORD shall renew their strength; they shall mount up with wings like eagles; they shall run and not be weary; they shall walk and not faint. Isaiah 40:31

Patience has become a rare virtue in this world of hustle and bustle. We have become a nervous, hectic, restless, and impatient people. Our pace is fast. Our patience is slow. What was once meant to be rest and recreation all too frequently spells exhaustion and depletion.

"Be still before the LORD and wait patiently for Him; fret not yourself over the one who prospers in his way, over the man who carries out evil devices," the psalmist reminds us (Psalm 37:7). "Be still, and know that I am God" (Psalm 46:10), counsels God in the great Psalm Luther loved so dearly. And over against His pending persecutions for us and for our salvation, the Lord Jesus reminded His disciples, "By your endurance you will gain your lives" (Luke 21:19). St. Peter includes patience in the fruits of the Spirit (2 Peter 1:6). And in today's verse, Isaiah points to the source and value of patience: wait upon the Lord. He has an hour and a season for everything. And until His hour comes, we must patiently wait on Him, knowing that all things work together for good to them that love God (Romans 8:28). Yet through such waiting we acquire new strength. Not only is old strength restored, but new confidence is given us—confidence that, because God has overcome all things for us in the death and resurrection of Jesus, He shall not abandon us now in this hour.

Dear Lord, in Your mercy grant to us a greater measure of patience. Teach us to wait on You. Amen.

The Wonders of God's Love

O LORD, rebuke me not in Your anger, nor discipline me in Your wrath. Be gracious to me, O LORD, for I am languishing; heal me, O LORD, for my bones are troubled. My soul also is greatly troubled. But You, O LORD—how long? Turn, O LORD, deliver my life; save me for the sake of Your steadfast love. Psalm 6:1–4

At times we are desperately disgusted with our own selves. With Paul we confess: "I do not do what I want, but I do the very thing I hate" (Romans 7:15). We make promises and fail to keep them; we say and repeat things we later regret; we resolve to amend our lives only to backtrack to the same old paths of sin.

How can God put up with such children? Must He not rid Himself of us? Will He receive us again, as we come, sobbing out our stories of failures and sins? This is why the psalmist prays, "O LORD, rebuke me not in Your anger, nor discipline me in Your wrath."

And the Lord, remembering that we are dust, receives us once more, removing our sins and healing us with His love. But why? Is it because He does not care one way or the other? Is He easygoing or weak? Never!

For His mercies' sake, God removes iniquity and blots out sin. Wonder of wonders, He abundantly pardons through Christ. His blood makes the foulest clean, and that every whit. There is peace, there is hope, there is joy—in Christ crucified. As long as we seek refuge in the sacred wounds of Jesus, God will not rebuke us, but deliver our souls from death.

O Lord, look upon me through Your Son's great sacrifice, which left nothing undone to restore my soul. For His sake have mercy. Amen.

Why Accidents and Catastrophes?

Or those eighteen on whom the tower in Siloam fell and killed them: do you think that they were worse offenders than all the others who lived in Jerusalem? Luke 13:4

When people suffer a great hardship or loss, it is easy to imagine that some particular sin must be at the bottom of it. They may ask: "Why did this have to happen to me?" Or: "What did I do to offend God?" To correct these wrong impressions, Jesus asked: "Or those eighteen on whom the tower in Siloam fell and killed them: do you think that they were worse offenders than all the others who lived in Jerusalem?" He answered immediately, "No." They were people like all the rest, perhaps some of them believers and some unbelievers.

It is the same today when a disaster strikes, whether it be a storm, flood, fire, bombing, or major accident. It is likely in every case that death strikes both believers and unbelievers. We are not to judge the righteousness or unrighteousness of those who suffer disaster.

Neither are we to question the justice of God when He permits catastrophes to happen. He deals only mercifully with His children. To be sure, the unbeliever who dies in an accident is punished by God, for his time of grace is abruptly cut off. The believer who dies in the same accident is swept from a troublesome life on earth into the glory of heaven, and death for him becomes a blessing.

Holy Spirit, give us penitent hearts, and keep us prepared for death and the Day of Judgment, for Jesus' sake. Amen.

Honest Confession

If we say we have no sin, we deceive ourselves, and the truth is not in us. If we confess our sins, He is faithful and just to forgive us our sins and to cleanse us from all unrighteousness. 1 John 1:8–9

One of the shortest words with the longest meaning is the word sin. Only three letters, but what a world of tragedy and sorrow it spells! There are those who deny the objective reality of sin—nothing really to worry about. There are others who water it down into a comparatively innocent and escapable thing—nothing really to be alarmed about. But there are others who very definitely see all of life's sorrows and tragedies in sin and who fear its consequences for time and for eternity.

St. John leaves no doubt where he stands on the question of sin. In unmistakable language, he labels those who deny or belittle sin as deceivers and liars. What is more, he is anxiously concerned about the forgiveness of sin and the escape from the penalties of sin. Yet when man honestly acknowledges his sins and confesses them to God, the assurance of forgiveness becomes his because of Jesus' suffering and death. Because Jesus died, forgiving *all* people, the penitent sinner is assured that yes, even he stands in the rich flood of God's pardon and peace.

Today, in the midst of the blight and ravages of sin round about us, let us humbly acknowledge and confess our transgressions to God, our Father, beseeching Him in the name of our Lord Jesus Christ to grant us forgiveness.

O God, forgive me all my sins for Jesus' sake, and grant me peace of heart and mind. Amen.

August

No Apologies

For I am not ashamed of the Gospel, for it is the power of God for salvation to everyone who believes, to the Jew first and also to the Greek. Romans 1:16

One of the greatest hindrances to the influence of Christianity in this world lies in the fact that followers of Christ are ashamed of their faith and of their religious convictions. An apologetic attitude, or one of shame, leads others to think little of the value of Christianity. We have every reason to be unashamed. We should be forthright in our high regard for the Gospel of Christ.

We are not ashamed of the Gospel because of Christ, its center and its power. Christ is the eternal Son of God, who assumed the human nature into His being to redeem sinful mankind. His words have brought more hope and more joy and more righteousness into the world than all the sayings of all the wise men of all the ages. To be identified with the followers of Christ is an honor.

The Gospel tells us of God's love for us, that, while we were sinners, Christ died for us. The Gospel does not overlook our transgressions, but it forgives them fully and freely. We might be ashamed of some cheap forgiveness that compromises the righteousness and the holiness of God, but we are never ashamed of the fact that God in Christ reconciled us to Himself and that He leaves us pardoned and justified, cleansed and sanctified.

Let me never be ashamed of You and Your Word, O Lord! Let them be my pride and joy always! Amen.

August

What Shall I Do with My Sins?

I acknowledged my sin to You, and I did not cover my iniquity; I said, "I will confess my transgressions to the LORD," and You forgave the iniquity of my sin. Psalm 32:5

What shall I do with my sins? "Forget them" is the casual advice of many. "Hide them" is my own natural reaction.

Easier said than done. My sin problem preys on my mind, brings regrets and recriminations, worries and tensions. I may be able to hide my sins from others, but how can I hide them from God?

David tried the hiding game, but failed. There was only one thing to do, and he did it: "I acknowledged my sin to You, and I did not cover my iniquity."

The first part of true repentance must be a frank and open confession: "I will confess my transgressions." Hiding, covering up, bluffing it out, has never helped. It can only harm, leading to emotional upsets and breakdowns. Like the prodigal in the parable, I shall never find inner happiness until I "arise and go to my father and I will say to him, 'Father I have sinned against heaven and before you'" (Luke 15:18).

Even more important is the second part of repentance: to believe with David, "You forgave the iniquity of my sin." I must know God not only as a God of stern justice, but also as a God of love, a sin-forgiving God, who woos me with the Gospel of His grace in Christ, whom He gave as my sin-bearer. "The LORD has laid on Him the iniquity of us all" (Isaiah 53:6). Trusting in that sin-atonement made *for me*, I am assured that my sins are really gone.

In the joy of Your salvation, O Lord, let my soul find peace. Amen.

August

What More Can We Ask!

I love You, O LORD, my strength. The LORD is my rock and my fortress and my deliverer, my God, my rock, in whom I take refuge, my shield, and the horn of my salvation, my stronghold. Psalm 18:1–2

Strange that we Christians should worry! As children of God's family we are so well protected. No fortification or hide-out made by man can give the security that we Christians find in the everlasting arms of God.

He is my strength. He sets the boundaries for the nations and keeps the sparrow from falling. This Almighty loves me, His child. Why worry?

He is my rock. Sands are unstable, and mire is slippery. But God is my rock when all falls and fails. Why worry?

He is my shield. He wards off those blows that would crush us and rob us of hope.

He is the horn of my salvation. The horns of the temple altar were placed there that man might hold fast and find safety. In the Savior's blood we find salvation. As we cling to the cross, no one can condemn us.

He is my stronghold. The stronghold permits me an overview of the entire situation. As I face many problems, I enter the stronghold for safety. Why, then, worry?

Heavenly Father, boundless is Your might and limitless is Your grace. So I come this day, leaning upon You and Your promises. Amen.

August

Thanks for Victory

But thanks be to God, who gives us the victory through our Lord Jesus Christ. 1 Corinthians 15:57

At every moment of our lives, both God and Satan are contending for our souls. God loves us and wants us to come back home to Him again. The devil hates us and wants to destroy us.

The first round in this battle went to Satan, when he misled our first parents into sin. Jesus reversed this when He died for us and rose again. This victory means that you and I have been freed from the guilt of sin.

When Jesus died and rose again, He also broke the power of sin. When sin gets hold of us, it does not readily let go again. We can see how true this is when we observe that we have an ugly temper, a cruel tongue, or when we are proud, greedy, envious, dishonest, lustful. The risen Christ, however, frees us from the force of evil and makes new people in Christ. The risen Christ has relieved us of the wages of sin, which is death, eternal death, everlasting separation from God.

When Jesus died on the cross, He paid the price. He now assures us, "Because I live, you also will live" (John 14:19). If we happen to have crippled bodies, sick minds, incurable diseases, we still have a glorious hope: one day we shall arise from our graves with bodies like the glorified body of the risen Jesus.

O blessed, glorious, and triumphant Christ, we thank You for the gift of victory. Help us by Your Spirit to apply the meaning thereof to our lives and to respond with conduct expressing gratitude. Amen.

Thus Says the Lord

The law of the LORD is perfect, reviving the soul; the testimony of the LORD is sure, making wise the simple; the precepts of the LORD are right, rejoicing the heart; the commandment of the LORD is pure, enlightening the eyes; the fear of the LORD is clean, enduring forever; the rules of the LORD are true, and righteous altogether. Psalm 19:7–9

What is truth, and where shall we find it? Can we be sure of the rightness of things? Upon whose authority do we call iniquity sin and say that mercy killing is wrong?

The Law of the Lord speaks, and the testimony of God's Word declares to us the truth. God's Law is timeless, not bound to certain centuries and races and people. The statutes and the Commandments of God are always right. No custom or public sentiment can make right what God has branded as sin.

And sin leads to judgment. We fear the courts of God because the sense of guilt haunts us. We have not—not one of us—observed this Law of God to the fullest in loving obedience to our Lord. So we are lost in sin.

But God does not want us to perish, so He made the way to restore the souls of men to His favor and grace. He gave His only-begotten Son, who in turn gave His life for our redemption, that by faith in His atoning blood we may be cleansed and saved.

Divine Lord, we cannot come into Your presence except through Jesus' blood and righteousness. Through Him we approach Your throne. Accept us, clothed in the garment of His holiness, and fill our hearts and minds with peace, for Jesus' sake. Amen.

August

The Christ Whom They Pierced

For dogs encompass Me; a company of evildoers encircles Me;
they have pierced My hands and feet—I can count all My
bones—they stare and gloat over Me; they divide My garments
among them, and for My clothing they cast lots. Psalm 22:16–18

Through the ages, man has been told to look on Him who
was pierced—Jesus—and by looking, be healed. That no one be
mistaken and look to the wrong person, the psalmist bids us to
note that He who is pierced also would have His garments
divided and for His vesture have lots cast. As Jesus of Nazareth
hangs on the accursed tree with two malefactors, the historian,
Luke, calls our attention to this bit of detail: "They cast lots to
divide His garments" (Luke 23:34).

We are to know from this seemingly unimportant fact
that Jesus, hanging on the middle cross, is the One whom God
had chosen from all eternity to be the Savior of mankind. When
Jesus bowed His head in death, you and I were freed from the
dominion of sin and the fear of judgment to come, for God was
in Christ, reconciling the world unto Himself.

To Him—this crucified Jesus—we must look, not merely
stare, believing Him to be God's anointed and our Redeemer.

Lord Jesus, Lamb of God, for sinners slain, we come to You with the
multitudes of our transgressions to be healed and saved. We are not
deserving of Your grace or worthy of Your love. Yet we come, because in
You only is salvation. You were pierced for our transgressions and bled
for our sins. Let Your holy, precious blood continually cleanse and heal
us. Draw many to Your redeeming cross, and let Your saving grace
cover the nations of the earth. Amen.

August

How God Remembers

*Make me to know Your ways, O LORD; teach me Your paths.
Lead me in Your truth and teach me, for You are the God of my
salvation; for You I wait all the day long. Remember Your mercy,
O LORD, and Your steadfast love, for they have been from of old.
Remember not the sins of my youth or my transgressions;
according to Your steadfast love remember me, for the sake of
Your goodness, O LORD! Psalm 25:4–7*

It is good to know that God does not remember our sins.
They have been many, heaping up as mountains from the days
of our youth. God remembers them no more because He has
placed them upon the shoulders of His Son, Jesus Christ. That's
Gospel truth: "The LORD has laid on Him the iniquity of us all"
(Isaiah 53:6).

It's good to know that what God remembers are His tender mercies, for we are ever and again transgressing against His
holy will. But in His unreachable goodness, God remembers
that we are dust, sinful by nature and surrounded by evil influ-
ences. But through the cross of His Son, our Redeemer, God's
love is boundless. Out of the sheer goodness of His perfect holiness, He loves us and saved us through Christ, the only
redeemer of mankind.

*Lord, eternal and gracious, merciful in Christ Jesus, teach us and all
mankind to know the greatness of Your love. In Your tender mercy blot
out our sins, and keep us in Your redeeming grace. Let our hearts
reflect Your love as we day after day meet our fellow men in the varied
walks of life. Teach us to be thoughtful and considerate, that all the
world may see Your transforming power in us and be drawn to Him
who gave His life that we may be Yours forever. Amen.*

The Bread of Life

Jesus said to them, "I am the bread of life; whoever comes to Me shall not hunger, and whoever believes in Me shall never thirst."
John 6:35

Some people eat heartily and yet are undernourished. They have hidden hungers their diet does not satisfy. Laboratories, after years of research, now offer them vitamins as the answer to their needs.

Many people are likewise undernourished spiritually. They seem to have everything that a person could wish for. But underneath it all there are unmet hungers that cry for attention.

There is but one answer. This is given us by our Savior in the words: "I am the bread of life." There is food, satisfying food for the soul, which has been starved by sin and ignorance, in the message, "Behold, the Lamb of God, who takes away the sin of the world" (John 1:29). There is food in the assurance: "He who did not spare His own Son but gave Him up for us all, how will He not also with Him graciously give us all things?" (Romans 8:32). There is food for the soul as we kneel at the altar and there hear the Savior say: "'Take, eat; this is My body.' And He took a cup, and when He had given thanks He gave it to them, saying, 'Drink of it, all of you, for this is My blood of the covenant, which is poured out for many for the forgiveness of sins'" (Matthew 26:26–28).

Lord Jesus Christ, Thou living Bread,
May I for mine possess Thee.
I would with heav'nly food be fed;
Descend, refresh, and bless me. Amen. (TLH 312:1)

The Joy of Believing

The LORD is my light and my salvation; whom shall I fear? The LORD is the stronghold of my life; of whom shall I be afraid? . . . Though an army encamp against me, my heart shall not fear; though war arise against me, yet I will be confident. One thing have I asked of the LORD, that will I seek after: that I may dwell in the house of the LORD all the days of my life, to gaze upon the beauty of the LORD and to inquire in His temple. For He will hide me in His shelter in the day of trouble; He will conceal me under the cover of His tent; He will lift me high upon a rock. Psalm 27:1,3–5

Mankind is haunted by a compelling fear. Nations remain continually suspicious of one another and feel they cannot ever trust even their closest neighbor. Even before the secrets of atomic or biological warfare had become known to man, all mankind lived in dread of tomorrow. The believer quells and subdues these misgivings by living trustingly each day. No one can separate us from God, not even death.

The world may stand against us, may rob us of all we have in earthly possessions, but this world cannot take away from us the salvation Christ has won for us. I live in His presence and in His everlasting arms, I know that somehow God will give me the necessary strength to face each new day. And if tomorrow shall be the last in this present turmoil, then I shall dwell all the days of eternity with Him who has redeemed me with His own blood.

You who are from everlasting, my God, enclose me with Your protecting grace, and preserve me in faith. Set my feet trustingly upon the sure rock of Your promises, and let me sleep each night unworried because of Your love in Christ Jesus. Amen.

August

Hosanna to the King

Rejoice greatly, O daughter of Zion! Shout aloud, O daughter of Jerusalem! behold, your king is coming to you; righteous and having salvation is He, humble and mounted on a donkey, on a colt, the foal of a donkey. Zechariah 9:9

This messianic prophecy was fulfilled when Jesus rode into Jerusalem and was hailed by the multitudes as the royal Son of David: "Hosanna to the Son of David! Blessed is He who comes in the name of the Lord! Hosanna in the highest!" (Matthew 21:9). The Messiah is both David's Son and Lord, King forever.

He is a king with a throne that is forever fixed in the heavens. The King, who sits on a throne at the right hand of the Father, is the final authority over all things in heaven and on earth. Our King is a king with a cross. He left His throne on high to come into this world that He might be nailed to the cross, "that whoever believes in Him may have eternal life" (John 3:15). He is a king with a crown. St. John, in his Revelation, sees the King "a golden crown on His head" (Revelation 14:14). But He has a crown also for all who are loyal to Him; His promise is: "Be faithful unto death, and I will give you the crown of life" (Revelation 2:10).

We rejoice that He is our King—crucified and risen and now ever-living! Let us praise God that we can live in His kingdom and serve such a king in everlasting righteousness, innocence, and blessedness.

O Lord Jesus, we pray You to come into our hearts, make them Your royal throne now, and someday gather us around Your throne in heaven, where we shall sing hosannas to You forevermore. Amen.

The Dead Shall Rise

Why is it thought incredible by any of you that God raises the dead? Acts 26:8

During His public ministry, Jesus raised three people from the dead. These were the daughter of Jairus (Luke 8); the youth at Nain (Luke 7); and Lazarus (John 11). Great men of God also have occasionally raised people from the dead by the power of God; for example, the prophet Elijah (1 Kings 17). Unbelievers both within and without the visible Christian Church have taken issue with these miracles and denied them. Either they brand the scriptural accounts as fables or they try to explain away the miracle by saying that probably the person in question was not really dead. Even the fact that, at the time of his resurrection, Lazarus had been in the grave three days will not deter these unbelievers. To all of them God says: "Why is it thought incredible that God raises the dead?"

Yes, why should it be thought unbelievable or impossible? Is not God the creator of the world? Is He not the giver of life and the Lord of life and death? Did not Jesus Himself rise from the dead after three days? The resurrection of Christ in itself is the guarantee of our own resurrection, and the resurrection of the persons of whom we are told in Scripture provides additional assurance that God's Word is true.

As Christians we rejoice in the hope of our resurrection. The knowledge of it takes the sting out of death for us. "O death, where is your victory? O death where is your sting?" (1 Corinthians 15:55). We shall rise to a glorious life with God and the angels in heaven. There God will provide, "the Lamb [who] will be their shepherd, and He will guide them to springs of living water, and God will wipe away every tear from their eyes" (Revelation 7:17).

Thank You, Lord, that by Your resurrection from the dead You have opened the way to mine. Amen.

Invocation

"Go therefore and make disciples of all nations, baptizing them in the name of the Father and of the Son and of the Holy Spirit."
Matthew 28:19

The name of God is indeed the name that is above all others. His name is sacred, but not so sacred that people may not speak or write it. The Christian knows and is convinced that his life becomes meaningful only when it is related to God. Every use of God's name, therefore, reminds the Christian of who he is, where he has come from, what he is doing in life, and where he is going after death.

It seems particularly appropriate that the Christian should begin everything with the name of God upon his lips or, at least, with the thought of God in his mind and heart. In this way the Christian keeps all his life in constant touch with God. It marks, as it were, everything the Christian does, says, or thinks, with the stamp of God.

Thus the mention of God's name when the Christian rises in the morning serves to keep the Christian in remembrance of the fact that breath, health, time, strength, sleep, and work belong to the purposes of God and that He gives them to His creatures in His wise and good providence. Again, the mention of God's name in prayer stirs the Christian's faith with gratitude that God has made Himself known through the life, death, and resurrection of His Son, Jesus Christ; in Christ we may come to God with all the boldness and confidence of forgiven children.

Keep Your name joyful and refreshing to us. In Jesus' name. Amen.

August

The Symbol of the Cross

And from Jesus Christ the faithful witness, the firstborn of the dead, and the ruler of kings on earth. To Him who loves us and has freed us from our sins by His blood. Revelation 1:5

In the Ajanta Caves in central India stands a great statue of Buddha. Shown lying on his side, the statue symbolizes the pathway of Buddhism—the quiet meditation of men, the desire to overcome all desires, tranquility, and rest.

What a striking contrast is found in the central symbol of the Christian faith: the cross! Here hangs the figure of the Son of God—His body convulsed in pain, His face twisted in agony, blood streaking His forehead. As His body sinks into death, He prays for forgiveness for His torturers.

The next time you gather for worship together with the whole Church, take note of how God's activity in Christ stands out. In a great doxology, St. John offers praise and glory "to Him who loves us and has freed us from our sins by His blood." This is the heart of the Christian faith: Not that we overcome our desires and achieve tranquility for ourselves, but that God loves us enough to act on our behalf! Faith does not revolve about my good intentions, the intensity of my prayers, or the generosity of my purse. It centers in God. God the Son absorbed all our pride, indifference, and lust into Himself and destroyed it in His death! Some may shy away from the biblical truth that we have been washed in His blood, but this core idea fully describes who we are in Christ. Our sin is destroyed by His death. In His death we have life!

May the blessing of God Almighty, the Father, Son, and Holy Spirit, rest upon us and our worship. Amen.

August

Absolution

And behold, some people brought to Him a paralytic, lying on a bed. And when Jesus saw their faith, He said to the paralytic, "Take heart, My son; your sins are forgiven." Matthew 9:2

Surprisingly, but appropriately, Jesus said "take heart" to the palsied man, first telling him that his sins are forgiven rather than telling him that he was healed. For there is nothing more cheering that sinful man wants to hear, and needs to hear, than the assurance of forgiveness through Jesus Christ.

When we perceive that sin separates us from God and that such separation is the source of all our unhappiness, tragedy, and despair, we know we have a problem on our hands. But what is the solution? We alone have created our problem, and it would seem reasonable that we alone should be responsible for working out our own salvation. Yet this is our predicament that we cannot bring ourselves into a right relationship to God, with whom we are, therefore, estranged.

Not only is Jesus Christ "God with us," He is also "God for us." In giving His life, He gave a holy sacrifice to reconcile the world of sinners to God. With complete confidence we can say: "We have peace with God through our Lord Jesus Christ" (Romans 5:1). This is the assurance that inspires good cheer in every man—the assurance that we are God's forgiven and restored children through the mercies of Jesus Christ.

Open our lives, good Lord, to the abiding joy of believing Your goodness in Jesus, our Savior. Amen.

August

Forgiveness with God

*If You, O LORD, should mark iniquities, O LORD, who could
stand? Psalm 130:3*

The Pharisees objected to Jesus' dealing with sinners. At
times they grumbled among themselves about it, and at times
they complained openly. "Why does He eat with tax collectors
and sinners?" (Mark 2:16). But Jesus went on His way undis-
turbed, helping sinners wherever He went. He Himself had
said, "The Son of Man came to seek and to save the lost" (Luke
19:10). He spent His entire earthly ministry seeking, admon-
ishing, forgiving, and strengthening souls who were formerly
lost.

What a blessing it is that Jesus loves sinners! If it were not
so, it would be better for us if we had never been born, "For all
have sinned and fall short of the glory of God," (Romans 3:23).
Truly, "If You, O LORD should mark iniquities, O LORD who
could stand?" The answer is *no one.* But the same God who sees
us and who knows every vileness and sin in us has also said;
"Come now, let us reason together, says the LORD: though your
sins are like scarlet, they shall be as white as snow; though they
are red like crimson, they shall become like wool" (Isaiah 1:18).
As the psalmist rightly said of God, "With You there is forgiveness" (Psalm 130:4), full and free forgiveness, and so we sinners
can lift our faces high. We rest securely in the arms of a forgiving God, who sent His own Son into death that we might be
forgiven.

*Lord Jesus, into whose name I have been baptized, I thank You for this
assurance of forgiveness. Amen.*

The End

"Heaven and earth will pass away, but My words will not pass away." Luke 21:33

We love this earth on which we live; it is so beautiful; it has so many attractive scenes. We delight in looking at its mountains, lakes, and rivers, these wonderful creations of our God. It is a pleasure to behold the beautiful flowers, shrubs, and trees that grow out of its soil. The heavens over our heads also shine in beauty! How the twinkling stars fascinate us, the lovely moon, the brightly shining sun, the multicolored clouds of ever-varying formations!

But listen! When the Son of man shall come for the last judgment, then both the earth on which we dwell and the canopy of the heavens at which we gaze with such a thrill shall pass away! The very thought might sadden us, and the sight of their destruction on the Last Day will shock us. Then woe will be to us if we possess nothing but the things of this visible earth and the star-spangled heavens above!

Yet blessed are they who then are Christ's by an abiding faith in Him! Despite the frightening destruction we shall be safe in the arms of Jesus. He will in that day take us to the eternal heaven of salvation that never shall pass away. We shall then be citizens of the new Jerusalem that abides forever. We shall forever rest in Abraham's bosom. We shall live endlessly with our God and our Savior.

In mercy, Jesus, bring us
To that dear land of rest!
You are, with God the Father
And Spirit, ever blest. Amen. (LW 309:4)

The King of Glory

Lift up your heads, O gates! And lift them up, O ancient doors, that the King of glory may come in. Psalm 24:9

Like all of the psalms, Psalm 24 is a hymn that was sung by God's people long ago. How joyous they must have been as they marched up to the temple-church on Mount Zion! How often the Lord had used His shining presence to rescue them from their enemies!

God's people today know this same joy because this God of glory sent His glorious Son, Jesus, to be our Rescuer and Deliverer. God the Son stepped out through the broad portals of heaven and quietly slipped into the narrow confines of our earthly life. "Lift up your heads, O gates!" Through the rough gate of a stable door, the King of glory comes in and becomes one of us so that through Him, the gates of heaven may be opened up for us.

Years after His birth, the old gates of Jerusalem likewise swung open for Him. A beast of burden carried the King of glory through. Not only did He ride a beast of burden, but He made a Himself a beast of burden, carrying before the eyes of all Jerusalem the timbers of a cross. But the people did not see another heavier weight upon His innocent shoulders—the burden of the guilt and evil of all people of all ages.

"Lift up your heads, O gates!" We Christians go joyfully through church doors today. There the Lord lets us hear His glorious Gospel. His Spirit uses this Word like a battering ram to open any doors of our heart the flesh wants closed to Him. By His powerful Word the King of glory enters in!

O Redeemer, come! Amen.

Saved by Blood

The blood shall be a sign for you, on the houses where you are.
And when I see the blood, I will pass over you, and no plague
will befall you to destroy you, when I strike the land of Egypt.
Exodus 12:13

Blood usually presents a picture of tragedy. When we see blood, we immediately think of wounds, of hurt, of death. In fact, some people become faint at the sight of blood. The Book of Exodus, however, shows that the sign of blood is the greatest and most wonderful token that has ever been given to man. It is the assurance of hope and deliverance.

When the children of Israel were ready for their deliverance from the slavery in Egypt, God gave them a sign of deliverance. The blood of a lamb was to be sprinkled on the doorposts as an indication of faith in God's promise, and thereby a means of escape from the judgment that God was going to bring upon the Egyptians by destroying every firstborn. This sign of the Passover was a symbol and a prophecy of the great deliverance that was to come through Jesus Christ, the perfect Lamb of God, who shed His blood that we might be delivered from the bondage of sin.

The Lord says, "Without the shedding of blood there is no forgiveness of sins" (Hebrews 9:22). Therefore Jesus died and shed His blood that we might have forgiveness and be saved. Rejoice, dear reader! "The blood of Jesus His Son cleanses us from all sin" (1 John 1:7).

O Jesus, spotless Lamb of God, cleanse us from our sins by faith in Your
blood. Amen.

The Lord's Anointed

Your throne, O God, is forever and ever. The scepter of Your
kingdom is a scepter of uprightness; You have loved righteous-
ness and hated wickedness. Therefore God, your God, has
anointed you with the oil of gladness beyond your companions.
Psalm 45:6–7

The psalmist speaks of the Anointed of the Lord, the
Messiah, our Lord Jesus Christ. He is established upon the
throne forever as God of very God. And this Anointed of the
Lord lived among us as one of our fellowmen. He took upon
Himself human form that He might establish Himself as victor
over Satan, who held us in bondage. He must ransom us with
His blood. That's why He dwelt among us and went to Calvary.
There Jesus defeated the powers of hell and proved that He still
was on the throne as the God of all eternity. Through His death
we are reconciled with God, and by faith His righteousness
becomes our own. "With His stripes we are healed" (Isaiah
53:5).

We live in His kingdom and His presence as children and
heirs of the household of the Eternal. So we need not hide from
God as long as we hide in the sacred wounds of His Anointed.

What difference that makes to the day through which I
pass! The Lord is my keeper. He will preserve my going out and
my coming home.

Lord, as preserver of my body and soul I lean upon You this day, as the
rock eternal. Guide my every step, and keep me from falling and injur-
ing myself. Above all, let Your grace preserve my soul from erring and
straying. Let that peace of Calvary take full possession of my heart and
put my mind at ease. Then Yours shall be the glory, the praise, and the
adoration now and always. Amen.

The Lion of the Tribe of Judah

Judah is a lion's cub; from the prey, my son, you have gone up.
He stooped down; he crouched as a lion and as a lioness; who
dares rouse him? The scepter shall not depart from Judah, nor
the ruler's staff from between his feet, until tribute comes to
Him; and to Him shall be the obedience of the peoples. Genesis
49:9–10

This remarkable and inspiring messianic promise was
spoken by Jacob to his son Judah. Princely power was to remain
in the hands of Judah, culminating in Shiloh, the Prince of
peace, which is Christ. The New Testament speaks of this Prince
as "the Lion of the tribe of Judah, the Root of David, has conquered, so that He can open the scroll and its seven seals,"
(Revelation 5:5).

It is for the purpose of exaltation that Jacob uses the term
"lion." He is picturing a man of majestic qualities. In Christ this
was fulfilled, for through Him all of Jacob's sons and all his
descendants were to come to glory, honor, and riches. Christ
was a man above all men, for in Him dwelt the fullness of the
Godhead bodily.

The symbol of a lion also indicates the courage and heroism of this prince. Christ is the fearless champion, who faced
the foes of God and man and fought the battles of His people.
He overpowered death and the devil.

The name "Lion of the tribe of Judah" also characterizes
Christ as a triumphant hero and victorious king. Christ's battle
for the souls of men was not in vain, for by His victory He
gained and maintained freedom and safety for His people.

Dear Lord, we thank You for the pardon, peace, protection, and power
we are daily receiving from Jesus Christ, that mighty conqueror of
Satan, sin, and hell. Amen.

Our Savior and Lord

They were filled with great fear and said to one another, "Who then is this, that even wind and sea obey Him?" Mark 4:41

Jesus and His disciples were in a small boat on the Sea of Galilee, and it was night. A great storm arose, and the disciples were frantic with fear. Moreover, the Master lay in the back part of the ship, sleeping peacefully as though there were no storm and no danger. The disciples woke Him and told Him that without a doubt they would perish in the waves. After chiding them for their weak faith, He calmed the sea with three small but mighty words: "Peace! Be still" (Mark 4:39). It was then that the disciples asked among themselves, "Who then is this, that even wind and sea obey Him?"

Indeed, who *is* this? He is a man, to be sure, but not the manner of man that we are. We are afraid when danger and sorrow threaten. We call out in fear, often losing hope and confidence. We recognize our weakness, our inability to meet the forces of nature and the dangers of life without assistance. Jesus is different. He has the raging sea in His power. He says, "Peace! Be still," and there is a great calm. Knowing that, we can trust in Him implicitly and depend on Him to make everything right. In danger, He protects; in sin, He pardons; in any kind of trouble, He is by our side with His almighty hand and His comforting Word, ready to speak the quieting words: "Peace, be still." Wonder of wonders! The Son of God is ever at our side to comfort and to save. We have nothing to fear.

Jesus, Savior, help us daily to find the sweet assurance of Your continual presence. Amen.

Saved by Hope

For in this hope we were saved. Now hope that is seen is not hope. For who hopes for what he sees? Romans 8:24

Everywhere we find some kind of hope. Young people hope for the time when they can go out and take their place in the world. People who are struggling with illness hope for the day of health. Those who are wrestling with a family problem hope for the day of its solution. Not all hope is alike. Some hope is futile and vain, for it rests on no solid foundation.

The Christian lives by hope with regard to his life and his eternal destiny. "For in this hope we were saved," says Paul. Yet this hope is not a mere wish. This hope is sure and certain, for it revolves around very definite and certain promises of the eternal God.

In this life the Christian already is saved by hope. He never accepts himself as he is, nor takes for granted that this is as far as he can go. The Christian is always looking up, living in the hope that God will help him in his infirmities and weaknesses.

The Christian's hope includes especially that which lies beyond the horizons of time. The Christian hopes for eternal life with God.

Our hope is based on the work of salvation through Jesus Christ. Jesus says: "I came that they may have life and have it abundantly" (John 10:10). He says: "Because I live, you also will live" (John 14:19).

Blessed Lord, keep aflame in me the light of hope. Amen.

Hope Thou in God

Why are you cast down, O my soul, and why are you in turmoil within me? Hope in God; for I shall again praise Him, my salvation. Psalm 42:5

Life is like a checkerboard. Every white space is surrounded by black. Even in the happy moments we realize that suffering or pain, tragedy or failure, grief or death are not too far away. And worst of all, powers on the outside seem to be making the moves. Life spins on but so often we don't feel in control of it.

Even men of God are moved onto the black spaces. The psalmist remembers pain and sorrow so great that he seemed to live on his tears. At the lowest point, however, he begins to talk with himself: "Why are you cast down, O my soul?" In his grief he gives his own answer—"Hope in God!"

Perhaps we shall soon be moved onto another black square. With God's help we shall give the same answer: "Hope in God!" This does not mean the problem will disappear or the pain will be lessened. But it does mean that even while the pain and grief grip us, we know we are in God's hand. For hope is less concerned with outside circumstances than with an inner faith in God. The darkness remains, but God's light shines into its very midst.

This is the comfort God provides to us by the cross. God did not remain aloof to our suffering. In His Son, He knelt down into its midst. In His suffering, He gave meaning to all our suffering. With His resurrection, He promises an end to our suffering and a bodily, eternal life with Him.

Grant us steadfast hearts, O Christ, to meet life's trials with cheerfulness and hope. Amen.

August

Contact Established

Through Him we have also obtained access by faith into this grace in which we stand, and we rejoice in hope of the glory of God. Romans 5:2

After World War I a painting was made to honor the Royal Corps of Signalers. The scene depicts a signaler who had been commissioned to crawl out under enemy fire to repair a snapped wire. His body is shown lying lifeless on the ground. But he had fulfilled his task. For he holds in his stiffened hands the two ends of the wire. Contact had been established. Beneath the painting there is one word: "Through!"

This is how the Bible portrays the work of Christ. The "wire" between God and mankind had snapped. In our sin we destroyed the contact of love and grace and went our own way. As God radioed His messages to us, we were unable to receive them. Somehow contact had to be established again.

Christ boldly went out into the battlefield of the world. "God sent forth His Son, born of woman, born under the Law, to redeem those who were under the Law, so that we might receive adoption as sons" (Galatians 4:4). The torturous journey meant pain and suffering. As the shells of the hostile world shattered His body, His hands brought together the two ends of the wire. Contact was established—through His death!

With contact established in Christ, communication between God and humanity now shall remain unbroken eternally. He speaks to us through His Word. He directs and strengthens us. We speak to Him in prayer, pouring out our need, confessing our sin. We worship and adore Him. "Through Him [Christ] we have also obtained access by faith."

We praise You, O Lord, for the death of Your Son, through whom we may now come to You in prayer. Amen.

August

But We Have a Perfect Savior

They have all fallen away; together they have become corrupt; there is none who does good, not even one. Psalm 53:3

It's rather disheartening to be told again and again that we are no good. But this truth must get into our hearts, lest we pass by the cross of Christ in our pride and self-righteousness. This holds true especially of us who are respectable, decent, and reputable. It is rather difficult for us to admit that we are sinners, that we too fail to meet the requirements of God's Law.

Paul, who later in life confessed himself to be the chief of sinners, thought himself well-nigh perfect in his youth. He was so much better than the mill run of the community. Not until he came face to face with Jesus on the Damascus road did Paul become conscious of the fact that he was a sinner who must be saved by grace and through the cross.

Not one of us can come into God's presence with clean hands and a pure heart. As we stand in the light of God's holiness, we must hide in shame and admit our guilt.

But we have our Friend and Savior! Let Him speak and plead for us! Thus we shall not fear the judgment of God. We will remain in His presence, for the blood of Jesus Christ has washed and cleansed us from all sin.

Eternal Savior of us all, lover of our soul, we come with You to the Father's throne, asking that You plead for us. We are not deserving of Your love. We are mindful of our daily transgressions, but we remember also Your sacrifice on Calvary. Restore us altogether and guide our footsteps in ways acceptable to You, Friend and Redeemer. Amen.

Sanctus

And one called to another and said: "Holy, holy, holy is the LORD *of hosts; the whole earth is full of His glory!" Isaiah 6:3*

Ever since men in ancient Babel decided to build a tower reaching from earth to heaven, people have not stopped being impressed with themselves. It is still news when some nation decides to build the biggest warship or passenger vessel. Many people likewise find a certain satisfaction in being part of a large city or congregation.

It is pathetic that, with all our concern for size, we do not often think of the greatness of God. Yet what is a more fitting subject for our imagination than the thought of Him, who is thrice holy, who rules kings and is subject to no authority, whose majesty fills the earth, who neither earth nor heaven can contain? Perhaps God's greatness staggers and frightens us.

But when we think of the greatness of God, let us not think only of the limitlessness of His nature. Incomprehensible as that may be, the most amazing thing about God is this, that God comes to us, makes Himself known to us, cares for us, dies for us, receives us into His fellowship. Think how God laid aside His greatness and glory and entered our human experience in the person of Jesus Christ. At Bethlehem and Golgotha, He plainly revealed God for us; He showed us who God is, what He is like. "Blessed is He," therefore, "who comes in the name of the Lord" (Matthew 21:9). Christ, our Savior, brings God to us in all the fullness of His power and love.

Thanks be to You, O Jesus, that by Your sacrifice You have made us God's own and that by faith in You we know God. Amen.

Our Communion with God

*"That they may all be one, just as You, Father, are in Me, and I
in You, that they also may be in us, so that the world may
believe that You have sent Me." John 17:21*

According to ancient mythology, the gods and their offspring frequently assumed human form and lived among men
in order to avenge themselves on men or to play capricious
tricks on unsuspecting persons. Over and against this, the Bible
makes it plain that God sent His Son to earth for quite another
purpose. Jesus Christ became man and died for man so He
might take away the sin that separated man from God. The
Gospel is the good news that Christ's mission was successful.
We were reconciled to God by the death of His Son and in Him
we have now received atonement.

The story of our salvation in Jesus Christ is not simply the
story of a penalty forgiven, of a barrier removed. It is those
things, of course, but it is also the story of our reunion with
God. Because Christ removed the barrier of sin that separated
us from God, we can live with God. This life with God is ours
already by faith, and Christ has promised that this life with Him
will never end. The time is coming when we shall enter more
completely into union with God, shall see Him face to face, and
know Him even as we are known to God. Meanwhile, however,
we are assured that nothing can tear us away from the love of
God, which is in Christ Jesus, our Lord.

*With saints, angels, archangels, seraphim, and cherubim, we laud and
magnify You for that blessed communion that we have with You now
and forevermore through the mercies of Jesus Christ. Amen.*

August

Nunc Dimittis

For I am already being poured out as a drink offering, and the time of my departure has come. I have fought the good fight, I have finished the race, I have kept the faith. 2 Timothy 4:6–7

There is nothing more certain in this world than the fact of death. Although a person may live an entire century or more, there is still no evading death. But the fear of death is increased by the uncertainty of how and when and where death will come. All we can know is that we live in the dominion of death. In our beginning is already written our end.

Still none of this is cause for despair in the Christian. We freely admit: "The time of my departure has come." Then, without bravado or boasting, we offer ourselves to death.

The secret of happy death is the faith we treasure in our heart. We look to the promise of God: "All things are yours, whether Paul or Apollos or Cephas or the world or life or death or the present or the future—all are yours, and you are Christ's, and Christ is God's" (1 Corinthians 3:21–23). On this promise we rest everything. That is the faith that overcomes the world. That is the faith that overcomes death and gains heaven by the grace of God in Christ Jesus.

Lord, now let Your servant depart in peace, according to Your Word, for my eyes have seen Your salvation. Amen.

Benediction

The grace of the Lord Jesus Christ and the love of God and the fellowship of the Holy Spirit be with you all. 2 Corinthians 13:14

God is the beginning and the end of all things. It is natural and proper to call upon the name of God before starting anything. It is equally natural and proper to await God's approval at the end.

The Gospel of forgiveness in Christ transforms every aspect of life. That which is cheap and ordinary, tawdry with shame and damaged by sin, He covers with grace. Always His grace is transforming, renewing, transfiguring. He alone can create beauty, goodness, and truth in us.

May it not be that our lives are dreary and dull, lacking harmony and sense, simply because God's grace is not blessing what we do, say, and think? If God is neither our end nor our beginning, what can we hope to make of ourselves? Left to ourselves, we can only bring all to ruin.

But in His goodness God reaches down toward us in Christ to save. He takes the good He has worked in us and makes it better. He takes that which is poor and sinful and makes it over into that which gives Him pleasure. His promise is sure: "My grace is sufficient for you, for My power is made perfect in weakness" (2 Corinthians 12:9).

Lord, bless us and keep us. Lord, let Your face shine upon us, and be gracious unto us. Lord, lift up Your countenance upon us, and give us Your peace. Amen.

Hiding from God

And they heard the sound of the LORD God walking in the garden in the cool of the day, and the man and his wife hid themselves from the presence of the LORD God among the trees of the garden. Genesis 3:8

Every person—in some way and at some time—finds himself trying to hide. He hides his life from his fellow men. He even tries to keep from his closest friends and loved ones some of the things he wants no one but himself to know. No one will deny a person the privilege of privacy. The mistake, however, that all of us are inclined to make is that we might try to hide certain things from God. Adam and Eve tried that as they cowered in the bushes of the garden.

The reason for their hiding, the reason for our hiding, is shame. Shame is caused by guilt; guilt is caused by sin. Adam and Eve had sinned against God, and they were afraid. They did not want to face God. They did not want to settle their difference with Him. They wanted to hide, to get away from God.

Many of us today are inclined to act in that same way. Instead of facing our sins and mistakes, we attempt to cover them up. But we cannot keep them from God! Our secret sins are already known to Him, even long before we commit them. The better thing by far is to confess to God our sins, our guilt and our shame. God is faithful! God has already forgiven you! This is the reason for Jesus' entry into the world, that covering ourselves with His righteousness, we might never need to hide from God again.

Cover me, O Lord, with Your righteousness and carry for me my shame. Amen.

Sonship

For in Christ Jesus you are all sons of God, through faith.
Galatians 3:26

The phrase, "the universal fatherhood of God," implies that all human beings without exception are God's children, that all have God as their Father. In a limited sense this is true, simply because God is the creator of all. Even the prophet said: "Have we not all one Father? Has not one God created us?" (Malachi 2:10).

However, in a higher and much more intimate sense only those are God's children who have believed the Gospel proclamation of our Lord's death and resurrection. According to today's verse, it is by faith in Christ Jesus that we are God's children. In John 1:12 we read: "But to all who did receive Him, who believed in His name, He gave the right to become children of God."

In ourselves we are so filthy through sin that we are not fit for this sonship toward God, for membership in His family. However, through faith in Jesus, we possess full forgiveness for all our sins and thus cleansing from all the guilt and all the filth of our transgression. That makes us acceptable to God and qualifies us to be His children.

This, in turn, means that we journey along under the protection, the love, the guidance, the direction, the blessing of the heavenly Father.

I thank You, Lord God, for including us in Your fellowship and allowing us to share Your love and grace with others. Amen.

Faith Comes by the Word of God

But how are they to call on Him in whom they have not believed? And how are they to believe in Him of whom they have never heard? And how are they to hear without someone preaching? Romans 10:14

"This is good, and it is pleasing in the sight of God our Savior, who desires all people to be saved and to come to the knowledge of the truth" (1 Timothy 2:3–4). The Bible is full of statements that show God's love for the sinner and His concern of the sinner's salvation. He wants the sinners in heaven, every one of them.

We Christians rejoice that we have come to the knowledge of salvation through faith in Jesus Christ. God's gift of faith brings with it a deep joy and gratitude for God's boundless mercy and for the sinner's salvation. But can we stop there, stop with our own joy? God gives us His Word that we may share the life-giving Bread with the spiritually hungry. They may be our relatives or friends or neighbors or they may be people whom we do not know personally at all.

As millions go back to school these days, we are reminded especially of our duty toward our own children. Is their education in home, church, and school such that it will strengthen their faith and train them in the art of Christian living? Witnessing of our God and Savior should begin in our own families, done so in the knowledge and the confidence that God's Word is powerful in itself. It is not dependent on our strength of faith or on our power to convince. It speaks, and eternal life results!

Dear Lord Christ, give us the willingness to proclaim the Gospel far and wide. Amen.

September

Peace

Therefore, since we have been justified by faith, we have peace with God through our Lord Jesus Christ. Romans 5:1

Peace with God is the second great gift in the treasure chest, Jesus Christ, and a most precious gift it is indeed!

Man desires to be happy, to be at peace with himself. But he will never be at peace with himself unless and until he has found peace with his God. The church father Augustine spoke so truly when he said: "Thou, O God, hast created us unto Thee, and our soul cannot rest till it rests in Thee." That truth ought to be quite apparent to us when we consider that God is our Creator and that we are His creatures. Peace with Him is the all-essential foundation for the peace within us, for peace with ourselves.

Really, there is one thing and one thing only that disturbs or mars or breaks our peace with God, and that is our sin. Inasmuch as our sins have been removed by Christ, there no longer is anything to deprive us of peace with God. Through our Lord Jesus Christ, we do have peace with God. Not an armistice, not a truce, not a ceasefire, or any other halfway thing, but peace, full peace, lasting peace. This peace we have now, in days good and evil, in the hour of our death, in the Day of Judgment, for all eternity.

O Lord Jesus, we hail You as our Prince of peace. Bless us with the peace of God which passes all understanding. In Your name we ask it. Amen.

"The Light"

Again Jesus spoke to them, saying, "I am the Light of the world. Whoever follows Me will not walk in darkness, but will have the light of life." John 8:12

Darkness expresses sin and wrongdoing, guilt and fear, sorrow and sadness, despair and the giving up of hope. Light expresses joy, gladness, peace, hope, wisdom, knowledge, enlightenment.

Man by himself and without Christ is in spiritual darkness; if he remains by himself and without Christ until his death, he will spend eternity in hell's "outer darkness. In that place there will be weeping and gnashing of teeth" (Matthew 8:12).

By dying for a world of sinners, Jesus earned for mankind forgiveness with the Lord, righteousness before God, acceptance by God, peace here, heaven hereafter. Thus Jesus created for man spiritual light in life, in death, for time, for eternity.

There is no contradiction between this word of Jesus: "I am the Light of the world" and this: "You are the light of the world" (Matthew 5:14). The moon has no light in itself, and still it can shine because the sun's light strikes it. Man has no spiritual light by himself, and yet the believer in Christ can shine because the Savior's light has fallen upon him. We reflect it as naturally and as passively as the moon reflects the bright light of the sun, and thus we become the light of the world.

Shine upon me brightly, O dear Jesus, and cause me to shine brightly on others. Amen.

The Promise of Recognition

"I am the good shepherd. I know My own and My own know Me." John 10:14

If the Scriptures did not picture Christ as our Good Shepherd, we would undoubtedly carry with us a much different picture of the life of sheep. We certainly would not wish to be referred to as sheep; we resent even now being known as "sheepish," and many characteristics of the flock are unappealing to us.

Pastors know that Psalm 23 and the parable of the lost sheep are among the most requested portions of Scripture by those who walk in the valley of the shadow of death. We like the picture because we like to see the Lord as the Shepherd. It is a figure He Himself chose. He wanted to assure us of His concern; unlike the hired man, He would not run away in time of danger. He cares. As a matter of fact, He laid down His life for the sheep when that was necessary.

How happy we are to hear again and again that He knows His own! He promises to recognize us and to give us the power to respond to Him. Earthly recognition may be a wrong quest; it may involve pride and self-seeking. Heavenly recognition by Christ is our hope, our assurance, our security already for this life. We are known to God today and forever.

Lead us, O Lord, our Shepherd, and never forsake us, for Your mercy's sake. Amen.

Our Salvation Is Sure

He who did not spare His own Son but gave Him up for us all, how will He not also with Him graciously give us all things? Romans 8:32

It is a sad but evident fact that Christians can lose their faith and become unbelievers. Sometimes we Christians think of this and ask: "What if this should happen to me?" Indeed, we should be daily and seriously concerned about our salvation, for we are admonished: "Therefore, my beloved, as you have always obeyed, so now, not only as in my presence but much more in my absence, work out your own salvation with fear and trembling" (Philippians 2:12). Yet we are also to have the sure confidence that the Holy Spirit will keep us in the faith until death.

St. Paul asks the question: "Who shall separate us from the love of Christ? Shall tribulation, or distress, or persecution, or famine, or nakedness, or danger, or sword?" (Romans 8:35). But he has hardly asked the question when he exults: "I am sure that neither death nor life, nor angels nor rulers, nor things present nor things to come, nor height nor depth, nor anything else in all creation, will be able to separate us from the love of God in Christ Jesus our Lord" (Romans 8:38–39). These are glorious words that can provide us with daily comfort in our struggle with the devil and sin. They reassure us and strengthen us when we despair in our weaknesses and failures. They make us happy and contented in Jesus' love. They are a small foretaste of the joys of heaven, spoken of in Psalm 16:11: "You make known to me the path of life; in Your presence there is fullness of joy." We are safe in God's hands and sure that, "He who began a good work in you will bring it to completion at the day of Jesus Christ" (Philippians 1:6).

Beautiful Savior, who has redeemed us by Your precious blood, strengthen our faith, and make us confident and sure of our eternal salvation. Amen.

Rags Yet Riches

And the people of Nineveh believed God. They called for a fast and put on sackcloth, from the greatest of them to the least of them. Jonah 3:5

Centuries ago it was symbolic of repentance to put on sackcloth. Here is the record of an entire city that wore sackcloth as a sign of their repentance. They had heard God's prophet, Jonah, warning them to repent or perish.

What a strange and unusual act for the people of Nineveh! These people were used to wearing expensive and beautiful clothing as symbols of their wealth. But now in the day of repentance, they are clothed in coarse, unattractive, and uncomfortable sackcloth. However, their rags are symbolic of a greater wealth than they had ever known. They are truly penitent people, people who are grieved because of their own wickedness. Like David of old, they could say: "I know my transgressions, and my sin is ever before me" (Psalm 51:3).

Even we Christians are continually tempted to count the things of this world as worthwhile and most valuable. But if we were to gain the whole world and lose our soul, we would be the poorest of men. The Holy Spirit brings us to the knowledge of our sins even as He brought the Ninevites to repent through the preaching of Jonah. He also creates faith for us, by which we are made able to believe Christ's pardon for us; and where there is pardon, there is also life and salvation. Each day should find us beneath the cross, rejoicing in the forgiveness that is ours in Jesus Christ.

Grant, O Lord, that our repentance may be sincere and not a sham lest we find ourselves repenting throughout eternity. Amen.

September

Sad Yet Glad

David said to Nathan, "I have sinned against the LORD." And Nathan said to David, "The LORD also has put away your sin; you shall not die." 2 Samuel 12:13

One of the most terrifying moments in the life of King David must have been when Nathan, the prophet, revealed to him that God was aware of his great sin. But it was also a sweet and blessed moment. David was relieved to make confession of his sin and to hear the prophet say, "The LORD has put away your sin; you shall not die."

How unhappy sins can make us once we have committed them! If we have ever tried to hide some ugly sin, we will recall how our conscience would give us no rest. It reminded us that we had sinned. It warned that someone might find out very quickly. It made for sleepless nights.

But we have also known the joy that was David's. We, too, have believed the Gospel message that our sins are forgiven before God. What a blessed relief to know there is no sin too great for God's mercy. David was truly sorry that he had permitted Satan to enter his heart and had fallen into such a terrible sin against God. Now the God against whom he had sinned was telling him that his sin was forgiven.

Our sadness is turned into gladness by this same announcement of God's pardon. We have sinned today, but God says to us, "[I have] put away your sin; you shall not die."

Give us wisdom, precious Jesus, to know that the only place to hide our sins is in You. Amen.

September

Grace upon Grace

And from His fullness we have all received, grace upon grace.
John 1:16

John says that Jesus is full of grace and truth. He also says that of His fullness we all have received grace for grace. Jesus is like a spring of water that never dries up. This spring is inexhaustible; it never loses anything, no matter how much we draw from it, but remains an infinite fountain of all grace and truth from God. The more we draw from it, the more abundantly it gives of the water that springs unto eternal life.

"Grace upon grace"—that means abundant grace, and more grace, and still more grace. That is what Jesus guarantees us. There is nothing we need quite so much as grace. Grace is undeserved favor. Grace presupposes our sin and our need for forgiveness. Yet grace also tells us that God has completely removed our sin not because we have merited a reward. Grace tells us that God has removed our sins despite our unworthiness.

We receive the blessings of grace from Jesus. He is the Fountain of grace. Because of what Jesus has done, we are rid of the burden of our sin. "I lay my sins on Jesus, / The spotless Lamb of God; / He bears them all and frees us / From the accursed load" (*LW* 366:1).

How happy we ought to be that God has given us such a gift. How grateful we ought to be for this gift of grace.

Nothing in my hand I bring;
Simply to thy cross I cling.
Naked, come to thee for dress,
Helpless, look to thee for grace;
Foul, I to the fountain fly;
Wash me, Savior, or I die! Amen. (LW 361:3)

The Holy Christian Church

*Even as He chose us in Him before the foundation of the world,
that we should be holy and blameless before Him. Ephesians 1:4*

God speaks of His Church and its members in most glorious terms. The Church is referred to as the Church of God, the family of God, the body of Christ, and even the bride of Christ. God calls us, the members of the Church, His "crown of glory" (1 Peter 5:4), "a royal diadem" (Isaiah 62:3), "My treasured possession" (Malachi 3:17).

Furthermore, God looks upon the members of His Church as being sinless, as saints. God wants His Church to be glorious, not having spot or wrinkle or any such thing, but holy and without blemish.

Do we actually measure up to this idea? Certainly, if we look upon our own hearts, on our own performance, we must admit and confess that we are sinners rather than saints. But God in His grace has rescued us. Christ has redeemed us. His precious blood cleanses us from all sin. We are now made holy. We are justified in the name of the Lord Jesus Christ and by the Spirit of our God. We were enemies of God. But Jesus by His merit has "reconciled in His body of flesh by His death, in order to present you holy and blameless and above reproach before Him" (Colossians 1:22).

In God's sight, as He sees us clothed in the garments of Christ's holiness, we by the grace of God have been made members of the holy Christian Church, the communion of saints.

Heavenly Father, thank You for the holiness of Jesus, which You have declared is mine. Amen.

God Is Our Helper

Have you not known? Have you not heard? The LORD is the everlasting God, the Creator of the ends of the earth. He does not faint or grow weary; His understanding is unsearchable. Isaiah 40:28

When the burdens of life become so heavy we do not see how we can carry on another day, we need the comfort only God can give. Sometimes this comfort is lacking, but only because of our sin. We seek to work out our difficulties without the divine help that is always at our beck and call, or we sink into deep despair and see no hope of help anywhere. For such a time there is no greater comfort than in the words: "Have you not known? Have you not heard? The LORD is the everlasting God, the Creator of the ends of the earth. He does not faint or grow weary; His understanding is unsearchable."

We may be weary; we may be so faint under our burdens that death would seem sweet relief. But not God. He is the Creator. He never wearies or sleeps. He is the everlasting God, who was there at the time of creation and who is here now, everywhere, in our homes, on the streets, in the fields, at our sickbed, in prison, wherever we may be. He is right there with His love and with the healing balm of His mercy. He wipes out our sins, corrects our mistakes, comforts us, lifts us up when we most need it. Therefore: "Fear not, for I am with you; be not dismayed, for I am your God; I will strengthen you, I will help you, I will uphold you with My righteous right hand" (Isaiah 41:10).

Dear Father in heaven, we thank You for the assurance of Your gracious presence. Increase our trust in You, and let us never doubt Your goodness, for Jesus' sake. Amen.

The Gospel of the Cross

Out of the depths I cry to you, O LORD! . . . If You, O LORD, should mark iniquities, O Lord, who could stand? But with You there is forgiveness, that You may be feared. Psalm 130:1,3–4

If the cry comes from the depths, then we must be lost somewhere in a deep pit. Sin puts us there. Sin blackens our soul, deadens our conscience, separates us from God. Sin puts us where we ought not to be.

Too many do not realize that they are in the depths. This cry for help did not come from the lips of Herod, secure for a while on his throne. Nor did it come from Pontius Pilate, who thought washing his hands in a ceremonial rite would absolve him from sin.

But those who know the destructive power of sin confess that they are helpless in their plight. No herb has been found to cleanse our soul; no scientific discovery to heal us from sin. We cannot stand before God, marked with our trespasses.

Out of that depth the psalmist cried for help. He did not despair. He believed he could get out of that pit. And how? "But with You there is forgiveness." God in His compassion reaches down and takes hold of us and lifts us to His heart.

That is the Gospel of the cross. The hands of His Son were pierced because He loved us so. His blood makes the foulest and saintliest clean. No matter how deep we have fallen, there is forgiveness with God because Christ died to lift us to Himself.

O Lord, count not our many transgressions against us. In Your mercy remove them all. Lift us to Your bosom, and give us peace of heart and mind through Jesus Christ, our Lord and Redeemer. Amen.

September

Christ, the Deliverer

Wretched man that I am! Who will deliver me from this body of death? Romans 7:24

St. Paul was greatly troubled by his sins. He confessed that there was nothing good in him. Often he could not bring himself around to performing that which he knew was the right thing to do. He often failed to do the good, but did the evil, all the while knowing better and wishing to do better. A constant battle was raging in him between the good and the evil. Paul was so distressed he cried out: "Wretched man that I am! Who will deliver me from this body of death?" What a picture of the great apostle! What a picture of the Christian!

We Christians go through the same experience constantly, and, like Paul, we often despair of ourselves. It is distressing for the Christian who wants to do right to have the same struggle day after day, falling and rising, only to fall again. We are upheld only by the grace and the mercy of God, which "are new every morning; great is Your faithfulness" (Lamentations 3:23).

The same apostle who was distressed because of his sins could exult: "Thanks be to God, who gives us the victory through our Lord Jesus Christ" (1 Corinthians 15:57). Here is the difference between the unbeliever and the believer: the Christian receives daily forgiveness in the return to Holy Baptism. By God's grace we rejoice in full and free forgiveness, and each day rise anew to the service of our Lord and Savior.

Redeemed, restored, forgiven,
Thro' Jesus' precious blood,
Heirs of His home in heaven,
Oh, praise our pard'ning God! Amen. (TLH 32:1)

September

Christ for Us

But He was wounded for our transgressions; He was crushed for our iniquities; upon Him was the chastisement that brought us peace, and with His stripes we are healed. Isaiah 53:5

Sir John Simpson, the man who discovered chloroform (among other things), was once asked which one of his discoveries he considered the greatest. He replied: "The greatest discovery I ever made is this, that I am a sinner and Jesus Christ is my Savior." By the mercies of God every sincere Christian has made this discovery.

Of course, we have not made this discovery by ourselves. God has revealed it to us through His Word and has given us the gift of faith that we might believe it. Ours is the heaven-born conviction that Christ is "for us." Isaiah declares: "*He* was wounded for *our* transgressions." St Paul states: "[*He*] gave Himself *for us*" (Titus 2:14). And again: "While we were still sinners, *Christ* died *for us*" (Romans 5:8).

Christ for us! This precious Gospel truth comforts us concerning our sin and guilt. Redeemed and reconciled through the sin-atoning work of Christ, we are the richly favored sons and daughters of our heavenly Father.

Christ for us! This assures us that His never-failing love surrounds us in every condition and circumstance of life. He has given us the assurance that our problems and perplexities must work together for our good. He has pledged Himself to direct our paths and to supply us with grace sufficient for every need.

Blessed Savior, who did live and die for us, grant that in heart and life we may find peace, joy, and strength in the confidence that You are always for us. Amen.

Man Inexcusable Apart from Faith

Therefore you have no excuse, O man, every one of you who judges. For in passing judgment on another you condemn yourself, because you, the judge, practice the very same things. Romans 2:1

Paul had shown in the first chapter of Romans that the heathen world was utterly sunk in sin and as such certainly could not hope to stand before God. The basic sin is always idolatry, and from that denial of God all the terrible manifestations of sin follow. But there certainly were also some fine, respectable people, religious people, people who had but one objective, and that was to please God and serve their fellow men. Did these also come under the sweeping condemnation of God as expressed by Paul? Is there not a difference that we can see and that God must also acknowledge?

Every time a man judges another, looks upon the worst of all sins and declares it to be the blasphemous thing that it is, he is condemning himself. He is merely showing that he has the wherewithal with which to judge, but shows nothing about his own keeping of the will of God. Not merely the knowers of the Law are what God wants, but the doers of the Law. This snatches from our greedy hearts every last vestige of homemade hope. Not a single one, not even the most religious, has even a shred of an excuse that he can hold up to God for his failure. Only God can excuse what we have done wrong; only God can forgive us our sins. That God offers us forgiveness, and that He does so for the sake of Jesus, is God's own true Gospel. He does abundantly so in Christ Jesus. He declares me righteous, gives me His own righteousness in Christ.

Father, I have sinned against heaven and in Your sight. Graciously forgive me all for Jesus' sake. Amen.

He Is Comforted

But Abraham said, "Child, remember that you in your lifetime received your good things, and Lazarus in like manner bad things; but now he is comforted here, and you are in anguish."
Luke 16:25

Among men it has always been an insoluble problem why the temporal goods and blessings are distributed so unevenly. In Psalm 73 Asaph thought about such things and was puzzled. In the story of the rich man and poor Lazarus, Jesus contrasted riches and poverty in glaring colors. He did not intend to solve, nor does He solve, the riddle of unequal distribution of material gifts. He simply took from material wealth its shining glamour and from poverty its impression of misery. Eternity will reveal what really are good things and what really are evil things. Earth's material advantage and disadvantage will not be the determining factors. On earth the rich man enjoyed what are good things materially.

The standard of the world—wealth, health, happiness—is only a relative standard of worldly prosperity. Heaven will be fullness of joy, and it will be perfect, created for us by the atoning blood of Christ. The full picture of heaven has not been yet revealed to us, but it can be summed up in these words regarding Lazarus: "He is comforted."

Dear Lord, let not the grandeur of this world detract from the blessings to come in heaven. Amen.

Scarlet and White

Come now, let us reason together, says the LORD: though your sins are like scarlet, they shall be as white as snow; though they are red like crimson, they shall become like wool. Isaiah 1:18

A court scene is portrayed in these words. Israel had spurned the mercy of God and had burdened its conscience with gross and grievous sins. Dark and sinister days had advanced upon the nation. In this crisis the summons of God goes forth: "Come now, let us reason together," or more perhaps, "Come, and let us take our case to court."

As the apostate people in Isaiah's day trembled before the divine tribunal and expected the inevitable sentence of doom, this startling verdict was pronounced: "Though your sins are like scarlet," that is, although they are hideous sins, "they shall be as white as snow." And then to reinforce the assurance, the promise is repeated: "Though they are red like crimson," the deepest red known to ancient Oriental art, "they shall become like wool," the pure, immaculate color of innocence, purity and holiness.

This expression of divine grace is not restricted to an ancient people. It is the imperishable foundation of our faith as well. We, too, have been selfish. We, too, have been materialistic. We, too, have grieved our Lord. For each one of us there is a personal summons in this dictum of divine love: "Come now, let us reason together."

And what is His verdict? God declares, "Glaring and revolting as your sins may be, standing out in the red and crimson of unpardonable guilt, the blood of Jesus Christ, My Son, cleanses you from all sin."

Blessed Lord, enable us by Your Spirit to lay hold on the things that belong to our eternal salvation through Christ, our Redeemer. Amen.

No Higher Ambition

That I may know Him and the power of His resurrection, and may share His sufferings, becoming like Him in His death.
Philippians 3:10

There is a beautiful story about Mrs. Einstein, the wife of the scientist who discovered the theory of relativity. One day, someone asked Mrs. Einstein, "Do you know all about relativity?" A satisfied smile played on the features of the kind old lady. "No," she replied, *"but I know my husband."*

Evidently Mrs. Einstein was not greatly troubled over the fact that she did not understand every detail about her husband's theory of relativity. It was enough for her that her husband knew it and that she knew her husband—that she was privileged to enjoy the love of so great a man.

And should we fret because we do not know all the mysteries of God? Richard Baxter spoke the Christian mind:

My knowledge of that life is small,
The eye of faith is dim;
But 'tis enough that Christ knows all,
And I shall be with him. (The Hymnal 1940 445:3)

Christ is our all. In Him are hidden all treasures of wisdom and knowledge. He governs all things—the course of planets, the fission of atoms, the fate of nations—in the loving interest of those whom He redeemed with His blood. To know Him, our God and Savior, is sufficient even though we do not fully understand the depths of who He is or what He has done for us.

Thou, O Christ, art all I want,
More than all in thee I find. Amen. (LW 508:4)

September

Thrice His

And they sang a new song, saying, "Worthy are You to take the scroll and to open its seals, for You were slain, and by Your blood You ransomed people for God from every tribe and language and people and nation." Revelation 5:9

A boy made a little boat, sailed it on a stream, and lost it. Later he discovered his boat in a secondhand store and bought it. Hugging it tightly, the boy looked at the boat and said: "Now you are twice mine: first I made you, and then I bought you."

And what does God say as He looks at us?

"I made you. I formed your body, and I gave you a soul. You are *Mine*.

"But I did more for you. When you got away from Me, choosing your willful way, I went after you. I would not let you go. I bought you with the blood of My only Son. You are *twice Mine*.

"Nor is that all I did for you. Although I had bought you at so great a price, you still resisted Me. You would not, could not, bring yourself to believe in your Savior. And so I brought you to faith through My Holy Spirit and Baptism and Gospel. I gave you a new birth. I made you My royal child. You are *thrice Mine*."

O Love that wilt not let me go,
I rest my weary soul in thee;
I give thee back the life I owe,
That in thine ocean depths its flow
May richer, fuller be. Amen. (The Hymnal 1940 458:1)

The Cross—God's Plan

"But how then should the Scriptures be fulfilled, that it must be so?" Matthew 26:54

What was most shocking about Buchenwald and the other Nazi torture camps during World War II was the evidence unearthed that the atrocities committed there were not the work of underlings, but were planned by top-level officials of a government that claimed a place in the society of nations.

The greatest atrocity in history—the crucifixion of Jesus—likewise was *planned*. God the Father planned it Himself.

Peter thought God's plans were being upset when a mob appeared at the gate of Gethsemane to arrest Jesus. He reached for his sword. Jesus stopped him, reminding him that if it were protection He needed, twelve legions of angels stood at His beck and call. Then Jesus added: "But how then should the Scriptures be fulfilled, that it must be so?"

Jesus *must* suffer and die because Scripture had foretold it. Scripture had foretold it because God had planned it. God had planned it because He wanted me to be saved. Jesus lived that He might die. He died that I might live.

Was it for sins that I had done
He groaned upon the tree?
Amazing pity, grace unknown,
And love beyond degree! (LW 97:2)

Redeeming Love, help me to see in Calvary's cross Your plan to save me from damnation. Help me to see my sins, repent of them, and find forgiveness in the cross. Amen.

I Will Not Leave You Comfortless

"I will not leave you as orphans; I will come to you. Yet a little while and the world will see Me no more, but you will see Me. Because I live, you also will live. In that day you will know that I am in My Father, and you in Me, and I in you. Whoever has My commandments and keeps them, he it is who loves Me. And he who loves Me will be loved by My Father, and I will love him and manifest Myself to him." John 14:18–21

A popular magazine once printed a picture of a young widow dressed in deep mourning standing before a symbolic figure of "Father Time." The caption read: "The mender of broken hearts." That is the only comfort the world has to offer those who mourn: Time supposedly heals all wounds.

The disciples of Jesus went out to His children in their distress. "I will not leave you as orphans; I will come to you." He still comes to us in His Word and by His Spirit to fill their hearts with such comfort and hope.

We all need comfort. There are many things that trouble and distress us. Our conscience accuses us. The ills common to all mankind also strike us. We fear that the future will bring us sorrow. We must suffer for His name's sake. Our burdens are heavy. Our hearts are sad. And the world has scant comfort to offer. The best it can do is to offer a vague hope that "better days are coming," or cynical advice to submit to the inevitable with a shrug of the shoulders and a resigned "So what!"

Jesus alone can offer comfort in the hour of need. "I will not leave you as orphans." He comes to us in His Word and comforts us through the Comforter, the Holy Spirit.

Holy Ghost, with joy divine Cheer this saddened heart of mine. Amen. (TLH 234:4)

Faith in Old Testament Times

Consider Abraham: "He believed God, and it was credited to him as righteousness." Galatians 3:6 NIV

Abraham's faith was more than merely that he believed there is a god. Abraham believed God. Mark this well! Abraham believed what God *told* him. This is the important thing in faith. We must believe what God tells us in His Word.

God told Abraham things that were not easy to believe. God said, "Sarah your wife shall have a son" (Genesis 18:10). Abraham was one hundred years old and his wife was ninety. Experience contradicted the Word of God. But Abraham believed God.

God also told Abraham that the world should be blessed in his Seed, a future descendant of Abraham. This, too, must have been difficult. How should the whole world benefit by anything one of his descendants might do—if indeed he were to have any? True, Abraham was a man of station. He had wealth. He had direct dealings with kings. Yet the possibility seemed remote that a son of his should bring blessings to the whole world. This Seed of Abraham is Christ, the world's Savior.

By faith in God's promises, Abraham was accounted righteous. Abraham's faith, then, was essentially not different from our faith. He believed God would send a Descendant who would bring God's blessing. We, too, believe this promised Seed has come and has brought the blessing of forgiveness and the promised hope of heaven.

Dear God, may we be true children of Abraham who believe Your Word to us. May we help Abraham's children after the flesh find Christ Jesus, the Savior of all nations. Amen.

Comforted Like Lazarus

"But first He must suffer many things and be rejected by this generation." Luke 17:25

Today's reading declares to you that your life right now looks nothing like what it shall be. Here is the story of a Christian man: "At his gate was laid a poor man named Lazarus, covered with sores, who desired to be fed with what fell from the rich man's table. Moreover, even the dogs came and licked his sores" (Luke 16:20–21).

Do not judge your place in the Church by anything you may or may not possess; do not judge your place in the Church by any health you may or may not be able to maintain; do not judge your place in the Church by anything at all you may experience in this life. Judge your place in the Church by the holy name that your crucified and risen Lord placed upon you at your Baptism. Look at your life through Lazarus's eyes, and see that you—like him—have been called "the one whom God has helped," which is the meaning of Lazarus's name.

Christ has died for you. Christ has risen for you. Christ has forgiven you all your sins. Christ has declared you sinless and holy and perfect because of all these things. None of this will be evident to your own eyes, any more than it was evident to Lazarus's suffering eyes. But this reading shows that your life, dear Christian, is now "hidden with Christ in God. When Christ who is your life appears, then you also will appear with Him in glory" (Colossians 3:3–4).

Give me patience, Lord, as I await Your final redemption. Amen.

September

The Power of the Holy Ghost

May the God of hope fill you with all joy and peace in believing, so that by the power of the Holy Spirit you may abound in hope. Romans 15:13

The Holy Spirit makes Christians. We confess with Luther: "I believe that I cannot by my own reason or strength believe in Jesus Christ, my Lord, or come to Him; but the Holy Spirit has called me by the Gospel, enlightened me with His gifts, sanctified and kept me in the true faith" (*Luther's Small Catechism*).

Every photographer knows that the image of a person whose picture he takes is transferred to the film by the power that is in the light. The film must be properly inserted, the speed of the camera minutely adjusted, the position of the subject carefully fixed, and the like, to ensure a good picture. However, unless the power of the light does its work, there will be no picture.

We can, of course, refuse to give the Holy Spirit an opportunity to do His regenerating work in our lives. We can refuse to use the means of grace, Word and Sacraments, through which the Spirit works. But even when we place ourselves face to face with Jesus by hearing and reading His Word and using Holy Baptism and the Lord's Supper, it is still the work of the Spirit of God, who supplies the enlightening and sanctifying power, that the righteousness and the likeness of Jesus Christ is transferred to our hearts and lives, and we are made and confirmed children of God.

O Holy Spirit, sanctify our lives, and make them holy and acceptable in the sight of God and man. In His name. Amen.

September

The Trial of Faith

So that the tested genuineness of your faith—more precious than gold that perishes though it is tested by fire—may be found to result in praise and glory and honor at the revelation of Jesus Christ. 1 Peter 1:7

Why should faith be tried or tested? For the same reason that gold is tried or refined: purification. Faith is purified and cleansed by fiery trials.

Faith is the work of the Holy Spirit. The Holy Spirit induces, persuades, brings a person to believe the Gospel. Man adds nothing.

Well, man might bring his own ideas along, but this dross must be burned away. Man has an awful time ridding himself of the idea that he himself can and must make a contribution of some kind in his approach to God. "Nothing in my hand I bring" is a nice, humble expression. Yet how often it seems to us that, after all, we *do* bring something to God. "For by grace you have been saved through faith. And this is not your own doing; it is the gift of God" (Ephesians 2:8). Still the idea lurks in our mind that we cannot really reach God unless we cooperate with the Holy Spirit.

Fiery trials clean out such ideas. Perhaps we must lose our health, our wealth, our family and friends, and almost our life before we *cling only to the cross of Jesus Christ* and trust solely in God's mercy. *His* life, *His* suffering, *His* death, and *His* resurrection form the basis of our claim to a final place in heaven.

Gracious Jesus, cleanse our lives by cleansing our faith even by fire if need be. Amen.

September

Facing Judgment—How?

And as he reasoned about righteousness and self-control and the coming judgment, Felix was alarmed and said, "Go away for the present. When I get an opportunity I will summon you." Acts 24:25

Felix reacted to the words of Paul. His conscience pierced him when Paul spoke of righteousness and temperance, and Paul's reference to the judgment to come made him tremble.

This verse illustrates that every person is accountable to God. At the bar of judgment each person will have to answer for himself to the Judge of all. What answer can he give when he stands there condemned already by his own conscience? No wonder the thought of a future judgment fills him with fear.

But praise be to God! Jesus has already endured our judgment for us. The chastisement of our peace was upon Him, and by His stripes we are healed. By faith we are made partakers of that peace and healing. So the judgment holds no terror for us.

We thank You, Lord Jesus, that You have freed us from the dread of the judgment to come. You have taken away the sins that would have condemned us. Give us Your Spirit that we may walk in holy obedience to Your Word and hold ourselves in readiness for the coming of Your great day. Amen.

"Abide in Me"

"Abide in Me, and I in you. As the branch cannot bear fruit by itself, unless it abides in the vine, neither can you, unless you abide in Me." John 15:4

"Lord, You have made us for Yourself, and we can find no rest until we rest in You," exclaimed St. Augustine, one of the great pastors and leaders of the Early Church. "I will give you rest," Jesus promised all those "who labor and are heavy laden," who come to Him with their burdens (Matthew 11:28). Repose can be achieved only in and with Him.

Jesus offers similar comforts in today's verse: "Abide in Me, and I in you. As the branch cannot bear fruit by itself, unless it abides in the vine, neither can you, unless you abide in Me."

Our Lord was here talking about the Christian faith, along with the Christian life and all that it implies, and He declared that only they can live Christian lives who abide in Him, believe in Him, and follow Him.

There are people who do not believe in Jesus as their Savior, but who live outwardly decent and respectable lives. These people sometimes declare that they are Christians, pointing, as proof, to their good conduct and kind deeds.

Jesus says that only they can live who abide in Him, their Savior. Our good life comes about only as result of our Lord's connection to us. He is our one and only source of the purity of forgiveness, and He freely supplies us with forgiveness and life through His Word and His Sacraments, just as a vine supplies its branches so they might live.

Grant us true faith, heavenly Father, that we may abide in Jesus always and bring forth the fruit of faith in lives of godliness. Amen.

September

Divine Torchbearer

"[The Holy Spirit] will glorify Me, for He will take what is Mine and declare it to you." John 16:14

This is a precious sentence. It sums up beautifully the activity of Him who does so much and who we know so little. The Holy Spirit glorifies Jesus.

The Holy Spirit is like a torchbearer at a native wedding. When a wedding procession passes through a city by night, the bridegroom, sitting on a bedecked horse, is accompanied by young men who hold up torches so the face of the bridegroom is illuminated.

So the Holy Spirit illuminates Jesus for us. He shows us, in the mirror of the Word, the face of our Savior. He makes bright and dear to us the Bridegroom of our souls. That is why we sing:

> *Holy Ghost, with light divine*
> *Shine upon this heart of mine;*
> *Chase the shades of night away,*
> *Turn the darkness into day.*
>
> *Let me see my Savior's face,*
> *Let me all His beauties trace;*
> *Show those glorious truth to me*
> *Which are only known to Thee. (TLH 234:1–2)*

I worship Thee, O Holy Ghost, I love to worship Thee: With Thee each day is Pentecost, Each night Nativity. Amen. (I Worship Thee, O Holy Ghost, verse 4)

Faith and Suffering

Yet if anyone suffers as a Christian, let him not be ashamed, but let him glorify God in that name. 1 Peter 4:16

The believer is here called Christian. The Bible uses this name only three times, here and in Acts 11:26 and 26:28. What glory for a sinner to be named after Christ! By true faith in Jesus Christ we are Christians.

Such honor and glory are not cheap. To be known as a Christian may cost us dearly. Everybody not a Christian who touches our lives will be of other opinions and ideas. Their manner of life will differ from ours. This in itself sets up a situation of tension. With continued exposure, clashes will occur. Such disunity becomes suffering and could take on violent form, even becoming physical.

When people revile us because we are believing Christians, we should not be dismayed. This is the price Christians must pay. This sort of suffering glorifies God. Of such suffering we must never be ashamed.

We thank Christ for suffering for us. His suffering established a right relationship again between us and God. His suffering removed from us the final suffering of damnation and hell. His suffering now makes our sufferings lighter, and we rejoice that we may participate with Him in them.

Dear Christ, when we glory, may it be only in Your cross. When we suffer, give us grateful hearts to be counted worthy to suffer for Your sake. Amen.

October

The Sermon in the Sacrament

For as often as you eat this bread and drink the cup, you proclaim the Lord's death until He comes. 1 Corinthians 11:26

When a sermon is delivered, the pastor does the preaching. But when the congregation comes to Holy Communion, the people also preach a sermon. By coming to Communion they declare a number of things about themselves, about God, and about the Lord's Supper.

What is the sermon in the Sacrament? Well, first of all, it declares: "We are sinful human beings. We need the forgiveness and life offered here in the body and blood of Christ."

The sermon in the Sacrament also declares that we have a Savior who forgives sin. He says to us: "This is My body, which is given for you. Do this in remembrance of Me. . . . This cup that is poured out for you is the new covenant in My blood" (Luke 22:19–20). We "proclaim the Lord's death until He comes" by joyously receiving the fruit of His death, namely, the personal assurance of forgiveness.

The sermon in the Sacrament also points out that we Christians are united with one another. "Because there is one bread, we who are many are one body, for we all partake of the one bread" (1 Corinthians 10:17).

The sermon in the Sacrament furthermore points to the glories of the life that is to come. It points to a risen Lord and to the heaven that is coming.

Finally, the sermon in the Sacrament declares that we who come intend to live a more consecrated Christian life with the help of God's Spirit.

Lord Jesus, grant that we come at all times worthily to Your Supper. Amen.

"This Is My Commandment"

"This is My commandment, that you love one another as I have loved you." John 15:12

An inner city rescue mission has posted this motto over its door: "Welcome to men and women who are welcome in no other place." The leader of the mission said: "We want to help those people particularly whom the world regards as 'not worth saving.' If the Lord Jesus had come to save those only who are 'worthy,' how many of us would be saved? 'While we were yet sinners, Christ died for us' (Romans 5:8 KJV)."

That mission understands our Lord's commandment: "That you love one another as I have loved you."

It is not difficult to love people who are lovable. Everyone loves a person who is kind, considerate, helpful, and who lives a decent, wholesome life. It is more difficult to love people who are mean and selfish, but it is most difficult of all to love those whose lives have been so ruined by sin that their outward appearance is repulsive and their minds and hearts are devoid of every decent impulse. Yet Jesus bids us love them with the same love with which He loved us.

We live solely because Jesus loves the unlovable. He recognized our needs of body and spirit, of time and eternity, and He gave His own self into death that He might help us. By His death He redeemed our bodies and souls from sin, death, and hell and saved us for a new and happier life on earth and for a life of perfect joy and peace in eternity.

O Lord, who has loved us with an everlasting love, fill our hearts and lives with love for our brethren. Amen.

October

"That Your Joy May Be Full"

*"These things I have spoken to you, that My joy may be in you,
and that your joy may be full." John 15:11*

Josef Haydn, the great composer, was asked why his
church music always sounded so happy and joyful. He replied:
"I cannot make it otherwise. I write according to the thoughts I
feel. When I think upon God, my heart is so full of joy that the
notes dance and leap, as it were, from my pen."

That is what Jesus meant when He said He had spoken
these things to His disciples in order that His own joy might
remain in them and their joy might be full and complete.

The world has its own prescription for happiness: "Eat,
drink, and be merry!" That is, make money, achieve fame, have
a good time, forget your troubles, and bear such as cannot be
forgotten with resignation! But that prescription does not result
in real happiness. The joys of the world are never full; at best
they last only a little while. The end is always despair.

A Christian's greatest joy is in the loving possession of
Jesus, in the fellowship he has with Jesus through His Word and
Spirit. This joy is really "full." It lifts a Christian above sorrow
and trouble, above the fleshly desire of momentary happiness,
and instills the deep joy of the Spirit. "You have sorrow now, but
I will see you again," promised Jesus, "and your hearts will
rejoice, and no one will take your joy from you" (John 16:22).

*Teach us, dear Lord, to understand and practice the things You have
spoken to us, that our hearts and lives may be filled with Your joy.
Amen.*

Bridging the Two Eternities

Knowing that you were ransomed from the futile ways inherited from your forefathers, not with perishable things such as silver or gold, but with the precious blood of Christ, like that of a lamb without blemish or spot. 1 Peter 1:18–19

No greater words than these are found outside Holy Scripture:

> I believe that Jesus Christ, true God, begotten of the Father from eternity, and also true man, born of the Virgin Mary, is my Lord, who has redeemed me, a lost and condemned person, purchased and won me from all sins, from death, and from the power of the devil; not with gold or silver, but with His holy, precious blood and with His innocent suffering and death, that I may be His own, and live under Him in His kingdom and serve Him in everlasting righteousness, innocence, and blessed-ness, just as He is risen from the dead, lives and reigns to all eternity. This is most certainly true. (*Luther's Small Catechism*)

The single, rising, gushing, deathless sentence from the pen of Luther bridges the two eternities.

"I believe that Jesus Christ, true God, begotten of the Father *from eternity*"—so it begins with Him who has no beginning. "That I may be His own, and live under Him in His kingdom and serve Him in everlasting righteousness, inno-cence, and blessedness, just as He is risen from the dead, lives and reigns *to all eternity*"—so it ends. He and I together with-out end. And in between—the manger, the cross, through which He "has redeemed me . . . purchased and won me . . . not with gold or silver, but with His holy, precious blood and with His innocent suffering and death." All this *for me*.

Thank You, Lord Jesus, for more than I can say or even summarize on my own. Amen.

Spiritual Poverty

"Blessed are the poor in spirit, for theirs is the kingdom of heaven." Matthew 5:3

No one enjoys or looks forward to being poor. In a land of plenty, it's considered a disgrace. We are constantly tempted to try and outdo one another in "keeping up with the Joneses" and in enjoying the good things of life.

Yet Jesus tells us to approach God as beggars. A beggar has no possessions of his own, but relies on the charity of others. So we must approach God. As beggars before God, we cannot rely on our own accomplishments, possessions, or works. We can only cast ourselves on the Lord's grace and mercy for help. This total reliance on God's grace and mercy is to remain with us all our life, whether we make a million dollars or live on state aid, whether we own a twenty-five room ranch house or live in the crowded ward of a welfare institution.

"For theirs is the kingdom of heaven." Those who come to the Lord as beggars receive more than an occasional coin. God gives them a great outpouring of eternal gifts: mercy, grace, complete pardon for all sins, and the guarantee of everlasting life, earned for them by their Christ and His cross and resurrection.

Humble us, O Lord, that in our spiritual poverty we may receive the riches of Your grace. Amen.

October

The Glorious Trinity

And one called to another and said: "Holy, holy, holy is the LORD of hosts; the whole earth is full of His glory!" Isaiah 6:3

Through trial and sin, the eyes of faith sometimes grow dim. We worry about the things of this life and grow very weary, and the cares of everyday life engulf us. So it is very refreshing to the soul to go back to the pages of the Holy Bible, realizing again that every word of it was breathed into the men of God by the Holy Ghost. And when we read prayerfully, the eyes of faith take on a new luster and we enlarge our thoughts about God.

"Holy, holy, holy is the LORD of hosts." The angels do well to cover their faces before Him as they approach His throne. And we do well to stand in awe and adoration before our God, who gave us life, who redeemed our lives from destruction, and who made us fellow citizens of the saints and members of the household of God.

In this life we shall always see through a glass darkly but it is possible to know God because Jesus Christ revealed God perfectly. In Christ God becomes known to us and we can only marvel over all that the Bible tells us about Him. Of course we know that the greatest thing about God, if indeed one thing is greater than another, is the love wherewith the holy God loved us in Christ Jesus our Lord.

O eternal and almighty God, protect us and keep us. O Jesus, lover of our souls, smile upon us and be gracious to us. O Holy Spirit, blessed Comforter, fill our hearts with the peace which passes understanding. Amen.

"In My Name"

"You did not choose me, but I chose you and appointed you that you should go and bear fruit and that your fruit should abide, so that whatever you ask the Father in My name, He may give it to you." John 15:16

"Help, dear St. Ann," cried young Martin Luther when a bolt of lightning struck near him and he fell, terrified, to the ground. St. Ann could not hear him or help him. Luther's prayer was spoken in vain, as he himself later realized.

A child of God addresses his prayers to his Father in heaven and to Him alone. Our Lord Himself taught us to pray "Our Father" and assured us that our prayers to our Father are heard by Him and are answered.

It is an amazing thought that every poor, sinful man can speak to Almighty God Himself and be heard by Him. Is it possible? There are so many of us, and we each of us are so unworthy of this honor!

Yet Jesus promises: "Whatever you ask the Father *in My name.*" Praying in the name of Jesus does not mean merely that our prayer must have the name of Jesus added to it. It means that we speak to God through faith in Jesus, our Savior. We trust that He will intercede for us with the Father; that He is the way, and the only way, to the Father's heart; that He is the key, and the only key, to the Father's storehouse of blessings.

Teach us, dear Lord, to pray, and to pray without ceasing in Your name. Amen.

Dry Bones

Then He said to me, "Son of man, these bones are the whole house of Israel. Behold, they say, 'Our bones are dried up, and our hope is lost; we are clean cut off.'" Ezekiel 37:11

The children of Israel had become unfaithful to the Lord. They had refused to listen to the warnings of the prophets of God. Instead they had supported those false prophets who had told them what they wanted to hear. They were a religious people, but they had chosen their own way to worship God and had followed after false gods. For these sins they had been punished. The armies of Babylon had taken Jerusalem, burned it to the ground, and led the people into captivity.

The prophet Ezekiel compares fallen Israel to a deserted valley covered with the bleached and dried bones of the dead in our reading for today. It would be difficult to find a picture of greater hopelessness and despair. Surely there was nothing that could be done for people who had fallen so low. But God promised that He would send His Spirit to these fallen sinners. By the working of the Holy Ghost they would once more become God's people. The dry bones would live again by the power of the Holy Spirit.

Dry bones may well be a picture of all men before they come to Christ. They are dead in trespasses and sins. They can do nothing to save themselves. They cannot even accept the water of life when it is offered to them. But in the vision of Ezekiel, the dry bones lived again when the prophet spoke to them the words of God. The words of the Lord still have the same power today. By the simple preaching of the Gospel, the Holy Ghost makes men alive in that they see themselves lost in sin, but saved by the Son of God.

Holy Spirit, grant us always the gift of life in Christ. Amen.

"The Lord Takes Thought for Me"

As for me, I am poor and needy, but the LORD takes thought for me. You are my help and my deliverer; do not delay, O my God! Psalm 40:17

According to our way of thinking, God must be very busy with the task of controlling and directing the affairs and the events of the world. He "upholds the universe by the word of His power" (Hebrews 1:3).

Since God has so many things to do, we might think that He would have no time to concern Himself with the life of each creature on earth. Yet the Bible assures us that God is interested in the welfare of every person on earth.

"The LORD takes thought for me." What a wondrous truth! Whenever we are burdened with problems and worries; whenever our hearts are filled with disappointments; whenever we seem to be without a friend in the world—each one of us should recall the cheering words: "The LORD takes thought for me."

The Lord thought about the sad situation into which our sins had plunged us and sent His Son to pay the penalty for our sins. Because His Son has redeemed us, God the Father lovingly thinks about each one of us and is deeply concerned about our bodily and spiritual well-being.

As children of God we can go about our daily tasks with the golden assurance of Scripture resounding in our hearts: "The LORD takes thought for me."

Lord Jesus, think on me! Keep me in Your grace. Amen.

October

Blind Eyes

The natural person does not accept the things of the Spirit of God, for they are folly to him, and he is not able to understand them because they are spiritually discerned. 1 Corinthians 2:14

Some people claim that years ago, when men did not know as much as they know today, it was easier to believe in the Bible. It is also said by some that if we want men to accept the Word of God, we must first revise it to make it fit better with the views of modern man.

There is nothing wrong with the Bible. There is something wrong with man. It is not the Bible that needs to be changed or converted. We cannot make a blind man see by improving the brightness of the sun. It simply is not true that people no longer believe the Bible because they are more intelligent than people were in days gone by. Men reject the Word of God because they are just as wicked as their fathers were. For in ancient times, too, men refused to believe the Word of God. Isaiah preached clearly about the Savior who was to come, but men would not accept his message. He had to complain, "Lord, who has believed what he heard from us?" (John 12:38). And it was not a group of twentieth-century college graduates, but first-century Athenians who laughed at Paul's preaching in Acts 17.

It will always seem like foolishness to human reason to say that God died on a cross and our crimes are paid for by the death of another. Christians believe this good news for only one reason: because the Holy Ghost has opened our blind eyes.

Heavenly Father, help us always to see that the foolishness of God is wiser than men. Amen.

We Have a Representative

My little children, I am writing these things to you so that you may not sin. But if anyone does sin, we have an advocate with the Father, Jesus Christ the righteous. 1 John 2:1

An advocate is a representative, an attorney, one who talks to the judge for us. Our Lord and Savior, Jesus Christ, is our eternal advocate before the eternal Judge on high. Of Him the Bible says: "Consequently, He is able to save to the uttermost those who draw near to God through Him, since He always lives to make intercession for them" (Hebrews 7:25).

He is the *only* advocate, the *only* One who has been divinely empowered to represent the sinner before the court of heaven. St. Paul says: "For there is one God, and there is one mediator between God and men, the man Christ Jesus, who gave Himself as ransom for all, which is the testimony given at the proper time" (1 Timothy 2:5–6). Through Christ, and through Christ alone, we have free access to the Father.

What a comfort in days of sorrow, particularly when our heart is weighted down with the heavy burden of guilt or shame, to know that we have a representative in heaven and to know that because He has died for us, He has won for us a place with the Father! He is indeed able to save us "to the uttermost."

Lord Jesus, be my advocate. Amen.

Celestial Music

And they sang a new song, saying, "Worthy are You to take the scroll and to open its seals, for You were slain, and by Your blood You ransomed people for God from every tribe and language and people and nation." Revelation 5:9

Music, like a genuine smile, is essentially the same in all languages. It exalts the soul. It sooths the ruffled spirit. It makes the heart feel more gentle, tender, discreet. Said Luther, "Music is one of the fairest and most glorious gifts of God, to which Satan is a bitter enemy; for it removes from the heart the weight of sorrow and fascination of evil thoughts. . . . I would have all arts, especially music, placed in the service of Him who gave and created them."

Handel, composer of *The Messiah*, exclaimed: "But what is all this compared to the grandest of all makers of harmony above?" Music is the speech of angels, an art of heaven given to earth and returning in perfected measure with us to heaven. One picture of the saints above is that they sing and that they love.

Out on Bethlehem's fields that first glad Christmas night, angels from the realms of glory thrilled the shepherds, wide-eyed with wonder, with their celestial melodies. It is the voice of rejoicing and salvation, and we shall join in the theme song of the Lamb that was slain and redeemed us to God by His blood!

Lord God, we join the angels and the community of saints in singing our praises to You. Amen.

"You Shall Not Die"

And the king said to Shimei, "You shall not die." And the king gave him his oath. 2 Samuel 19:23

As king, David held the power of life or death over Shimei, a relative of King Saul. Shimei's earlier actions made him worthy of death. He had cursed David openly and publicly. According to ancient law this act was punishable by death. But David showed kindness to Shimei and assured him that he would not die for his sin.

Not long before this David had heard these same words from the prophet Nathan. Having been brought to the knowledge of his sins of adultery and murder, David confessed, "I have sinned against the LORD" (2 Samuel 12:13). Thereupon the prophet assured him, "The LORD also has put away your sin; you shall not die" (2 Samuel 12:13). Having received forgiveness from God, he could also show mercy to Shimei.

For all of us, Jesus, the Son of David, has procured forgiveness of sins and pardon from eternal death. While any sin we commit is deserving of death and damnation, we receive, instead, mercy and forgiveness. This is true because Christ has redeemed us from the curse of the Law (death), when He went into the jaws of death for us. Death has lost its sting, its power to destroy. Because Christ died and rose again, we, too, shall live.

Lord Jesus, Lord of life and death, cheer us with the hope of a blessed immortality. Amen.

Angels

For He will command His angels concerning you to guard you in all your ways. Psalm 91:11

Isaiah in a vision saw the Lord "sitting upon a throne, high and lifted up; and the train of His robe filled the temple. Above Him stood the seraphim. Each had six wings: with two he covered his face, and with two he covered his feet, and with two he flew. And one called to another and said: 'Holy, holy, holy is the LORD of hosts; the whole earth is full of His glory!'" (Isaiah 6:1–3). Angels praise God, in accordance with His Word: "Bless the LORD, O you His angels, you mighty ones who do His word, obeying the voice of His word" (Psalm 103:20).

Angels also serve us. The prophet Elisha and his servant were surrounded by the Syrian army at Dothan. The servant was frightened. Elisha prayed. "So the LORD opened the eyes of the young man, and he saw, and behold, the mountain was full of horses and chariots of fire all around Elisha" (2 Kings 6:17).

"Are they not all ministering spirits sent out to serve for the sake of those who are to inherit salvation?" (Hebrews 1:14).

What a comfort to the Church of the living Christ and to His believers that He shall give His angels charge over us to keep us in all our ways, to defend us and our children against all the powers of evil, and finally to carry our souls to the mansion that Christ Jesus, by His death and resurrection, prepared for us in our Father's house.

Give Your angels charge over me, O Lord, to guard me in all my ways. Amen.

October

Christ the High Priest

He himself bore our sins in His body on the tree, that we might die to sin and live to righteousness. By His wounds you have been healed. 1 Peter 2:24

On the great Day of Atonement in the Old Testament, a lamb without blemish was slain. The high priest, with the twelve precious stones engraved with the names of the twelve tribes of Israel on his breast, took the blood of the lamb into the Holy of Holies. There he sprinkled the blood on the mercy seat, the golden cover of the Ark of the Covenant. In the Ark lay the two tablets of stone on which was written the Law of God. This sacred act reminded the people of their sins and of God's grace and pardon. The high priest sacrificed, prayed, and blessed the people.

The high priest was a living prophecy of Christ, the one and only mediator between God and man. The Lamb of God sacrificed Himself on the altar of the cross. His blood cleanses us from all sin. "For by a single offering He has perfected for all time those who are being sanctified" (Hebrews 10:14). "If anyone does sin, we have an advocate with Father, Jesus Christ the righteous. He is the propitiation for our sins, and not for ours only but also for the sins of the whole world" (1 John 2:1–2).

O Christ, O Lamb of God, we thank You that by Your atoning grace You have restored us to God in heaven. Keep us steadfast in faith that we fall not from Your loving care. Amen.

A Well

As he looked, he saw a well in the field, and behold, three flocks of sheep lying beside it, for out of that well the flocks were watered. The stone on the well's mouth was large. Genesis 29:2

Only those who have experienced real thirst can appreciate the value of a well. When Jacob, weary and thirsty, came near Haran, he spied a well and rejoiced. Two thousand years later, the woman of Samaria told Jesus: "Our father Jacob . . . gave us the well" (John 4:12). Jacob's well provided thirst-quenching relief to all who sought it out and used it.

Are we in our day thankful to our heavenly Father for the bountiful supply of drinking water that we enjoy in the corporate worship of the church? How grateful are we for the spiritual wells in our churches? Here Jesus offers us the same spiritual water He gave to the woman of Sychar when He said: "Everyone who drinks of this water will be thirsty again, but whoever drinks of the water that I will give him will never be thirsty forever. The water that I will give him will become in him a spring of water welling up to eternal life" (John 4:13–14). To Israel God said through Isaiah: "With joy you will draw water from the wells of salvation" (Isaiah 12:3). The Gospel of God's redeeming love in Christ is an ever-flowing fountain of living water. "Come, everyone who thirsts, come to the waters" (Isaiah 55:1). "The Spirit and the Bride say, 'Come.' And let the one who hears say, 'Come.' And let the one who is thirsty come; let the one who desires take the water of life without price" (Revelation 22:17).

In Christ, the deepest thirst of the soul is fully quenched, and by His power we shall remain satisfied by this well of life to all eternity!

Lord Jesus, teach us to appreciate the water of life in the Gospel of Your forgiving and sanctifying love. Amen.

Our Holy Gospel

Now I would remind you, brothers, of the gospel I preached to you, which you received, in which you stand, and by which you are being saved, if you hold fast to the word I preached to you— unless you believed in vain. 1 Corinthians 15:1–2

What is the Gospel? Suppose you were to write down the answer, what would you write? Suppose someone in spiritual distress was to ask you, what would you say? For our own good and the good of others, and especially for the honor of Christ, we ought to have in heart and mind an adequate answer to the question: "What is the Gospel?"

The word "gospel" is derived from the words *good spell*. The word "spell" is an old English word meaning story or news. The word gospel means good news. It is the good news that Jesus is our Prophet, Savior, and King.

The Gospel is the good news that our sin debt has been paid in full by Christ crucified and that we stand pure and justified before God through faith in His Son.

This Gospel is the best of all blessings, for it is the power of God for salvation for every believer. It is God's power to cover our sins, to give hope and life to the sinner, to impart that peace which passes all understanding.

God's Word promises that we who have received the Gospel in faith, who stand on the Gospel, and who continue in it will be saved. Only the Gospel can do that. Therefore we ought to prize and cherish the Gospel, rejoice in it, cling to it, and proclaim it to others. It is God's promise of a forgiving Savior and an open heaven.

Lord Jesus, good and gracious Savior, we thank You sincerely for the good news of forgiveness, life, and salvation. Now help us to welcome You as our Savior-King and to serve You in all goodness, through the Holy Spirit. Amen.

October

Don't Say It

Keep your tongue from evil and your lips from speaking deceit.
Psalm 34:13

A very old woman kept an inflamed and festering sore in the depths of her personality. There she had harbored what she considered were unkind words spoken by someone in an unguarded moment fifty years before. Now, near the close of life's journey, she was unforgiving and resentful.

What careers have been ruined, what cherished plans shattered, what graves dug by cruel and thoughtless words! Our words, once uttered, may go on either singing or sobbing, healing or hurting, inspiring or depressing to the end of life's day. Whether we appreciate it or not, the words we utter reveal what we really are, and thus we pass judgment on ourselves.

One who for long years has studied human behavior gives this deliberate judgment: "No man is better than his gossip. He may preach like an archangel, he may work like a Trojan, he may give like a prince; but it is by his gossip that he must be judged."

The tongue merely utters what lies within. If the fountain be impure, the flow of water must necessarily be so. It is impossible to have a tongue that speaks words of healing unless the heart is clean and pure.

Thank God there is such a cleansing. "The blood of Jesus His Son cleanses us from all sin" (1 John 1:7). He has pardoned you and forgiven all your sins! Then, when the heart is clean, the tongue shall speak words that encourage, cheer, and help.

Forgive us, gentle Savior, the sins of our tongue and give us a greater measure of Your Spirit that what we say may not hurt but heal. Amen.

October

Only One Lord and Savior

I, I am the LORD, and besides Me there is no savior. Isaiah 43:11

There is only one God. Israel knew and professed to believe this. We also know this and confess it. But in Israel many denied their professed faith by joining idolatrous practices of the heathens around them. Even so today. Many members of Christian churches recite the Apostolic Creed on Sundays, professing faith in the Triune God, but during the week they engage in idolatrous practices of a subtler kind, by joining in prayer directed to some nondescript "god" who does not really exist and by giving first place to other interests. When St. Paul came to Athens, his heart was stirred at the sight of the altar dedicated "to the unknown god" (Acts 17:23), and promptly he made known to them the true God and Jesus, our Savior and judge.

Only *one* God; only *one* Savior; only *One* who *has* delivered mankind from the power of sin and Satan. In this mighty forty-third chapter of Isaiah, the Lord is beautifully blending Law and Gospel; He seeks to impress His people with His majesty and holiness on the one hand and with His love and redeeming grace on the other. Marvelous and merciful God! He spared not His own Son; on Him He laid the iniquities of us all. In Christ we have redemption through His blood! Wondrous love! "There is salvation in no one else, for there is no other name under heaven given among men by which we must be saved" (Acts 4:12).

O God, forgive us the idolatry of our wayward hearts. Have mercy upon us for Jesus' sake. Sanctify us by Your Spirit. Amen.

The Heaven of God

"He will wipe away every tear from their eyes, and death shall be no more, neither shall there be mourning nor crying nor pain anymore, for the former things have passed away." Revelation 21:4

By the blood and suffering of our Lord Jesus Christ, God has taken us from the way of sin and set our feet on the road to heaven. By faith in our blessed Savior we are now pilgrims on a road that leads upward to paradise. The earth is not our home. We walk through it as a pilgrim through a strange land, a part of the life around us, and yet always free, so free that nothing can harm us and nothing can dismay us. We are citizens of heaven, whose eyes of faith already see the dawn of God's eternal day.

In the modern world there are too many things on earth that draw our thoughts away from heaven. Our daily work, our troubles, our difficulties, turn our eyes downward. It is good, therefore, to see God's heaven in nature. As we see the glory of the sky on a clear summer night, it speaks to us of the glory of heaven, our eternal home.

When our Lord ascended into heaven and the disciples stood gazing after Him, two angels appeared and said: "Why do you stand looking into heaven? This Jesus, who was taken up from you into heaven, will come in the same way as you saw Him go into heaven" (Acts 1:11). This is our sure faith. Here God has given us a life to live, work to do, burdens to bear, but through them all we can see the heaven our Savior bought for us. He has gone before; we follow. His home is our home.

Lord Jesus, keep our eyes fixed, we pray You, on the eternal home You have prepared for us. Amen.

The Upper Room

"And he will show you a large upper room furnished; prepare it there." Luke 22:12

On the night that Jesus was betrayed, He gathered His disciples in an upper room to institute the Lord's Supper. The Passover meal preceded the giving of the Sacrament. Why? Because the next day Jesus was to be the real Passover Lamb of God, offered for the sin of the whole world. Out of the Passover covenant would come the new testament covenant of grace, in and through which Christ gives His body and blood.

Having finished the meal, Jesus took the bread and the cup, saying: "Take eat; this is My body. . . . Drink of it, all of you, for this is My blood" (Matthew 26:26–28). He gives Himself that you and I might have forgiveness of sin and our soul find peace. "With His stripes we are healed" (Isaiah 53:5). Through this Sacrament Jesus seals to us the full forgiveness of all sin.

In giving us the Lord's Supper, Jesus gave us the way in which we show forth His death until He comes. Every time the church administers the Lord's Supper, it confesses that Jesus is coming again. Each Communion urges us to make ready for His return. Washed and cleansed through the Lord's Supper, we live in His grace and can look forward to His return without fear, for there is no condemnation to them who are in Christ Jesus.

Friend of sinners, make our hearts ever ready to receive Your supper worthily and to go on our way with the joy of forgiveness in our hearts. Amen.

Asleep in Jesus

Then David slept with his fathers and was buried in the city of David. 1 Kings 2:10

Notice the euphemism in today's verse: "David slept with his fathers." Why not simply say, "David died"? Does describing death in gentle terms take away its terror?

Let's face death's realities, like David did. He saw death approaching and said, "I am about to go the way of all the earth" (1 Kings 2:2). Even in the prime of life he said, "There is but a step between me and death" (1 Samuel 20:3).

But God also faced the reality of death. Because He faced it and defeated it for us in His Son Jesus, it has lost its fear for us. "Therefore, just as sin came into the world through one man, and death through sin, and so death spread to all men because all sinned" (Romans 5:12). But God did something about the reality of death. When Jesus, God's Son, died on the cross, He conquered death, that is, He took away death's power to destroy and condemn. And when Jesus rose again from the dead, He established for all time the glorious hope of resurrection and life eternal.

And so the euphemism. This is not mere sugarcoating, but the reality created for us in Christ. Christians do not die, but they fall asleep in Jesus. This isn't merely polite language; this is the expression of the faith that the dead in Christ will awaken unto life everlasting. We weep and lament when lifelong ties are broken by death. But we do not sorrow as those who have no hope. Our hope is in Jesus, the conqueror of death and hell.

Lord, keep us ever mindful of the approach of death. Increase our faith that we may fall asleep in You. Amen.

Conquering Through Christ

God raised Him up, loosing the pangs of death, because it was not possible for Him to be held by it. Acts 2:24

It was Pentecost in Jerusalem. As the news spread through the city of the wonders that had just happened, a crowd of people gathered about the apostles. Peter stepped forward and began to speak. His theme was Jesus, "a man attested to you by God with mighty works and wonders and signs" (Acts 2:22). Peter reminded his listeners of what they had done to Him. Out of spite and hate they had killed Him.

But death, mighty as it is, could not hold Him. Here was One mightier than death. At last death had met its master.

Sin cannot hold those who have been joined to Christ, for Christ has freed them from sin and its guilt. Satan cannot hold them, for Christ has delivered them from his power. The trials of life cannot hold them down, for through Christ they endure their troubles, declared to be "more than conquerors" (Romans 8:37). Death cannot hold them, for through Christ they, too, shall burst the bonds of death and rise to everlasting life.

Since it was not possible for death to hold Christ, it is not possible for any power to stop the onward march of His Gospel and His kingdom. Men have tried to silence the voice of the Gospel, but it will not be stilled. They have tried to destroy His Church, but it will outlast all their feeble efforts and remain the Kingdom eternal.

O Christ, give us grace to conquer through You. Amen.

Christ the King

On His robe and on His thigh He has a name written, King of kings and Lord of lords. Revelation 19:16

Jesus is "the blessed and only Sovereign, the King of kings and Lord of lords" (1 Timothy 6:15). He has all power and authority in heaven and on earth. Nation might rise against nation. Ungodly rulers might cause confusion and disaster. Our Savior King, however, has the destiny of individuals and of nations in His almighty hand. We are safe under His loving care.

God put all things under His feet and gave Him to be the Head over all things to the Church. The Church, the true believers in Christ, is God's chief concern. In His Church, in His kingdom of grace, Jesus rules with His grace by His Holy Spirit through the Gospel and the holy Sacraments. Gladly we ought to hear and believe His holy Word and lead godly lives according to it.

Jesus redeemed us that we might be His own, live under Him in His kingdom of grace, serve and obey Him, and finally be received into His kingdom of glory. "To Him be the dominion forever and ever. Amen" (1 Peter 5:11).

Lord Jesus, True and Living Head, grant us a greater awareness of what it means to live in Your kingdom. Amen.

Too Good to Be True

For you did not receive the spirit of slavery to fall back into fear, but you have received the Spirit of adoption as sons, by whom we cry, "Abba! Father!" Romans 8:15

Often the Gospel of salvation seems too good to be true. As we reflect on these wonderful promises, we are tempted to ask, "Can this really be so?"

Yet, because the Spirit works by powerful persuasion, and because He creates within us the very gift of faith by which we believe, each and every Christian is able to believe each and every amazing promise of the Gospel with genuine certainty and conviction. The power to believe is not the product of logic, based on experience, nor is it a blind groping by man for some defense against the storms of life. The Gospel is the power of God, and, therefore, we can rely on its message with all our life and strength.

Through His Word, the Sacraments, divine worship, prayer, Christian fellowship—through these means the Holy Spirit instructs and nurtures us in the amazing truth of the Gospel. We receive the assurance that God is, indeed, our loving Father and we His beloved children, heirs with Christ of eternal life.

Spirit of Adoption,
Make us overflow
With Thy sevenfold blessing
And in grace to grow. Amen. (TLH 229:6)

My Wonderful Baptism

For as many of you as were baptized into Christ have put on Christ. Galatians 3:27

As the young boy made his way up the steps to bed, he remarked to his mother, "Mommy, my hands are clean now. The dirt's washed down the drain. All gone."

Human hearts, like human hands, get dirty every day, dirty with the sins of pride, selfish thoughts, and selfish deeds. We see how dirty our hearts are when we hold them up to the mirror of God's Law.

Human hearts, like human hands, should be washed regularly. Martin Luther wrote in the *Small Catechism* that the Old Adam in us, our sinful self, should by daily contrition and repentance be drowned and die with all sins and evil lusts.

Many of us had our first spiritual cleansing when we were baptized. It was at our Baptism that God washed away our former evil nature and gave us a new life. It was at our Baptism that God planted in us a new faith in Him.

It is important for us Christians to think of our Baptism daily. The thought of our Baptism reminds us of a loving God, who for the sake of His Son Jesus Christ daily forgives us all our sins. It reminds us that God washes them down the drain when we confess our sins. They're all gone; washed onto Jesus.

Because of the new life that Christ gives to us in Baptism, we rise daily to live before Him "in righteousness and purity forever" (*Luther's Small Catechism*).

Lord, help us to think often of our wonderful Baptism. Amen.

Faith Grows

We ought always to give thanks to God for you, brothers, as is right, because your faith is growing abundantly, and the love of every one of you for one another is increasing. 2 Thessalonians 1:3

Holy Scripture declares repeatedly that faith in Christ is a living, growing thing. St. Paul thanks God because the faith of the Thessalonians is growing exceedingly. Holy Scripture is just as clear in stating that we grow through the Word of God. St. Peter puts this truth very graphically when he urges us to be like newborn babes in our desire for the pure milk of the Word that we may thereby grow (1 Peter 2:2).

It is good for us to remember these simple truths of Scripture not only on Sunday but also in our daily use of the Word in family and private devotions. Our relationship with God is a friendship that becomes strong and deep by association. When we read the Holy Scriptures, we are associating with God, listening to Him speak. How we respond to God through prayer, meditation, and praise depends upon what we have heard God say to us. Reading and hearing the Word is fellowship with God, togetherness with Him. Because this is true, Bible reading and study ought never to be dull and uninteresting. It is always a means whereby our faith grows. It is always the cultivation of our friendship with God. It is always listening to Him who loves us eternally.

When Christians live impoverished spiritual lives, the reason is easily seen. They are neglecting or not fully using the Word of God. God alone can give us faith. God alone can make it grow. He gives us faith and causes it to grow through His Word with the power of the Holy Spirit.

Divine Savior, increase our faith day by day. Amen.

October

The Threatening Blackout

For in it the righteousness of God is revealed from faith for faith,
as it is written, "The righteous shall live by faith." Romans 1:17

Not many sermons in the Christian Church may truly be called *Gospel* sermons. This writer once read a volume containing fifty sermons written by as many prominent preachers of our day. Under every sermon in which I found as much as one single Gospel statement, I made a cross. When I finished, I counted the crosses. There were *three*.

As I put the book away, there came to mind the words of Luther's hymn:

O Lord, look down from heav'n, behold
And let Thy pity waken;
How few are we within Thy fold,
Thy saints by men forsaken!
True faith seems quenched on ev'ry hand,
Men suffer not Thy Word to stand;
Dark times have us o'ertaken. (TLH 260:1)

What is needed today—in the pulpit and out of it—is a renewed, sustained, everlasting emphasis on this truth: Man is justified—is declared just before God—for the crucified Redeemer's sake. "This article," says Luther—and his words are as true today as they were in the days of the Reformation—"is the chief thing and the cornerstone, which alone begets, strengthens, preserves, and protects the church of God, and without it the church cannot exist for one hour."

Preserve Your Church, dear Savior. Send out Your light. Amen.

October

The Open Bible—Our Reformation Heritage

Now these Jews were more noble than those in Thessalonica; they received the word with all eagerness, examining the Scriptures daily to see if these things were so. Acts 17:11

It happened in Berea on the apostle Paul's second missionary trip. There Paul told the Jews about Jesus, declaring that He was the promised Messiah and Savior. After listening to him, the people went home and "[examined] the Scriptures daily to see if these things were so." Paul's word was not enough. Did his teaching agree with the Scriptures? To them the Scriptures were the highest authority. Having searched the Scriptures, they believed the Gospel Paul taught—not because he spoke it, but because the Scriptures taught it.

It was Martin Luther who, by the grace and guidance of God, opened the Bible again after it had almost become a closed book. It was Luther who put the open Bible back into the hands of the people so each man was free to search the Scriptures for himself. It was Luther who restored the Bible as the supreme authority and only rule in matters of faith and life. It was Luther who, after great spiritual struggle, discovered in the Bible the key to the soul's forgiveness and peace with God. That key is the truth that a sinner is forgiven and justified alone by the grace of God, through faith in Christ, without the deeds of the Law. It was this good news that Paul preached in Berea, that the Bereans discovered in the Scriptures, and that Luther rediscovered and restored to the world. This same good news guards and sustains God's people yet today.

O Lord, keep us by Your grace in Your saving truth. Amen.

Our Reformation Heritage

So Jesus said to the Jews who had believed in Him, "If you abide in My word, you are truly My disciples." John 8:31

Today is the festival of the Reformation. Whether we shall continue to enjoy the priceless blessing of Luther's Reformation—the doctrine of salvation by grace through faith—depends upon whether we continue in the living Word of the living Christ: "If you abide in My Word, you are truly My disciples."

The Church is to continue in Christ's Word. And who is the Church? The Church is you and me. The Church is everyone who gathers in faith around God's Word and His Sacraments. You and I are to continue in God's Word if we are to remain His disciples.

What has our record been in this respect? Are we familiar with our Bible or has it become a stranger to us? Are we regular, conscientious, and attentive in our use of Word and Sacrament as they are dispensed to us at church? How zealous have we been in our personal searching of the Scriptures? We shall not long remain "free" if we neglect "the truth," and we shall not long remember "the truth" if we do not diligently continue in God's Word.

Luther once said that the Gospel is like a traveling shower; it does not remain long in one place. History has shown his words to be all too true. Let us on this day, then, pray in repentance that God would not take His Word and Spirit from us. Such prayers God loves to hear for the sake of His Son Jesus, who died to set us free.

Lord Jesus, grant that I may remain ever faithful to Your Word. And grant that through Your Word I may be forever free. Amen.

Sons of God

See what kind of love the Father has given to us, that we should be called children of God; and so we are. The reason why the world does not know us is that it did not know Him. 1 John 3:1

"In the mercy of almighty God, Jesus Christ was given to die for us, and for His sake God forgives us all our sins. To those who believe in Jesus Christ, He gives power to become the children of God and bestows on them the Holy Spirit. May the Lord, who has begun this good work in us, bring it to completion in the day of our Lord Jesus Christ. Amen." These are familiar, comforting words from the liturgies of the various hymnals available to our church body!

"Children of God." What an honor! What a privilege that we, once children of wrath because of our sins, should now, by faith in Jesus Christ, be called children of God! "And so we are!" Now we are no longer strangers to God and foreigners, but fellow citizens with the saints and of the household of God. We belong to those of whom Jesus said, "No longer do I call you servants, for the servant does not know what his master is doing; but I have called you friends, for all that I have heard from My Father I have made known to you" (John 15:15).

Through our adoption as children of God, we have the assurance of forgiveness of all our sins, peace with God, the privilege of prayer, the comfort of His companionship, a sure guide for living, and the pleasant prospect of an eternal home. "See what kind of love the Father has given to us, that we should be called children of God."

Father in heaven, we thank You for Your love. Help us to be loyal children of Your household. Amen.

The Greater Savior

"For the Son of Man came to seek and to save the lost." Luke 19:10

One day, relates Luther, the devil came to him and said: "Martin, you are a great sinner; therefore you are damned."

"Stop," cried Luther, "one thing at a time! It is true; I am a great sinner. What next?"

"Therefore you are damned," growled the devil.

"No," answered Luther, "that is poor reasoning. I am a great sinner; *therefore I am saved*, for it is written: 'Jesus Christ came into the world to seek and *to save that which was lost.'*"

"So," concludes Luther, "I cut the devil's head off with his own sword, and he went away mourning because he could not cast me down by calling me a sinner."

Our sins are not trifles. One look at Calvary ought to make us hate every sin. But the same hill also tells us that the devil is lying when he says our sins are too great to be forgiven. Great as our sins may be, we have a greater Savior. "The Son of Man came to seek and to save the lost"—*me*. Fling that at the hellish Goliath you see in your temptations!

O Lord God, count not our many transgressions against us. In Your mercy, remove them all. Lift us to Yourself, and give peace of heart and mind through Jesus Christ, our Lord and Redeemer. Amen.

Unsearchable Love

And to know the love of Christ that surpasses knowledge, that you may be filled with all the fullness of God. Ephesians 3:19

In this well-known passage from the Letter to the Ephesians, St. Paul exhausts the possibilities of human language in an effort to describe the love of Christ. He adds a fourth dimension to the usual three when he prays that you "may have strength to comprehend with all the saints what is the breadth and length and height and depth, and to know the love of Christ that surpasses knowledge, that you may be filled with all the fullness of God" (Ephesians 3:18–19).

The human mind simply cannot fathom a love so deep, so divine, that it could tear the eternal Son from the bosom of the Father and cause Him to suffer and to die for a world of sinners. Such love, indeed, surpasses knowledge.

Men sometimes make the mistake of trying to understand the great truths of our salvation—the truth of God's love, the truth of Christ's atonement, the truth of full and free forgiveness through faith in His atoning blood.

We need not understand the solar system to be armed by the light of the sun. We need not know the chemical formula for a drop of water to be refreshed by a cooling spring. Nor need we fathom the mind of God to know that He loves us and that through Christ we have become His own. For that we need merely trust—through the faith that He Himself has given to us—His eternal Word of promise.

Why Thou couldst ever love me so, And be the God Thou art, Is darkness to my intellect, But sunshine to my heart. Amen. (Frederick William Faber)

Does God Mean Me?

"All that the Father gives Me will come to Me, and whoever comes to Me I will never cast out." John 6:37

Martin Luther once said that he was glad God never mentioned him by name in any of the Gospel promises. If the Bible had ever said that Christ came into the world to save Martin Luther, he could not have been sure that *he* was the Martin Luther who was meant, for the world has had other Martin Luthers.

The great Reformer found his greatest comfort in the fact that the Gospel promises are general, universal, and all-inclusive. "For God so loved the world, that He gave His only Son, that whoever believes in Him should not perish but have eternal life" (John 3:16).

That "whoever" was Luther's source of assurance. That, he was sure, included him. And likewise a host of other Gospel promises. "Whoever comes to Me I will never cast out." That "whoever" included Martin Luther.

And that "whoever" includes us. In our weaker moments we may doubt that God's promises are really for *us*. We may think that *our* particular sins are too great, too numerous, to be included in the Gospel's offer of forgiveness, that we have strayed too far, sinned too often! We *cannot* be included!

But there stands that word—"whoever!" "Whoever believes." Yes, that does include each of us. "Though [my] sins are like scarlet, they shall be as white snow; though they are red like crimson, they shall become like wool" (Isaiah 1:18).

Thank You, dear Jesus, that Your promises include even me. Amen.

"Keep Them from the Evil"

"But now I am coming to You, and these things I speak in the world, that they may have My joy fulfilled in themselves. I have given them Your word, and the world has hated them because they are not of the world, just as I am not of the world. I do not ask that You take them out of the world, but that You keep them from the evil one. They are not of the world, just as I am not of the world." John 17:13–16

The world hates Jesus, and the world hates the followers of Jesus. Neither He nor they are of the world.

Some people might think that the best way for us to escape the hatred of the world is for God to take us and all Christians out of the world. That would be the simplest way to escape from the world's hatred. But that cannot be. The followers of Jesus have important business in the world. They are to make Jesus known to men and so save out of the world as many as possible. Necessarily that brings them into contact with the world and exposes them to the world's hatred. But such is the will of God.

So Jesus prays instead that God would keep His disciples from the evil one. Satan would repeat in every Christian's life the victory he once gained in Eden. He would lead astray God's children and so win them for himself again. We know how powerfully he tempts us, how utterly lost we would be were it not for the protecting power of God. Jesus has pleaded for this protection, and therefore we always are sure of it. Although we be sifted as wheat, our faith will not fail because it is not ours. God has given it to us and God cannot fail!

You know how weak I am, O Lord. In every trial be my strength and my confidence of faith. Amen.

Not Another Gospel

I am astonished that you are so quickly deserting Him who called you in the grace of Christ and are turning to a different gospel—not that there is another one, but there are some who trouble you and want to distort the gospel of Christ. Galatians 1:6–7

It is quite common to hear people say that there are various ways to get to heaven and it does not matter much which way we select. Statements like this have a tremendous appeal because of the tolerance and broadmindedness they seem to reveal. Yet it is certain from today's verse that St. Paul did not share this kind of tolerance. He refuses to concede that there can be another gospel in the sense that it is on the same level of truth and authority as is the Gospel he preaches. There can be another gospel only in the sense that some people are perverting the Gospel of Christ. St. Paul could not have claimed that there is only one true and saving Gospel in a more emphatic way. This Gospel is the one he received from Christ and this Gospel he is preaching to the Galatians.

There are in fact only two religions in the world, one that lives by the Gospel of Christ and the other that rejects this Gospel. This is just another way of saying that every person believes either that he has been saved by the merits of Christ or that he must and can save himself. For the supreme question: How can we be saved? There is only one right answer—the answer of God, "Believe in the Lord Jesus" (Acts 16:31). There is not another gospel. There is no salvation possible for man except that which Christ fully achieved when on the cross He took away the sin of the world.

Father in heaven, let no one rob us of the hope of Jesus' Gospel. Amen.

This Is Success

For to me to live is Christ, and to die is gain. Philippians 1:21

Bud Fisher, a cartoonist who was the highest-paid newspaper contributor in the world at one point, once said: "Success is getting what you go after."

Of course, but what is worth going after? Monetary success? But at what point are you successful? A million dollars? Ten million dollars? Is fame the mark of success? Does seeing your name in lights mean you're successful? *What is success?*

Paul, God's beautiful fool, answered the question with a word: Christ. "For to me to live is Christ."

Call that success, call it glory, call it whatever you wish, we find ourselves in understatement. Paul's very heartbeat was connected with his Christ. Because Christ loved, a man yearned. Because Christ spoke, a man learned. Because Christ taught, a man preached. Because Christ died, a man lived. Because Christ is, Paul was and will be with Him forever in heaven. Consequently Paul was also—in every sense of the word—a success.

To give ourselves—our believing, loving selves—to Christ; to spend ourselves lavishly, utterly, in Christ and in Christ's service; to share in fullness Paul's magnificent obsession, "For to me to live is Christ"—this is success.

Jesus, your boundless love so true
No thought can reach, no tongue declare;
Unite my thankful heart to you,
And reign without a rival there. Amen. (LW 280:1)

Just for Today

"Therefore do not be anxious about tomorrow, for tomorrow will be anxious for itself. Sufficient for the day is its own trouble."
Matthew 6:34

St. Paul wrote, "Do not be anxious about anything" (Philippians 4:6). This, of course, is nothing other than a repetition of what Jesus Himself said: "Do not be anxious about tomorrow."

How difficult it is, however, for many people to live just for today. They load upon themselves the heavy weight of all their yesterdays and add to that the unreal fears of tomorrow. The problems of each day are enough to engage the best that is in us. The Lord knows how much we can bear and gives us no more, and with the challenge of each situation He has promised to give us the strength to meet it. When people do the foolish thing of loading on themselves something that is no longer a reality, or has not yet happened and may never occur, they are doing something to themselves that the Lord does not want them to do.

Our sins, our neglects, and our failures of yesterday are already forgiven by the Lord who died for us all. Let us believe that they are forgiven, and let them lie forever in the silence of the dead yesteryears. The burdens of tomorrow do not confront us yet, and perhaps they never will. Whatever problems and tasks we shall have tomorrow shall also be met with the strength that God Himself has provided us in Christ.

Lord, increase our faith, that we may live cheerfully with You every day. Amen.

November

By Faith Alone

Now it is evident that no one is justified before God by the law, for "The righteous shall live by faith." Galatians 3:11

In today's verse, the apostle Paul chides the Galatian Christians for backsliding. He had preached the message of the saving Gospel to them, but they had allowed themselves to be misled by false teachers, who taught that observing the Old Testament ceremonial laws was necessary for salvation. To disprove this, the apostle, recalls the words from the prophet Habakkuk, "The righteous shall live by his faith" (2:4).

Some misuse this passage by saying, "The righteous shall live by faith, if it is a working faith, or a faith formed by charitable works." But to speak of a faith formed by charitable works is to speak in a manner contrary to Scripture. If charitable works could form faith, Christ and His benefits would be lost to us.

Today's Bible passage makes a clear declaration to us. It is by faith that we are saved. Works have no part in our salvation. Neither does the Holy Spirit work faith in us because we have performed so many good works. It is "by grace you have been saved through faith" (Ephesians 2:8) that we are made God's children and heirs of eternal life. Let us comfort one another with these words, "I am sure of this, that He who began a good work in you will bring it to completion at the day of Jesus Christ" (Philippians 1:6).

Lord Jesus, strengthen and preserve in us the faith that You have begun Your Holy Spirit. Amen.

November

The Change

Therefore, since we have been justified by faith, we have peace with God through our Lord Jesus Christ. Romans 5:1

Many years ago today a baby was born whose entire life was changed when he learned the words, "Justified by faith." As a child, as a youth, as a student, he had been trained to be afraid of God. His sins troubled him; they deserved punishment. God must be angry.

Could he win God's favor? He would set his life aside for the service of God in a cloister. He would try to gain God's favor by humbling himself, by fasting, by praying. Many of the things he tried were good in themselves. His one great mistake was to think that such things must be done in order to satisfy an angry God.

Through the Bible he discovered that God is merciful to troubled sinners and forgives them because Jesus carried the sins of the whole world. A cross had been placed on His back to carry to Calvary's hill, a cross made heavy with the sins of man. He now calls to all the world to come to Him and receive forgiveness. Anyone who would look to that cross with faith and love would be declared a saint of God, would be justified, counted holy.

That message changed the entire life of Martin Luther. He became the great preacher of justification by faith, the benefactor to whom we owe many precious liberties. He learned that service of God is an act of grateful love, not an attempt to win God's favor.

Lord Jesus, keep us in this saving faith. Amen.

Do Not Tempt God

They tested God in their heart by demanding the food they craved. They spoke against God, saying, "Can God spread a table in the wilderness?" Psalm 78:18–19

The people described in the Psalm repaid God's kindness with ingratitude. They were always ready to receive, never ready to give in return. No sooner were the gifts received than the Giver was forgotten. One minute they were healed, the next minute they threw the crutches at the doctor.

Many people are like that today. They accept God's gifts, breathe His air, enjoy His food, receive His blessings, but do not want Him as their God. They want what He gives, but they don't want what He loves. This is like saying: "God, I don't care what You say or what You want. I'll go my way, and You go Yours." We are all tempted to be like that.

The roots of unbelief remain the soil of our heart. We who are the children of God through faith in our divine Redeemer ought to pray in fervent earnestness: "I believe; help my unbelief" (Mark 9:24). Such prayers God joyfully answers by giving the gift of faith, which trusts in Jesus, His crucified and resurrected Son.

Holy Spirit, help us to live with faith and peace and joy in our heart every minute of life. Since our feet have been planted on the path of eternal life, give us power to thank and praise You with hands and hearts and voices. In Jesus' name we ask it. Amen.

November

Access

Through Him we have also obtained access by faith into this grace in which we stand, and we rejoice in hope of the glory of God. Romans 5:2

"Who shall ascend the hill of the LORD? And who shall stand in His holy place? He who has clean hands and a pure heart, who does not lift up his soul to what is false and does not swear deceitfully" (Psalm 24:3–4). This leaves me out. I cannot measure up to such requirements. My hands have been stained by sin. Many evil thoughts have revealed the foulness of my heart.

Still I long for the right to approach God, to bring my troubles to Him, to seek His help.

Even the noblest of men have had their times of weakness. Noah's heart was not always pure. Abraham swore deceitfully. Jacob's hands were not always clean. John lifted his soul to vanity. Paul's hands were stained with blood. Even Mary's heart was not pure. How can any of them be a help to me?

The Hebrew singer pointed the way to returning to God's presence. "If You, O LORD, should mark iniquities, O LORD, who could stand? But with You there is forgiveness" (Psalm 130:3–4). Paul says it is by our Lord Jesus Christ that we have access through faith, not faith in ourselves, but faith in Christ, who asserts that He is the Way.

Having this access, let us make use of it. Let us come boldly to the throne of grace that we may obtain mercy and find grace to help in the time of need.

Lord Jesus, I come just as I am. Accept and keep me in Your grace. Amen.

November

A Coffin in Egypt

So Joseph died, being 110 years old. They embalmed him, and he was put in a coffin in Egypt. Genesis 50:26

"A coffin in Egypt." The reference is to the coffin in which Joseph was placed when he died in Egypt at the age of 110 years. No doubt it was as fine a coffin as could then be made, for Joseph had been a great man, next in authority to Pharaoh. His body had been given an embalming in which the Egyptians excelled. Yet the massively constructed and beautifully decorated coffin could not hide a gruesome fact—the fact of death!

The tragedy of this last statement in Genesis appears most clearly in contrast to the first chapter. The very opening words read: "In the beginning, God" (Genesis 1:1). The last words read: "a coffin in Egypt." Between those two statements we have in miniature a history of humanity.

Genesis 1 reveals God's eternal existence, His unlimited wisdom and power. It tells the story of the creation of this vast and complex universe with man as God's highest creature. It is a story of life, of activity, of happiness. All that God made "was very good" (Genesis 1:31).

The Genesis account ends on a note of death. Yet there are gleams of life and glory in the rest of the story. The coffin that held Joseph's bones did not remain in Egypt. At Joseph's request, his earthly remains, like those of his father Jacob, were interred in Canaan, the land of promise. These requests of Jacob and Joseph were expressions of faith in the coming Messiah, of confidence in God's faithfulness to keep His promises, and of the blessed expectation of resurrection to a new life and companionship with God and with their fathers. All this was later accomplished for them—and for us—in Christ, who has "abolished death and brought life and immortality to light through the gospel" (2 Timothy 1:10).

Heavenly Father, grant us resurrection and life, through Christ! Amen.

God's Purpose

"And that you may tell in the hearing of your son and of your grandson how I have dealt harshly with the Egyptians and what signs I have done among them, that you may know that I am the LORD." Exodus 10:2

This statement of God's purpose occurs repeatedly in the Exodus story of the ten plagues that the God of Israel brought upon Pharaoh and the Egyptians. By these miracles, the living God was demonstrating His wisdom, power, and justice. His purpose was to fortify the faith of the Israelites in the God of their fathers, and at the same time to prove to Pharaoh and his people that the gods of the Egyptians were dumb and dead idols and that their magicians were deceivers from whom they could expect no help.

"That *you* may know" or "that *they* may know," and other variations of this phrase, occur repeatedly in the prophecy of Ezekiel and in other books of the Bible. The Lord of heaven and earth, the God of wisdom and power, of truth and justice, of mercy and grace, often intervenes in the regular course of nature to demonstrate not only that He is the supreme Ruler, about whom men of all nations and all times must learn to know, but also that He is the God of patience, mercy, and love. In thus revealing Himself, He seeks to humble proud men and to uplift the fainthearted, to call sinners to repentance, and to strengthen the believers. As Jesus said to the scribes when He healed the paralyzed man, God acts "that you may know that the Son of Man has authority on earth to forgive sins" (Mark 2:10).

Lord, teach us to recognize Your purpose in Your dealings with us. Forgive and bless us for Jesus' sake. Amen.

November

The Great Salvation

For he took his life in his hand and he struck down the Philistine, and the LORD worked a great salvation for all Israel. You saw it, and rejoiced. Why then will you sin against innocent blood by killing David without cause? 1 Samuel 19:5

This is the voice of Jonathan, David's bosom friend, rehearsing David's great act of slaying Goliath and saving God's people from destruction. Unmindful of his own safety, David literally took his life in his hands when he went out against the well-armed giant. Nor did he perform this act of heroism to gain honor and distinction for himself, but to protect God's honor and the welfare of God's people.

As Jonathan magnified the performance of David, so men and angels at all times likewise sing praises of Jesus, the Son of David, because of the great salvation He wrought for all people. Jesus put His life into His hands. "The Good Shepherd lays down His life for the sheep" (John 10:11). "He humbled Himself by becoming obedient to the point of death, even death on a cross" (Philippians 2:8). "Even as the Son of Man came not to be served but to serve, and to give His life as a ransom for many" (Matthew 20:28).

Our salvation in Christ is the ever-recurring theme of Christian worship. It lifts conscience-stricken sinners from the depth of despair, assuring them of forgiveness and pardon. It brings joy to the sad and lonely, assuring them that a loving heavenly Father has not forgotten them. It strengthens the dying for their last journey into the valley with the promise of eternal life, where they will join the angels in the song to the Lamb, "You were slain, and by Your blood You ransomed people for God" (Revelation 5:9).

Lord Jesus, make us mindful every day of the great salvation You have wrought for us. Amen.

The Lord Be with You!

Saul was afraid of David because the LORD was with him but had departed from Saul. 1 Samuel 18:12

Saul was afraid of David for two reasons: the Lord was with David, and the Lord had departed from Saul. Actually there was no real cause for fear in the first reason. Saul should have been thankful for this demonstration of divine love. But Saul viewed this development with fear because by his unbelief he had caused God to depart from him. And therein was real cause for fear. There is nothing more dreadful and hopeless than to be rejected by God. On the other hand, there is no greater joy and comfort than to be assured that God is with us.

This assurance we have through Jesus, the Son of David and the Son of God. Our sins and transgressions give God every right to reject us, as He rejected Saul. If there are any doubts about that statement, then listen to Jesus cry out on the cross, "My God, My God, why have You forsaken Me?" (Matthew 27:46). Bearing the sins of the whole world, Jesus was forsaken of God.

The dying Jesus is the evidence of God's anger toward sin, but the living Jesus is the proof of God's love and forgiveness. Because He was rejected by God in our stead, we need never be rejected. On Sunday, in churches everywhere, ministers of God will address people with the words, "The Lord be with you." By faith in Christ we believe that this is not just a pious wish, but a glorious fact!

Lord Jesus, give us grace to live in the constant assurance that God is with us. Amen.

Make My Heart Sincere!

*Search me, O God, and know my heart! Try me and know my
thoughts! And see if there be any grievous way in me, and lead
me in the way everlasting! Psalm 139:23–24*

These words are an admission of David's part that outward appearances can be deceiving, that God is not impressed
by outward appearance, and that it is more important to have a
clean heart and a pure mind than to give merely the outward
appearance of piety and holiness.

How very necessary it is for us to say this prayer every day!
Oh, how we like to impress others with our knowledge, our
bravery, our possession, our accomplishments, yes, even with
our godliness and devotion! Is our heart sincere? Are we seeking to glorify God or ourselves?

Only God can give us a pure heart and noble thoughts.
Only God can turn us from the wicked way and lead us in the
way everlasting. We have the right to pray for this gift of sincer-
ity because Jesus has cleansed our hearts and thoughts with His
purifying blood. His death and resurrection have opened to us
the "way everlasting" that leads to God.

*Order my footsteps by your Word
And make my heart sincere. Amen. (LW 392:2)*

Our Champion, Jesus

And David said to Saul, "Let no man's heart fail because of him. Your servant will go and fight with this Philistine." 1 Samuel 17:32

This Philistine was a huge and powerful man named Goliath. Every day this mighty man of the army of the Philistines would challenge anyone from the army of God's people, Israel, to do battle with him. The outcome of such a battle would determine the supremacy either of the Philistine army or the army of God's people. Every day the sight of this giant struck great fear into the hearts of the Israelites. Before any military progress could be made, Goliath had to be eliminated.

Finally, David, moved by the Spirit of God, offered to fight Goliath. Trusting in the Lord for strength and courage, and depending upon his marksmanship with the sling, he went out and killed the giant. This heroic feat was the turning point in Israel's campaign against the Philistines.

"Your servant will go and fight with this Philistine." Jesus, the servant of God, the Son of David, likewise went into battle against the champion of evil, Satan. Although He was despised, rejected, and crucified, Jesus conquered the old evil foe. Now our hearts need not fail us when we are called upon to fight the giants of malice and hatred and lust, or any other sin. Our champion, Jesus, is ever at our side, granting us victory after victory against any evil that assails us.

Lord Jesus, help us to see our helplessness in the struggle against sin. Fight for us and give us the victory in every battle. Amen.

An Occupation Changed

And so also were James and John, sons of Zebedee, who were partners with Simon. And Jesus said to Simon, "Do not be afraid; from now on you will be catching men." Luke 5:10

Simon Peter was a fisherman by profession. Night after night he plied his humble trade on the Sea of Galilee, thereby supporting himself and his family. One night, the memory of which must have stayed with him a long time, he with his companions, James and John, had taken nothing. They rowed up and down the narrow beach of the lake, letting down their nets and drawing them up again, but with no success. It was a night of fruitless toil. The next morning they met Jesus on the shore. He borrowed their boat to use as a pulpit and after the sermon told the disciples to row out into the deep and let down their nets for a draft of fishes. Although conditions were unfavorable, they enclosed a multitude of fish. Peter was so astonished that he said to Jesus, "Depart from me, for I am a sinful man, O Lord" (Luke 5:8).

Each sinner might likewise feel Peter's desire to be away from Jesus on account of the realization of sin in the presence of His holiness and perfection. Yet Jesus will not depart from us: He has come to us, He has lived for us, and He has died for us precisely because He wants us to be where He is.

Cast me not away from Your presence, O Lord. Amen.

Jesus Christ

"And there is salvation in no one else, for there is no other name under heaven given among men by which we must be saved."
Acts 4:12

"See what kind of love the Father has given to us, that we should be called children of God" (1 John 3:1). It is our duty to thank and praise Him, to serve and obey Him (*Luther's Small Catechism*).

Yet we ungrateful children constantly offend God in thought, word, and deed. Nevertheless He loves us unworthy children with an everlasting love. "For God so loved the world, that He gave His only Son, that whoever believes in Him should not perish but have eternal life" (John 3:16).

When this Son of God was about to take unto Himself our human nature, the angel of the Lord appeared and told Joseph that his espoused wife, Mary, would bring forth a son and that he should call His name Jesus, "for He will save His people from their sins" (Matthew 1:21). Jesus is our Savior.

In the Old Testament the coming Savior was often referred to as the Messiah, the Christ, the Anointed One. We are told by Isaiah that the Spirit of the Lord God anointed the promised Redeemer to preach the Gospel of salvation and to deliver us out of the slavery of Satan.

Oh, that we would more zealously hear, learn, and keep God's holy Word, that we would love God and our Savior more!

Jesus, the very tho't of Thee
With sweetness fills the breast;
But sweeter far Thy face to see
And in Thy presence rest. Amen. (TLH 350:1)

The Two Natures in Jesus Christ

"That all may honor the Son, just as they honor the Father. Whoever does not honor the Son does not honor the Father who sent Him." John 5:23

The ancient heretic Arius denied that Jesus is God. His heresy was condemned in AD 325, when at Nicea the Nicene Creed was adopted, which emphasized the deity of our Savior—"God of God . . . begotten, not made, being of one substance with the Father."

Under Theodosius the Great, later in the Fourth Century, the Arian heresy spread through the Roman Empire. The emperor Theodosius decided to make his son Arcadius partner with him on the throne. When the bishops came to extend congratulations, the esteemed bishop Amphilochus passed by the prince. The emperor asked indignantly: "What, do you take no notice of my son, whom I have made of equal dignity with myself?" Amphilochus looked the emperor in the eye and said: "What must the eternal God think of you, who have allowed His coequal and coeternal Son to be degraded in His proper divinity in every part of your empire!"

At the Baptism of Jesus, God the Father said: "This is My beloved Son!" (Matthew 3:17). Jesus is the true God and eternal life. All power is given Him in heaven and earth. This eternal Son of God, in the stream of time, for our salvation adopted a human nature into His Person. What a comfort to know this divine truth and to confess with Luther: "I believe that Jesus Christ, true God, begotten of the Father from eternity, and also true man, born of the Virgin Mary, is my Lord, who has redeemed me" (*Luther's Small Catechism*).

Dear Jesus, help me always to believe rightly. Amen.

Blessed

But He said, "Blessed rather are those who hear the word of God and keep it!" Luke 11:28

The Church is fast approaching the last Sunday of the Church Year. According to an old Lutheran custom, the last Sunday of the Church Year is still observed by some congregations as Memorial Sunday. It is good to remember those who have fallen asleep in Christ. It is good to recall God's mercies upon them and their own participation in the building of Christ's kingdom.

For all the saints
who from their labors rest,
All who by faith
before the world confessed,
Your name, O Jesus, be forever blessed!
Alleluia! Alleluia! (LW 191:1)

It is also good to review our own record of the past year. How have I attended worship to hear of God's mercy and receive the proclamation of His grace? How many did I needlessly miss? How did I prepare myself for worship? How did I hear and how did I respond? The remembrance of the those who have preceded us into eternal life not only gives us opportunity to imitate their works of faith and piety, but also to rejoice that we have been saved from death and damnation in the same way as the saints of heaven have been saved: by the death of Jesus for our sins. Because He lives, we, too, shall taste eternal life with the entire company of heaven.

For all Your mercies, dear heavenly Father, I thank You. For my shortcomings I beg Your forgiveness in Christ. In His name I pray that Your Spirit may make me faithful in all things. For Jesus' sake. Amen.

A Little While!

"A little while, and you will see Me no longer; and again a little while, and you will see Me." John 16:16

"Will my sorrows and troubles never end?" Many ask this question—the bereaved, the sick, the lonely, the poor, the imprisoned.

Troubles seem endless when we hold the clock and calendar before our eyes. But look at them through God's eyes, and they do not seem so long and hard. God tells Christians, "Your hurts last only a little while; I will end them and turn them into joy." This is what is meant by the psalmist's words, "Weeping may tarry for the night, but joy comes with the morning" (Psalm 30:5).

"A little while." The disciples found it was only a little while from the sorrow of Good Friday to the joy of Easter morning. Likewise, from God's viewpoint, the years between His leaving the earth and His final coming back are only "a little while." To God, the 2000 years since Christ's ascension are like a weekend. Let's remember this too. When death separates our spirit and body, our spirit goes at once to Jesus. In heaven with Him, we will not fearfully count the months and years. Also, our bodies asleep in the grave will not know of the stream of time flowing by. When Jesus awakens us and reunites our bodies and souls, we will feel like saying, "Lord, it seemed like only a little while. You came quickly indeed!"

Jesus, give us endurance and patience for a little while! Amen.

November

Thank God for His Faithfulness

To declare Your steadfast love in the morning, and Your faithfulness by night. Psalm 92:2

We count our many earthly blessings this Thanksgiving season. But suppose today we were hungry, cold, sick, lonely, and afraid. Even then we would still owe God thanks and praise for revealing Himself to us in the person of His Son and for the salvation worked for us in Him.

In Psalm 92, David praises God because He is the living, everlasting, almighty God. But most of all, David thanks God for His faithfulness.

The Bible word "faithful" sends us a clear picture. A father carries his little boy. The son looks up at him confidently; he relaxes and leans his whole weight on those strong arms.

God, our heavenly Father, is faithful. He supports us with loving care. We can depend on Him and His Word. By faith we lean the full weight of our being on Him. He will not let us down.

This faithful God always keeps His Word. Again this year, His promises came true, for he sent us summer and winter, seedtime and harvest. But these blessings would mean little if God had not also made good His greatest promise of a Savior.

Across the centuries, men kept asking, "Lord, how long?" And God did not put their trust to shame. In the fullness of time He sent forth His Son. In Jesus, therefore, all the promises of God stand firm and sure.

Lord, keep us from leaning upon ourselves or depending on the stuff of this world. Help us to rest only on You. Amen.

November

God Reigns

Your throne is established from of old; You are from everlasting.
Psalm 93:2

As Thanksgiving approaches, we recall the fruits of the closing year: the abundance of harvests, profits in enterprise, health of body, harmony in the family, peace within our boundaries, all reasons for thanksgiving! But if this is the whole story, then we must divide our people into classes of fortunates and unfortunates in setting up our Thanksgiving program.

During the past years many have experienced losses. Especially do we recall destructive hurricanes and floods as well as drought and early frost. Even in more prosperous areas individuals have experienced disappointments, ill health, lack of employment.

We must learn to link our thankfulness not to blessings received, as we measure them, but rather to Him from whom all blessings flow. Come weal or woe, thank God that He reigns. They point to the great Flood of history, in which God showed us that man's strength, however destructive man may be in setting himself against God and His holy will, does not approach the power of God. If man is set upon destroying God's world, God is able to be far more destructive in His judgments. But God's throne will remain unmoved. He will continue to reign. Out of man's disorder He will reestablish order. Man's wickedness can be wiped out; God's holiness will remain. When man has done his worst, a perfect world will yet emerge. God's pledge of this truth is the empty tomb.

Creator God, keep us ever faithful to Your will and Word. Amen.

November

Come, Lord Jesus!

He who testifies to these things says, "Surely I am coming soon."
Amen. Come, Lord Jesus! Revelation 22:20

These words from the last chapter in the Holy Bible are the last words of Jesus Christ, our incarnate Savior, to the Church and to the world at large. In these last words He calls Himself the Alpha and Omega, the Beginning and the End, the First and the Last. Only God can talk like that. And Jesus is God. From everlasting to everlasting He is God. By Him the universe came into being in the beginning, and by Him it shall come to its end on the day appointed. And He is the Beginning and the End of the revelation of God. He has revealed the one true and only God, the ever-blessed Holy Trinity. He has made known to man the counsel of God's salvation. He is the God of the holy prophets and apostles. He calls all men to repentance and faith. He promises grace and every blessing to all that obey Him. He threatens the plague of the judgments of God to all who falsify His Word by adding thereto or taking away therefrom. He calls to all the world to make ready for the Last Judgment. He will surely come. Amen. Yea, He will come. Meanwhile His Holy Spirit, through the Church, cries to the world, "Come." All who thirst for pardon and life shall come. His everlasting salvation is free; let the weary and heavy laden take it without money and without price.

With the Church we answer: "Come, Lord Jesus!" We desire to see Him who loves us and gave Himself for us and washed us from our sins in His own blood. Until He comes, He assures us of His grace and love.

The grace of our Lord Jesus Christ be with you all. Amen.

Names Written in Heaven

Nevertheless, do not rejoice in this, that the spirits are subject to you, but rejoice that your names are written in heaven." Luke 10:20

Jesus had sent out seventy men as advance messengers to prepare the way for Him. Reporting to Jesus about their experiences, they exclaimed, "Lord, even the demons are subject to us in Your name" (Luke 10:17). The Savior's reply was, "But rejoice that your names are written in heaven."

What does it mean to have one's name written in heaven? Whether an actual book is kept in heaven and names are inscribed upon its pages is beside the point. Having our name written in heaven means we are the children of God and are recognized as such by the heavenly Father.

True, sometimes we feel as did St. Paul when he cried out: "Wretched man that I am" (Romans 7:24). But as we hear the life-giving proclamation of the Gospel, that Christ died and rose to write our names into the book of heaven, we exult with St. Paul, "Thanks be to God through Jesus Christ our Lord" (Romans 7:25). With Jesus to protect and keep us, all the demons of the kingdom of darkness cannot remove our names from the Book of Life.

O my Savior, help afford
By your Spirit and your Word!
When my wayward heart would stray,
Keep me in the narrow way;
Grace in time of need supply
While I live and when I die. Amen. (LW 285:5)

November

Key of David

And I will place on His shoulder the key of the house of David.
He shall open, and none shall shut; and He shall shut, and none
shall open. Isaiah 22:22

When municipal authorities wish to honor some distinguished visitor, they sometimes present him with the "key to the city" to signify that he is welcome wherever he goes. So God, in this prophecy in Isaiah, says He will give all royal privileges to His chosen One. Christ will have authority to open doors and to shut them.

Jesus spoke to His disciples about "the keys of the kingdom of heaven" (Matthew 16:19). The exercise of this power by the Church is based upon our Savior's office of Prophet, Priest, and King. It is only because Christ has opened the door to heaven by His atoning work that the Church can do anything at all. If He were not the door, there would be no door. If He had not opened the way, no man could go along it. The Church proclaims a truth that is not hers but His; she offers a life that is the life of her Lord.

The mood of Advent is one of longing and expectation. Many selections from the Old Testament are read, recalling the yearning of Israel for the coming of the Redeemer. The Church of the New Testament time also expresses this hope of the return of the great King, who will finish His work of deliverance. To those who have rejected Him He will lock the door forever, but those who have acknowledged Him as their Lord He will lead through the everlasting doors into glory. In the meantime what He says is true for us: "I am the door. If anyone enters by Me, he will be saved and will go in and out and find pasture" (John 10:9).

O Scepter of Israel, bring us at last into Your heavenly mansions.
Amen.

November

Great David's Greater Son

In those days and at that time I will cause a righteous Branch to spring up for David, and He shall execute justice and righteousness in the land. Jeremiah 33:15

Jesus, the Savior, was promised to come from a noble lineage. According to Jeremiah He was to be a son of David's royal line, a true man. No man in history can establish his family tree as definitely as Christ. In Matthew chapter 1 we have the genealogy of Jesus Christ from Abraham, through David, to Joseph, the foster father of Christ. In Luke chapter 3 we have His genealogy through Mary, His true mother according to the flesh.

What a message of cheer and encouragement for fainting hearts at the time of Jeremiah, when Israel was already in captivity! These words also give us courage for our times.

Great David's greater Son does not come with empty hands. It is said that "He shall execute justice and righteousness." He will present a plan of salvation, the covenant of grace. "He shall execute . . . righteousness in the land." Christ's righteousness, exercised for us and our salvation during His life on earth, is the only righteousness which avails before God. He will bring safety, for "in those days Judah will be saved and Jerusalem will dwell securely" (Jeremiah 33:16). True security may be had only from God through Christ.

Stir us, O God, to dedicate ourselves during this Advent season to be loyal subjects of great David's greater Son. Amen.

November

Our Blessed Hope

Waiting for our blessed hope, the appearing of the glory of our great God and Savior Jesus Christ. Titus 2:13

Advent is a meaningful word when applied to our Lord Jesus. Advent means coming.

1. *He came.* "The saying is trustworthy and deserving of full acceptance, that Christ Jesus came into the world to save sinners" (1 Timothy 1:15). He finished the work He came to do. He fulfilled the Law. He bore its curse. He paid the penalty—all this for us, for all men. Redemption is finished—redemption from sin, death, and the power of the devil.

2. *He comes.* Through Word and Sacrament He still comes to us in our churches, in our homes, in our hearts. "Behold, I stand at the door and knock. If anyone hears My voice and opens the door, I will come in to him and eat with him, and he with Me" (Revelation 3:20). When He thus comes to us, He blesses us with the treasure of His grace: forgiveness, life, and salvation. Do we sincerely and earnestly pray Him to abide with us?

3. *He will come again.* "I will come again and will take you to Myself, that where I am you may be also" (John 14:3). Thus Jesus spoke to His first disciples. He gives the same promise to us. That is the "blessed hope" with which the apostles cheered the early Christians.

The grace of God that brings salvation has appeared unto us in the person of His Son, Jesus! As we contemplate this Gospel proclamation, may our preparation in these Advent weeks be inward more than outward, spiritual more than material, so our Christmas festivities may rightly be a preparation for and a foretaste of the eternal Christmas in heaven.

Come, Lord Jesus, make Your advent into our churches, our homes, our hearts. Bless us with Your redeeming love and save us by Your grace. Make us Yours forevermore! Amen.

Forgiveness

In Him we have redemption through His blood, the forgiveness of our trespasses, according to the riches of His grace.
Ephesians 1:7

Among the things God gives us in Christ, there is chiefly the forgiveness of our sins. That is exactly what you and I and every mortal needs more than anything else. Everyone is filthy with sin: the most despicable inmate of the penitentiary, the most moral man on earth, the mightiest sovereign in any land; in short, everybody. In that respect, "there is no distinction" (Romans 3:22). You and I are sinners.

Sin places us under the wrath of a holy God, gives us a bad conscience here, and damns us for all eternity hereafter.

Yet from this sinful misery Jesus is our Savior. Did not the Christmas angel announce to the shepherds: "Unto you is born . . . a Savior" (Luke 2:11)? Had not an angel said to Joseph: "Call His name Jesus, for He will save His people from their sins" (Matthew 1:21)? Later Jesus Himself declared that He had come to minister to men by giving His life as a ransom. Hence He gave His life on the cross in atonement for our sins, paid with His blood to purchase forgiveness for us.

That forgiveness covers all our sins, and that fully. "The blood of Jesus His Son cleanses us from all sin" (1 John 1:7). "As far as the east is from the west, so far does He remove our transgressions from us" (Psalm 103:12).

Lord Jesus, we thank You for the great blessing of forgiveness. Amen.

December

Christ our Priest

For you were bought with a price. So glorify God in your body.
1 Corinthians 6:20

Conquerors have ever demanded tremendous sums of money of their defeated foes. Not all the gold in the universe is a sufficient ransom for a single human soul. "Knowing that you were ransomed from the futile ways inherited from your forefathers, not with perishable things such as silver or gold, but with the precious blood of Christ, like that of a lamb without blemish or spot" (1 Peter 1:18–19). "He was wounded for our transgressions; He was crushed for our iniquities; upon Him was the chastisement that brought us peace, and with His stripes we are healed" (Isaiah 53:5). Indeed, the precious blood of Jesus Christ, God's Son, cleanses us from all sin.

As we meditate on the price that was paid for our redemption, we marvel at the grace of God, which has caused Him to lay our sins on His innocent Son. We stand in awe at the love of our Savior for us unworthy and guilty sinners, for He takes us to His bosom and assures us: "I, I am He who blots out your transgressions for My own sake, and I will not remember your sins" (Isaiah 43:25). This, our great High Priest, offers up the sacrifice of Himself for us and for our salvation.

In our weakness and in our sin we come to You, our Father, through our compassionate and faithful High Priest, Jesus Christ. Amen.

The Morning Star

"I, Jesus, have sent My angel to testify to you about these things for the churches. I am the root and the descendant of David, the bright morning star." Revelation 22:16

Those who have traveled all night in their car may have noticed, toward dawn, a star of unusual brilliance appearing in the sky as a herald of the new day. This star is used in the last book of the Bible as a symbol of our Lord Jesus Christ and the new era ushered in by Him. Certainly there was a heavenly brightness to be seen in Him. St. John says in his Gospel that He is the Light. Luther says that the coming of His Spirit into the soul of a man is like a light being turned on so this man sees things he had never seen before. Most of all, the love of God shines in his heart "to give the light of the knowledge of the glory of God in the face of Jesus Christ" (2 Corinthians 4:6).

The advent of our Lord meant that a new day dawned for the world. Men presently began to number the years from His birth. His religion changed human institutions. There is no area of life that has not been affected by the words He spoke, the life He lived, the death He died. In our part of the world we owe our ideas of liberty, justice, charity, the dignity and rights of man, and the place of women in society to His influence. No one could have suspected, when His star first appeared in the eastern sky, how bright would be the day that would follow and how all-pervasive its light.

God promises to every man "who conquers" (Revelation 21:7) that He "will give him the morning star" (Revelation 2:28). This can only mean that He will give Christ to such a one. "Awake, O sleeper, and arise from the dead, and Christ will shine on you" (Ephesians 5:14).

Lighten our darkness, we beseech You, O Lord, that we may see You clearly. Amen.

The Rose of Sharon

I am a rose of Sharon, a lily of the valleys. Song of Solomon 2:1

The Song of Solomon is a long poem that most commentators believe expresses the mutual love existing between Christ and His Church. Each addresses the other by endearing names, a practice that has had ample imitation in the devotional literature of Christianity. It is an old custom for the faithful to apply to Jesus all the lovely titles they can think of. In the passage quoted above the Lord uses such a title in speaking about Himself. He is the Rose of Sharon.

Roses are some of the world's most beautiful flowers, and in ancient times were best grown in the fertile region between Joppa and Carmel, which was called Sharon. To call Jesus the Rose of Sharon is to say that He is our beautiful Savior. And in His case it is certainly true that "a thing of beauty is a joy forever." His loveliness increases in our eyes the longer we look at Him.

In the season of Advent the Church longs for the consummation of their union with Him who is "the most handsome of the sons of men" (Psalm 45:2). The keynote of the season is the word *come*. When Christ does come again, we shall behold in His own person all the loveliness we have believed to be in Him while He was veiled from our sight. This will surely come to pass, for it has already been the experience of men, as St. John says: "We have seen His glory" (John 1:14).

Lord, teach us greatly to desire Your beauty, that our lives may be as lovely as Yourself. Amen.

A Sacrifice

He entered once for all into the holy places, not by means of the blood of goats and calves but by means of His own blood, thus securing an eternal redemption. Hebrews 9:12

This statement in the Letter to the Hebrews may strike the modern Christian as rather strange and foreign, for in our churches we are no longer required to worship in the manner of the Jews of the Old Testament. We worship through our prayers, our hymns, our gifts, and our listening to the sermon and Scripture readings.

Yet it is important to remember that sacrificing was a highly important element of Old Testament worship. The shedding of the blood in these sacrifices served as a signpost that pointed to the time when Jesus Christ would be slain, the Messiah and the Lamb of God.

The high priest's role was also important. Once a year he entered the Holy of Holies in the temple at Jerusalem. He would sprinkle some of the blood of the sacrificed animals upon the Ark of the Covenant. This was the rite by which the Jews obtained forgiveness.

In the New Testament, Jesus Christ becomes not only the Sacrifice for all people, but also the High Priest. He has made the sacrifice and He pleads for us before God. He is both Priest and Lamb.

Accept, O Lord, our gifts of love to You, which are but a poor sacrifice in the light of Your sacrifice upon the cross. Amen.

December

Christ's Exaltation

For in Him the whole fullness of deity dwells bodily. Colossians 2:9

When our thoughts are directed to Jesus, we dare not stop at Bethlehem's lowly manger nor at the foot of His cross. Our knowledge of Him is incomplete if we look at our Savior only in His state of humiliation.

Even in His humble state on earth He was the "one Lord Jesus Christ, the only-begotten Son of God, begotten of His Father before all worlds, God of god, Light of light, Very God of very god, begotten not made, Being of one substance with the Father, By whom all things were made." In Him dwelt all the fullness of the Godhead bodily. Yet on His way from the manger to the cross He did not always and fully use His divine qualities, such as His omnipotence, omniscience, omnipresence.

Now, however, ever since He descended into hell and rose from the dead, He always makes full use of His divine majesty.

This is a glorious comfort for us. Jesus, the exalted King of glory, rules and governs the universe and leads and protects His Church, His believers, through this present valley of the shadow of death to final victory and eternal glory.

Lord Jesus Christ, King of kings and Lord of lords, rule our hearts and lives now and always. Amen.

December

Come!

"Come to Me, all who labor and are heavy laden, and I will give you rest . . . rest for your souls." Matthew 11:28–29

More gracious words were never spoken on this earth than these, which fell from the divine lips of Jesus Christ. Here is an invitation without limitation. The words: "All who labor and are heavy laden" do not restrict His offer of help to the feeble, the aged, the sorrowing. The word *all* includes everyone. In reality, *all people*, whether they realize it or not, are *burdened* with sin and guilt, are laboring under the severe requirements of the Law of God and under its condemnation as guilty transgressors.

Come to Me! Here is an invitation without strings attached. No condition is imposed; no requirements are added. The Savior of all men stretches out His arms of divine love to embrace all humanity. Many in the darkness of heathenism, hearing these words for the first time, have exclaimed: "This is too good to be true!"

This most gracious invitation and promise, "*Come* . . . and I will give you rest . . . rest for your souls," has sadly lost much of its sweetness and power for many who have grown up in Christendom! Jesus is *the only one* who gives rest for our souls by the assurance of pardon and peace in His shed blood. And this He has already accomplished for us in His dying and His rising again.

Jesus, just as I am, I come to You for cleansing in Your blood, for peace in my heart, for rest in my soul! Amen.

December

No Difference

The righteousness of God through faith in Jesus Christ for all who believe. For there is no distinction: for all have sinned and fall short of the glory of God. Romans 3:22–23

When the aged emperor of Austria-Hungary died some years ago, his body was carried to the gates of the crypt of the Royal Church in Vienna. In answer to the knock at the gate came the question "Who is there?" Back came the answer "His Serene Majesty, the Emperor of Austria." The voice within replied, "I know him not. Who is there?" Back came the answer "The Apostolic King of Hungary." Once more the voice within said, "I know him not. Who is there?" This time the answer came back, "Our brother, Franz Joseph, a sinner." Then the gates opened, and the emperor was laid with his fathers.

This historical incident aptly illustrates the basic teaching of Scripture that in judgment before God all men are sinners. None is better than another. Neither birth, nor class, nor color counts. "For there is no distinction: for all have sinned and fall short of the glory of God." It is not what my wife, or husband, or parents, or children think of me. It is not what my associates and fellow citizens think of me. Before God I am a sinner.

But thanks be to God, although I am a sinner I am saved and received into heaven! Jesus came to take my place before the judgment seat of God. He fulfilled the Law perfectly for me. He suffered that I might live!

Good God, I thank You that in Jesus' blood, rich and poor, high and low, saint and sinner and even I can have a place in Your kingdom. Amen.

December

A Mighty Preacher of the Gospel

The next day he saw Jesus coming toward him, and said, "Behold, the Lamb of God, who takes away the sin of the world!" John 1:29

John the Baptist was more than a preacher of the Law. Yes, John brought men to the conviction of sin by a fearless preaching of repentance. His message, however, did not stop there. He knew of a means whereby this repentance was to be effected and men's hearts made happy in the assurance of sins forgiven and their life brought under the influence of moral power from on high. The King was drawing nigh, who was mighty to save and to deliver. John knew Jesus to be the incarnate God and the true sacrificial Lamb, prefigured in all the sacrifices of the Old Testament church.

He pointed the anxious minds and discouraged hearts to the King of grace, who in His infinite love would become the Lamb of God and by His holy sacrifice atone for the sins of men and win for them pardon and peace, acceptance with God, and entrance into the home of eternal glory. John knew of no way to escape from the coming wrath than Jesus, the sin-atoning Savior.

This Gospel is the power with which God has entrusted His Church. By it the Spirit of God turns men's hearts from sin to the Savior, from anxiety of heart and despair of soul to faith and the joy of salvation, from the love of sin to the service of God, from spiritual death to spiritual life. Thus the Church is the greatest power for good in the world, and certainly the Church ought to lift up its voice with strength in the wilderness of the world and cry to the groping and anxious children of men, "Behold, the Lamb of God, who takes away the sin of the world."

Continue to turn my heart, O Holy Spirit, away from sin and toward the Lamb of God. Amen.

Christ, Our Priest, Born to Save

For it was indeed fitting that we should have such a high priest, holy, innocent, unstained, separated from sinners, and exalted above the heavens. Hebrews 7:26–27

The reason for celebrating Christmas is contained in these words: "When the fullness of time had come, God sent forth His Son, born of woman, born under the Law, to redeem those who were under the Law, so that we might receive adoption as sons" (Galatians 4:4). Christ is our Priest, born to save us.

In the Old Testament days the priests served as mediators who offered sacrifices to God for the people. Because they were sinners, they had to offer sacrifices also for themselves. Sacrifices were symbolic and pointed to the sacrifice of Christ.

As our High Priest, Christ wrought our salvation by His blameless life and by His innocent suffering and death. He fulfilled the Law for us and paid the penalty for our sins.

Christ was not only the Priest, but He was also the Sacrifice. He is called "the Lamb of God" (John 1:29) as well as "High Priest." Because He was "holy, innocent, unstained, separated from sinners, and exalted above the heavens," He needed not to offer up sacrifices for Himself. His sacrifice was altogether in the interest and for the benefit of man. "There is one God, and there is one Mediator between God and men, the man Christ Jesus" (1 Timothy 2:5).

We thank You, Lord, for Jesus, our Advocate, who even now speaks on our behalf at Your throne because He died for our sins according to the Scriptures. Amen.

December

Christ, Our Prophet, Born to Teach

"The LORD your God will raise up for you a prophet like me from among you, from your brothers—it is to Him you shall listen." Deuteronomy 18:15

The prophetic office of Christ is at work whenever we read or hear the Gospel message.

In Old Testament days the work of the prophets among the children of Israel consisted of teaching the people the Word of the Lord. Moses, Isaiah, Jeremiah, and Daniel were among the prophets of God. In our text Moses is speaking of the coming of Christ, the great Prophet.

During His days in the flesh, Christ was known as the great Teacher. No one ever taught as He did. He was the great Prophet.

What did Christ teach? He told the people that "the kingdom of God is at hand" (Mark 1:15) and that they were to repent of their sins and accept Him as the Messiah. The burden of His teaching was: "The Son of Man came to seek and to save the lost" (Luke 19:10). As our Prophet, Christ through His Church still makes known what He has earned for us as our Priest. "Go therefore and make disciples of all nations" (Matthew 28:19), is the great Prophet's directive to His children.

The anniversary of Christ's birth merits so great a celebration because of the message Christmas proclaims: "Unto you is born this day in the city of David a Savior, who is Christ the Lord" (Luke 2:11).

Lord, may we accept Your Word in faith and make it known to our fellow men. Amen.

December

Christ, Our King, Born to Rule

"Say to the daughter of Zion, 'Behold, your king is coming to you, humble, and mounted on a donkey, and on a colt, the foal of a beast of burden.'" Matthew 21:5

Christ was born our Savior at Bethlehem that we might "live under Him in His kingdom and serve Him in everlasting righteousness, innocence, and blessedness" (*Luther's Small Catechism*). Christ is a king. He is the King of kings and the Lord of lords.

The work of a king is to rule and govern. Among the children of Israel in Old Testament days were David, Solomon, and others, who were anointed with oil to signify that they had been set apart for their royal office.

Christ is the Anointed of God whose kingdom far surpasses the kingdoms of the world. As our Creator, together with the Father and the Holy Spirit, Christ rules the world and upholds all things. All creation is subject to Christ's power and providence.

But He also rules in the kingdom established in the human heart. Jesus dwells in the heart of each one of His children. He rules with His love and grace. He preserves His own for His heavenly kingdom.

Christ became the King of His children by His work of redemption. The Wise Men spoke correctly of the child born at Bethlehem as a king. Someday soon this King will deliver us from every evil and will draw us unto His heavenly kingdom!

O holy Child of Bethlehem,
Descend to us, we pray;
Cast out our sin,
And enter in,
Be born in us today. Amen. (LW 59:4)

The Work of the Holy Ghost

But you will receive power when the Holy Spirit has come upon you, and you will be My witnesses in Jerusalem and in all Judea and Samaria, and to the end of the earth." Acts 1:8.

In Baptism we passed from death to life. When Jesus came to the city gate at Nain, "a man who had died was being carried out, the only son of his mother" (Luke 7:12). No human power could restore life to the young man. The young man was utterly helpless, lifeless, dead. The Lord had compassion. He said: "Young man, I say to you, arise" (Luke 7:14). This word of our almighty Savior caused the young man to sit up and to speak.

Spiritually we once were helpless, lifeless, dead in trespasses and sins. With our human intelligence, reason, and strength, we could not come to Jesus Christ, our Lord, or believe in Him as our only Redeemer. "No one can say 'Jesus is Lord' except in the Holy Spirit" (1 Corinthians 12:3).

But God had compassion on us. In Baptism we passed from death to life. He not only redeemed us with the blood of His Son, but also brought us to spiritual life, a life that carries us to eternal life. "Not because of works done by us in righteousness, but according to His own mercy, by the washing of regeneration and renewal of the Holy Spirit" (Titus 3:5). Thank God, we have passed from death to life!

Come, Holy Ghost, Creator blest,
Vouchsafe within our souls to rest;
Come with Thy grace and heav'nly aid
And fill the hearts which Thou hast made. Amen. (TLH 233:1)

December

Creed and Faith

Because, if you confess with your mouth that Jesus is Lord and believe in your heart that God raised Him from the dead, you will be saved. For with the heart one believes and is justified, and with the mouth one confesses and is saved. Romans 10:9–10

Creeds are not highly thought of in our day. They receive little attention in many circles and religious groups. In fact, they are regarded by many Christians as stumbling blocks in the pathway of Christian progress. "Not creeds, but deeds" has been their cry and slogan.

Now, just what is a creed? The word comes from the Latin "credo," which simply means "I believe." A creed, then, at least in its simple form, is no more than a statement of faith. Whatever I believe is my creed. Wherever there is faith in the heart, a confession of that faith is sure to follow. A creed is but the inevitable result of faith. Where there is faith, there must be a creed. On the other hand, a man may profess a faith that is not in his heart. In such a case his creed is a fraud. Furthermore, his faith may contain elements of error. He may be falsely instructed. If his belief, however sincere, is not based on the truth of God's Word, his creed will be faulty.

Note how the holy apostle in today's text intertwines faith and creed. If you believe in your heart that God the Father raised up His Son, Jesus Christ, from the dead and will confess such faith with your mouth, you will be saved. This confession arises only out of the faith that comes as a gift from God. Creeds themselves—the "I believe" that every Christian speaks—are made possible only by the God who first spoke to us and gave His Son to us for our eternal salvation.

Lord Jesus, by Your Spirit move us ever to base our faith on Your Word and gladly to confess this unchanging faith before men. Amen.

December

Alpha and Omega

"I am the Alpha and the Omega," says the Lord God, "who is and who was and who is to come, the Almighty." Revelation 1:8

Soon we shall celebrate the Christmas festival, the birthday of Jesus. He "was conceived by the Holy Spirit, [and] born of the Virgin Mary," and that marked His beginning as a member of the human race (*Luther's Small Catechism*). Yet it was not His beginning. He told the Jews: "Truly, truly, I say to you, before Abraham was, I am" (John 8:58). He was living when the foundations of the world were laid. He is the living Word. The opening verses of John's Gospel say of Him: "In the beginning was the Word, and the Word was with God, and the Word was God. He was in the beginning with God. All things were made through Him, and without Him was not any thing made that was made" (John 1:1–3).

He is the true God, and as such He never began to be; for He always was. He is Alpha (the first letter in the Greek alphabet). And He is Omega (the last letter). He always will be, even after the destruction of this earth on Judgment Day. He is "the same yesterday and today and forever" (Hebrews 13:8).

How comforting this must have been to John when he had to endure his lonely exile on the Isle of Patmos! When we are experiencing a Patmos of one kind or another, let us recall Jesus' words in Revelation 1:8 and thus comfort and cheer our soul!

We adore Thee, "Lord Jesus Christ . . . God of God, Light of Light, very God of very God, begotten, not made, being of one substance with the Father, by whom all things were made; who for us men and for our salvation came down from heaven" (LW Nicene Creed page 141). Amen.

A Sudden Arrival

"Behold, I send My messenger and he will prepare the way
before Me. And the Lord whom you seek will suddenly come to
His temple; and the messenger of the covenant in whom you
delight, behold, He is coming, says the LORD of hosts." Malachi
3:1

The first Christmas came to the world suddenly, but not unexpectedly. For centuries people had waited for its coming. When Christ came in the darkness of the night, however, He arrived in a way that no one could have anticipated. Heaven interrupted the shepherds in the fields and took the Wise Men from their studies and shook the cruel Herod who had established his throne by blood. The promised Lord and Savior came to His temple—the Church—with a thrilling suddenness.

During this season, we talk and read about Christmas for weeks. Unfortunately for many people, this dulls their appreciation of the true meaning of Christmas. The Lord doesn't appear to them as being all that important. That is, they do not see in Him the only Savior and Redeemer, who, fulfilling a promise, came suddenly in the fullness of time to offer forgiveness to the world. For some people the true peace and joy of Christmas will break through when they understand that Christmas is the birthday of their Savior.

Happy and blessed are the people who prepare their hearts in true repentance! Just as surely as the Redeemer of the world came at the first Christmas, so He also comes to you through His Word. And He shall come for you yet again to fulfill and complete every promise He has spoken to you in His Word.

Come, O Lord Jesus, and enter into our lives with Your peace. Amen.

December

Emmanuel

"Behold, the virgin shall conceive and bear a son, and they shall call His name Immanuel" (which means, God with us).
Matthew 1:23

The Evangelist explains that this Hebrew word means "God with us." It is a very significant name. Many of our churches have taken it for their own. It is used in the first stanza of that Advent hymn: "Oh, Come, Oh, Come, Emmanuel." It is a name which is expressive of the basic Christian teaching of the deity of Jesus Christ.

When our Lord began His ministry long ago, there were at least some who understood who He was. They said that "God has visited His people" (Luke 7:16). Later on there was a great controversy about it. Some said that Jesus is godlike, but refused to acknowledge that He is God made flesh. The Council of Nicaea in 325 officially settled the argument by adopting the creed that calls Jesus "God of God, Light of Light, very God of very God."

We believe Jesus of Nazareth to be the eternal Word, the second Person of the Holy Trinity, come among us as a man. This, indeed, is what Christmas is all about. "The Word became flesh and dwelt among us" (John 1:14). There can be no real celebration of Christmas without faith in this truth. Here is something altogether wonderful, beautiful, and glorious. With the shepherds and the Wise Men we kneel before the Child and adore Him as our Lord and God.

Be with us always, O Lord, as You have ever been with Your own. Amen.

God's Early Promise to Help

"I will put enmity between you and the woman, and between your offspring and her offspring; He shall bruise your head, and you shall bruise His heel." Genesis 3:15

God's desire to keep man in communion with Him became evident as soon as man sinned in the Garden of Eden. In their perfection Adam and Eve enjoyed full communion with God. But when they fell into sin, they hid themselves. God sought them out and declared upon them the curse of sin. However, He was also quick to show the way back, for He spoke of the promised Savior in His words to Satan. The offspring of the woman refers to Christ, who in due time came to destroy the works of the devil by fulfilling the Law for us and atoning for our sins.

Aware of this promise, Eve, at the birth of her firstborn, said: "I have gotten a man with the help of the LORD" (Genesis 4:1). She thought her son was the promised Savior. While Eve was mistaken, she did well to remember God's promise of a coming Savior. Already in the dawn of history man yearned for the Christmas message.

It is wonderful to realize that the idea of Christmas was not an afterthought with God. As soon as man had sinned, God promised deliverance from sin.

As we approach the coming anniversary of our Savior's birth, let us turn our thoughts to this early promise of a Savior for our fallen race. This will enlarge our thinking about Christmas and will lead us to realize that God wants all people in communion with Him.

We thank You, gracious Lord, for coming so soon to man's rescue in his desperate need. Amen.

Starlight

I see Him, but not now; I behold Him, but not near: a star shall come out of Jacob, and a scepter shall rise out of Israel; it shall crush the forehead of Moab and break down all the sons of Sheth. Numbers 24:17

The psalmist says, "The heavens declare the glory of God" (Psalm 19:1). The many stars that sparkle like precious gems in the great blue dome of heaven show forth the glory of God. They speak of His greatness, of His power, of His wisdom. And in their course they give guidance to the wayfarer struggling in the darkness of night. Starlight has ever been a blessing to man.

But there is a more wonderful Star—a much greater Light—that blesses the earth. The prophet Balaam spoke of this Starlight centuries before it ever shone. He foretold the coming of Jesus Christ, who was to be the Starlight of the ages, the glory of God, the Savior of all men. When Jesus was born in Bethlehem, He showed forth a light that no other star could, and He made known a glory of God that no heavenly body had ever made known.

Jesus showed forth the glory of God's love that whoever believes in Him shall not perish but have eternal life. Jesus is the true guide that shows the way. As the Magi were guided by the star to Bethlehem, so through Jesus we too are brought across the wilderness of time to the lasting joy of our heavenly home. He, then, is the most wonderful Starlight that has ever shone, for He is the Light of the world and the Light of eternal life.

Jesus Savior, pilot me Over life's tempestuous sea. Amen. (LW 513:1)

December

The Church

So we, though many, are one body in Christ, and individually members one of another. Romans 12:5

St. Paul prays for the Church, the communion of saints: "For this reason I bow my knees before the Father, from whom every family in heaven and on earth is named" (Ephesians 3:14–15). The members of this family, despite the sad divisions in Christendom, are those in whose hearts Christ lives by faith and who are "rooted and grounded in love" (Ephesians 3:17). They are the "children of God" (Romans 8:16), "heirs of God" (Romans 8:17), and "fellow heirs with Christ" (Romans 8:17). The believers in Christ are "fellow citizens with the saints and members of the household of God" (Ephesians 2:19).

> *The saints on earth and those above*
> *But one communion make;*
> *Joined to their Lord in bonds of love,*
> *All of His grace partake. (TLH 478:1)*

Who the actual believers and members of the Church are, only the Lord knows. Yet it is comforting to be assured by God's Word that the Spirit of God that dwells in us bears witness with our spirit that we are the children of God.

This Church, purchased with the blood of Christ, He will build and defend against all its enemies. Even the gates of hell shall not prevail against it.

O Holy Spirit, keep us steadfast in the faith. "Now to Him who is able to do far more abundantly than all we ask or think, according to the power at work within us, to Him be glory in the Church and in Christ Jesus throughout all generations, forever and ever. Amen" (Ephesians 3:20–21).

December

Forgiveness Is Certain

"She will bear a son, and you shall call His name Jesus, for He will save His people from their sins." Matthew 1:21

The angel of the Lord appeared to Joseph and said: "Joseph, son of David, do not fear to take Mary as your wife, for that which is conceived in her is from the Holy Spirit. She will bear a son, and you shall call His name Jesus, for He will *save His people from their sins*" (Matthew 1:20–21).

"And an angel of the Lord appeared to them, and the glory of the Lord shone around them, and they were filled with fear. And the angel said to them, 'Fear not, for behold, I bring good news of a great joy that will be for all the people. For unto you is born this day in the city of David a Savior, who is Christ the Lord'" (Luke 2:9–11).

"In this is love," writes St. John, "not that we have loved God but that He loved us and sent His Son to be the propitiation for our sins" (1 John 4:10). "In this the love of God was made manifest among us, that God sent His only Son into the world, so that we might live through Him" (1 John 4:9).

No matter how long we have sinned, or how horrible our sins were, or how stubbornly we refused the grace of God, the birth of Christ assures us of the love of God for us sinners. For the Son of God left the throne of His glory: "And being found in human form, He humbled Himself by becoming obedient to the point of death, even death on a cross" (Philippians 2:8).

Come, mighty Judge, our Savior, and make us free from every evil! Amen.

Light of the World

"I am the light of the world." John 8: 12

"You are the light of the world. A city set on a hill cannot be hidden." Matthew 5:14

There is no contradiction in these two statements; rather, they complement each other. The second statement is an offshoot of the first.

The world lies in darkness: intellectual, social, spiritual darkness. Sin has so darkened the human mind, Satan has so blinded human reason that even in secular matters men grope about for solutions of difficulties and fail to find them. Witness the succession of wars and the failures to establish a more abiding peace.

Against this backdrop, Christ asserts that He is *the* Light of the world, *the* Light that men need before all other light. He has proved Himself to be this very Light. By the truth of His teaching He has illumined men's minds and liberated them from the darkness of ignorance and error and unbelief. The light of God's wisdom and of God's love shines through Christ into the lives of men.

And so Christ says to His disciples: "You are the light of the world." Later, at His ascension, Christ withdrew His visible presence, but He left His Word and His Spirit with His disciples. Wherever they went, they carried the Light of Christ into the darkness of the world. That is still the privilege and the task of Christ's disciples. His light must shine through us. Christ also added: "In the same way, let your light shine before others, so that they may see your good works and give glory to your Father who is in heaven" (Matthew 5:16).

Enlighten me more and more, O Christ, and enable me to let Your light shine in the dark places on earth. Amen.

The Eternal Power of Christmas

For unto you is born this day in the city of David a Savior, who is Christ the Lord. Luke 2:11

The hearts of Christians throughout the world are dwelling during these sacred hours upon the wondrous story of that first Christmas eve. And what a resplendent spectacle is unfolded before our wondering eyes in the simple language of that story! Lowly shepherds in shepherds' garb, dumbfounded, stupefied, bewildered: *they* form the first Christmas audience. An angel of God, in all the glory and brilliance of heaven, the first Christmas messenger. A choir of angels, the first Christmas chorus. And the words "Unto you is born this day in the city of David a Savior, who is Christ the Lord," the keynote of the first Christmas sermon ever preached to dying sinners.

The eternal power and divine eloquence of this simple yet tremendously important message has perpetuated the Christmas festival and still electrifies the hearts of Christians whenever its language is repeated. "Unto you is born . . . a Savior!"

Unto *you*, you who were born in sin, you whose life is a record of transgression and iniquity and therefore under the wrath of an offended God, "Unto *you* is born this day in the city of David a Savior," a Redeemer, an Emancipator, which is Christ the Lord, the promised Messiah, the Emmanuel, the God-with-us, the mighty God!

As long as that message remains true—and it will remain *forever* true—Christmas will never lose its power. Christmas will never cease to bring its peace and hope and joy into the souls of men—that peace, that hope, that joy of which the angels sang—that peace, that hope, that joy which—thank God—are ours today.

Thank You, heavenly Father, for the gift of Your Son. Amen.

The Sign of Christmas

Therefore the Lord Himself will give you a sign. Behold, the virgin shall conceive and bear a son, and shall call His name Immanuel. Isaiah 7:14

O Holy Night, the stars are brightly shining.
It is the night of the dear Savior's birth!
(Placide Clappeau, translated by John S. Dwight)

It is Christmas Eve. Throughout the Christian world there is excitement and joy. It is the night on which the eyes of young and old sparkle with holy excitement. It is Christmas! Yet someone will surely say, What is the big deal about a baby in a manger? There are always voices of doubt, skepticism, and unbelief. Maybe doubts even enter our mind in the presence of so great a mystery as this: God in a manger!

Centuries before Christ was born, God gave a sign that the whole world might know when it would be Christmas. The prophet Isaiah says, "Therefore the Lord Himself will give you sign. Behold, the virgin shall conceive and bear a son, and shall call His name Immanuel." Never before and never since has such a miracle taken place. A virgin gave birth to a son. The sign of the virgin, then, is the sign of Christmas. By it we know that the child of Bethlehem is not just a human child but is, as the angel said, "the Son of God" (Matthew 26:63). Therefore, His name is truly Immanuel, that is, "God with us" (Matthew 1:23). So we say in faith: "I believe . . . in Jesus Christ, His only Son, our Lord, who was conceived by the Holy Spirit, [and] born of the Virgin Mary" (*Luther's Small Catechism*). Yes, it is Christmas. God came to us in human form, to live with us and die for us.

Lord we thank You for this sign of Christmas. Amen.

The Mystery of Bethlehem

Great indeed, we confess, is the mystery of godliness: He was manifested in the flesh, vindicated by the Spirit, seen by angels, proclaimed among the nations, believed on in the world, taken up in glory. 1 Timothy 3:16

The mysterious light that shone over the fields of Bethlehem more than two thousand years ago directed the shepherds to the greater mystery in the manger. They saw only a human baby; but informed by God through the angel, they worshiped this child, the newborn Savior. The mysterious star that aroused the interests of the Wise Men of the East directed them to the Christ Child in Bethlehem. They were mystified. But, enlightened by the Spirit of God, they worshiped Him and presented to Him their gifts of adoration.

Yes, what occurred in Bethlehem was a mystery, which event also the angels desired to look into. Even to the virgin mother this birth remained a deep mystery. When the angel made the startling annunciation to her, she quite naturally asked: "How will this be?" (Luke 1:34). The explanation she received was: "The Holy Spirit will come upon you, and the power of the Most High will overshadow you; therefore the child to be born will be called holy—the Son of God. And behold, your relative Elizabeth in her old age has also conceived a son, and this is the sixth month with her who was called barren. For nothing will be impossible with God" (Luke 1:35–37).

The doctrine of the virgin birth is today denied by many, but we Christians believe and confess it. We must, for it stands at the heart of our faith. Without it, the divinity of Christ must be denied, along with the entirety of our salvation.

Rather than denying our Lord's virgin birth, let us rejoice over this mystery and thank God for revealing it. In the Christ of Bethlehem let us ever worship "[God] manifested in the flesh." Let us join the virgin mother in declaring:

"My soul magnifies the Lord, and my spirit rejoices in God my Savior" *(Luke 1:46–47). Amen.*

Eternal Blessings

"Lord, now You are letting Your servant depart in peace, according to Your word; for my eyes have seen Your salvation." Luke 2:29–30

On the day after Christmas, also known as Saint Stephen's Day, we look around and see so many things brought about by our Christmas celebration. There are toys—perhaps some of them already broken—scattered around, the gifts that don't quite fit, the leftovers from the Christmas dinner. There are pleasant memories of associations and remembrances by friends and loved ones. But Christmas brings more than earthly celebrations; it brings us heaven itself.

St. Stephen was the first follower of Jesus to die a martyr's death. As he was dying, he beheld the heavens open and Jesus in all His glory. He was able to say, "Lord Jesus, receive my spirit" (Acts 7:59). He could say this because he believed in Jesus, the Savior born in Bethlehem. He, like Simeon (Luke 2), had seen the Lord's salvation.

On this day that remembers St. Stephen, we can join with him and with Simeon in the prayer, "Lord, now You are letting Your servant depart in peace, according to Your word; for my eyes have seen Your salvation." Thus the true value of Christmas consists in bringing us the peace of forgiveness and complete oneness with God by faith. The peace on earth, of which the angels sang, is the peace of salvation in the heart and the soul of man. The final consequence of Christmas will be for us a glorious entrance with all the saints into the Kingdom above.

Lord Jesus, give us Your peace by faith in You, that through You we come to endless peace. Amen.

December

"His Glory"

And the Word became flesh and dwelt among us, and we have seen His glory, glory as of the only Son from the Father, full of grace and truth. John 1:14

What did Christmas and its celebration tell us about Jesus Christ? Did He shine forth more brightly to us? Were we drawn more closely to Him, our wonderful Savior? Did we get a glimpse of His glory?

St. John, perhaps, beheld more of the glory of Jesus than any other disciple. At least he wrote more about the wonderful glory than any of the others did. John tells us, "We have seen His glory"; then he describes that glory. He points out that Jesus is true God and that as such He has all the might and the majesty of the everlasting God. Such glory Jesus displayed in His mighty works. But the glory of Jesus, as St. John says, is also "grace and truth." To know the truth brings joy! The all-important truth Jesus revealed tells us that He is the Way. Included in that truth is the grace of God. The word *grace* means "unmerited favor." Jesus is the gift of God to the world. God loved us so that He saved us by sending Jesus to be sacrificed in our stead. In Jesus we know love, unmerited love, the true grace of God.

Praise God! We know Jesus not only as God but, above all, as our loving Savior; and this wonderful love of Jesus and His blessed truth give us life eternal! "Whoever believes in Him should not perish but have eternal life" (John 3:16).

Lord Jesus, You are the Truth, the Life, and the Way. Lead us by faith in You to the full glory of heaven. Amen.

December

The Peace of Bethlehem

"Glory to God in the highest, and on earth peace among those with whom He is pleased!" Luke 2:14

We may assume that the little village of Bethlehem was a quiet and peaceful place in which to live—just the kind of a place we like to dream about in the hurly-burly of our modern life. Yet in Bethlehem there was "weeping and loud lamentation" (Matthew 2:18) when Herod had his soldiers kill the baby boys after he heard of the birth of a new-born "King of the Jews" (Mark 15:26). The peace of which the angels sang at the birth of Christ was not of this world; not civic or political peace, not industrial or social peace. It was not even the "small town," easy-paced peace that so many in our day have come to desire. It was divine peace, a peace between holy God and sinful man, a peace that God was offering to Jew and Gentile alike in the precious gift of His beloved Son.

The "Prince of Peace" (Isaiah 9:6) is one of the great titles given to Christ in prophecy. This peace between God and man Jesus proclaimed in the days of His flesh. He bestowed it upon highly respectable Nicodemus and the publican Zacchaeus on identical terms: repentance and faith. He secured it by His holy life and sacrificial death. He sealed it by His triumphant resurrection and ascension. Now, "we have been justified by faith, we have peace with God through our Lord Jesus Christ" (Romans 5:1). And the words Jesus spoke to the innermost circle of His disciples are recorded of us: "Peace I leave with you; My peace I give to you" (John 14:27). In this peace we shall live eternally, no matter what trial and travail we must endure for a while here on earth.

Dear Savior, bless us with Your peace, now and evermore! Amen.

December

Kept by the Power of God

Who by God's power are being guarded through faith for a salvation ready to be revealed in the last time. 1 Peter 1:5

During World War II several men in the U. S. Air Force had to take refuge in a small rubber boat out on the vast waters of the Pacific Ocean. For days they drifted without food or water. But they were kept not only from being engulfed by the waves, but also from dying of a tormenting thirst under the blazing sun of a clear South Pacific sky. Christians will readily agree that these men were "kept by the power of God"; and the men themselves acknowledged this fact. They were later rescued and brought to the homeland they so dearly loved.

For us Christians, heaven is our home. But because we are Christians, we must wage a hard warfare, undergo many afflictions, and pass through the deep waters of affliction. Often our strength fails us; at times we are driven almost to despair. How can we persevere? How can we endure to the end? How can we reach the homeland? Here is God's answer: "[You] . . . by God's power are being guarded through faith." The Holy Spirit, whom Jesus gives us as our Teacher, Counselor, and Comforter, strengthens us through the Gospel and the Sacraments. Through these means of grace He nourishes our souls unto eternal life. As we prayerfully meditate upon such a passage as this first chapter of First Peter, in which we are assured of our undefiled, unfading, and imperishable inheritance in heaven, we are being drawn heavenward. Thus we are kept by the power of God through faith unto salvation that will be revealed to us at the end of days.

Dear Father, keep us in Your grace through faith in Jesus Christ. Amen.

December

The Glory of Bethlehem

And an angel of the Lord appeared to them, and the glory of the Lord shone around them, and they were filled with fear. Luke 2:9

Many an otherwise insignificant village has become famous because it was the birthplace of some illustrious person. Micah foretold that the little village of Bethlehem would be the birthplace of that Ruler "whose origin is from of old, from ancient days" (Micah 5:2). The glorious light from heaven that shone round about the shepherds indicated the far greater glory that had come to Bethlehem in the miraculous incarnation of the eternal Son of God—conceived by the Holy Ghost and born of the Virgin Mary.

Every year thousands of pilgrims visit Bethlehem, but many fail to see its real glory. The Christ of Bethlehem was and still is the Light of the world. His light shines for us in the Gospel record. If we study and in faith accept that record, we shall be able to say with the first disciples: "We have seen His glory, glory as of the only Son from the Father, full of grace and truth" (John 1:14). In faith and love we follow this Light of the world. The Holy Spirit comes to us through the divine Word, enlightening our hearts and minds so we "will not walk in darkness, but will have the light of life" (John 8:12).

O holy Child of Bethlehem,
Descend to us, we pray;
Cast out our sin,
And enter in,
Be born in us today. Amen. (LW 59:4)

Lord, Have Mercy upon Us

"But the tax collector, standing far off, would not even lift up his eyes to heaven, but beat his breast, saying, 'God, be merciful to me, a sinner!'" Luke 18:13

This year is now finished. The record is complete. We like to recall the good and pleasant things of which we are proud. We like to forget the unpleasant and the disturbing things. Our mistakes are so often relegated and suppressed into a forced forgetfulness. We do not like to own up to our sins. But, try as we might, we cannot escape our faults and transgressions. We must settle our account with God, who justly judges. We should not leave this year behind without doing just that.

How shall we close this year in peace? Like the publican in the temple, we would be wise to throw ourselves upon the mercy of God. Our heavenly Father has prepared the way for us in Christ Jesus, who "was wounded for our transgressions; He was crushed for our iniquities" (Isaiah 53:5). All that was wrong in this past year, and in every year before that, was paid for by the Lamb of God on the cross of Calvary. Because of His payment for our sins by faith, we have forgiveness.

Jesus sweetly and tenderly calls us, "Come to Me, all who labor and are heavy laden, and I will give you rest" (Matthew 11:28).

Lord, have mercy upon us.
Christ, have mercy upon us.
Lord, have mercy upon us. Amen.